Playing the White Man's Games

PLAYING THE
WHITE MAN'S GAMES

Don Marks

J. GORDON SHILLINGFORD
PUBLISHING INC

Playing the White Man's Games
First published 2014 by J. Gordon Shillingford Publishing Inc.
©2014, Don Marks

Cover and interior design by Relish New Brand Experience
Printed and bound in Canada on 100% post-consumer recycled paper

We acknowledge the financial support of the Manitoba Arts Council
and The Canada Council for the Arts for our publishing program.

Images courtesy of: Bain News Service, British Library, Library
and Archives Canada, Official Marine Corps, O-Pee-Chee/
Hockey Hall of Fame, *Winnipeg Tribune*/University of Manitoba
Libraries Archives

LIBRARY AND ARCHIVES CANADA CATALOGUING IN PUBLICATION

Marks, Don, 1953-, author
       Playing the white man's games / Don Marks.

Includes index.
ISBN 978-1-927922-01-9 (pbk.)

       1. Native athletes--Canada--Biography. I. Title.

GV697.AIMI95 2014   796.092'271   C2014-903696-5

Table of Contents

Acknowledgements

There are always three kinds of people I want to thank for helping me create a book like this—the people who help by providing research, information, stories and other specific and general content, the friends who support you through the process and provide feedback to your ideas and approaches, and then those people who are just out there providing inspiration and living examples of the good spirit I would like this book to be a part of. Most of this is personal and of little interest to the general reader so I will keep this short.

In regards to the content of this book, there is such a wealth of information nowadays on the internet that it is misleading to source material in some sort of standard or academic way. I researched the subject matter as widely as I could, I read as many stories about the people I was writing about as possible, and I interviewed them, their families, friends and associates as much as I could. I made very broad notes, and then tried to write up this material with a fresh voice. And then I checked my facts against available research. To the many voices on the internet or YouTube and all of the other wonderful places we can find information about anything we need or desire, I thank you wholeheartedly. To writers such as Michael Brown, Tom Farrey, Lee Allen, Martin Kaufman, G. Neri, Mike Shropshire, Len Hayward, Kenny Moore, Charles Enman and others who wrote articles about the heroes here, I thank you, and if there is a sentence which reads just like you wrote it, it is because your prose was so striking it just burnt into my memory as is (I would never claim to have a photographic memory like Sheldon Cooper). And if anybody wishes to use the information that I have provided in this book in a good way, feel free to do so, and it is not necessary to source, credit, thank or acknowledge me in any way.

To my friends and colleagues, thank you, especially Gary Zubeck for the research, writing and editing help, and Dennis Nanowin, Clay O'Bray and Ken MacDonald for their especially close friendship during this time (and Chris Mcleod and Milton Tootoosis for their professional advice and support). To the many other friends and colleagues I have enjoyed throughout my life, I offer my general gratitude and appreciation without running the risk of leaving anybody out.

A very special colleague and friend throughout my life has always been Marion Ironquil Meadmore—this dynamo from Peepeekisis First Nation who was the first Treaty Indian woman to be called to the bar, a founder of the Friendship Centre movement in Canada and a key driving force behind Indian self-government and indigenous sovereignty worldwide. Always five years ahead of her time, she has shown me how to dream and she has honoured me by involving me in her forward-thinking initiatives. Marion's tireless energy, stratospheric intelligence and never-ending idealism inspires me, but mostly, she makes me work as hard as I can every day; just to try and keep up to people like her.

And to my Guardian Angel on Earth, Kathleen Richardson, whose way of living and thinking and believing is a source of inspiration to me every day, if not every hour, thank you.

And just to say that I kept some sort of company with writers whose work inspires me, I want to thank the late great Hunter S. Thompson, and the people who are responsible for the Golden Age of Television we are experiencing and that I am honest enough to say has most inspired me. To people like David Simon, who gave us *The Wire*, and David Chase (*The Sopranos*), Aaron Sorkin (*The West Wing* and *The Newsroom*), and all the folks who provide us with art and entertainment like *Breaking Bad*, *Fargo*, *Orange is the Next Black* and *Boardwalk Empire*, I thank you for inspiring me to try and emulate your craft. Even if I don't come close, I appreciate your work.

Preface

This book is the natural extension/evolution of *They Call Me Chief: Warriors on Ice*, which told the fascinating stories of First Nations hockey players who overcame incredible obstacles to achieve success in the National Hockey League. *They Call Me Chief* was well-received and provided the confidence to write a similar book featuring the stories of other indigenous sports stars.

First Nations/Native American athletes have definitely achieved their most widespread success in hockey, but the most significant achievements made by native people in sports overall belongs to Jim Thorpe, whose exploits in track and field, especially at the Olympics, and on the football field, made *Time* magazine name him "Athlete of the Half-Century" (1900-1950) and caused the American Congress (as well as the ABC television network) to proclaim him "Athlete of the Century." To rise above names like Babe Ruth and Lou Gehrig, Jesse Owens and Muhammed Ali, Wayne Gretzky and Michael Jordan, is an enormous accomplishment and it raises interest in other Native American athletes who have achieved similar success in other sports.

Like *They Call Me Chief*, this book will not focus on statistics (which can be found so easily on the internet nowadays), I searched beyond the field of play to find deeper meaning behind what happened in the lives of these athletes/entertainers. And I made no secret of the fact *They Call Me Chief* was designed like an advertisement which used hockey to draw the attention of a large sports audience and then diverted that attention towards information about First Nations people; their history, culture and issues, because this was such a big part of the story for these athletes, similar to the way an advertisement uses an attractive model to attract attention and then divert that attention to a product.

I wanted to entertain and empower people with this information. It was not my goal to convince people whether or not the "cause of native people" is right or wrong. Certainly I have my opinions and the reader is free to agree or disagree. I have tried to avoid preaching or lecturing or arguing. There is nothing better than an informed exchange which benefits both sides with the power of new information and perspectives. The Elders teach by guiding people gently to a higher understanding, and I hope my writing emulates that approach.

I agree with those who maintain that nobody has justice unless we all have justice, and that nobody is free unless we are all free. And so we work together for justice and freedom. Information creates awareness and understanding, and sometimes this creates empathy and support, which builds unity, and sets us on our way to economic and social justice and equality.

Freedom.

But the bottom line for this author is to entertain you, the reader.

We succeeded with *They Call Me Chief*, mostly because we didn't sacrifice the exciting elements of sports—the intense competition, the secrets to success, the fascinating inside stories which resulted in some of the biggest victories and most agonizing defeats that the hockey world has ever known. Complementing this with their life away from the field of play, along with the history, culture and issues which are tied to their heritage, found us a wider audience, including many people, particularly women, who told me "they don't generally follow sports."

It turns out we found a winning formula so we're going to stay with it, with these new stories about remarkable athletes who found a way to success, and into our hearts and minds, while remaining true to their spirit and heritage.

Most of the star athletes in *They Call Me Chief* are Canadian because the book is about hockey, which is Canada's national sport. Many of the athletes in *Playing the White Man's Games* are from south of the 49th parallel, because we have expanded our scope to globally popular sports like track and field, football and golf, where indigenous athletes have made the most impact.

The athletes in this book hail from nations which extended from Canada to the United States and back again long before these countries existed. The 49th parallel meant nothing to Native Americans or the First Nations of North America and they retain free access across the border through the Jay Treaty.

In my mind, it doesn't matter which side of the border the tribe a native athlete is affiliated with is located. They are the First Nations of the Americas.

Canadian readers who are interested in good stories that include "First Nations" history, culture and current affairs, will enjoy meeting the athletes who are featured here, as will American readers who are likewise interested in "Native American" issues, activities and personalities.

So for the sake of this book, we can make that border disappear, just like it was in the old days.

But just like before, there is that old bugaboo about "What to call Indians?" Native Americans seems to be the favoured, politically correct term in the United States, while First Nations is becoming common in Canada (the term "aboriginal" finds less favour year by year north of the 49th parallel, while "indigenous" is being used more widely throughout the world).

I have always maintained that the most appropriate names to use are the names the people call themselves; the names they prefer to be called. We used up a lot of ink and paper in *They Call Me Chief* explaining the history and rationale pertaining to this question and we offer recaps of that throughout this book.

Suffice to say, the name "Indian" is still commonly used in the U.S. as well as the term "Native American." First Nations seems to be acceptable everywhere, especially in Canada, and we see the words "native" and "indigenous" used by the people and their organizations quite often. So I will stick to those words in this book except when the person is Metis or Inuit.

I do not mean to offend anyone and I am sorry if I use a name you do not care for. I can only say that the names I use are commonly used by the people themselves, or some of the people some of the time, but not all of the people all of the time.

My purpose is to tell the stories of some remarkable athletes no matter what names we use.

They Call Me Chief missed out on some truly outstanding native athletes because of space limitations. I have included some of these stars in Chapter 11 because they also provide some amazing stories and achievements. I apologize for lumping these remarkable athletes together and not providing the most complete story of their lives and their accomplishments.

Still, the summaries and highlights from the careers of baseball stars like Aflie Reynolds, Charlie Bender, Joba Chamberlain, Kyle Lohse and Jacoby Ellersby, and Olympic kayaking gold medalist Alwyn Morris, and figure skater Naomi Lang, make for some interesting and enjoyable reading.

I have tried to support the stories we tell with factual research from information which is available. If I got something wrong, I apologize. As much as sports relies on cold, hard statistics to tell the stories, sometimes numbers can get stretched in the telling and re-telling. It's like the size of that fish you caught. It grows an inch with each new audience.

This book is more about the stories than the stats anyways, but even then sometimes I am going to get it wrong because it was given to me wrong. I hope I have kept that to a minimum.

Books like this aren't intended to be factual texts or investigative journalism. They are mostly entertainment for your reading pleasure and they should accentuate the positive and downplay the negative. I have strived to be accurate but I may have gotten some things wrong. Really, what's the big harm?

They're great stories. They're mostly true.

Enjoy.

Jim Thorpe

1

The World's Greatest Athlete— Anytime, Anywhere

Jim Thorpe, Sac and Fox Nation, was unanimously voted Athlete of the first half century by *Time Magazine* and the Associated Press, and the Athlete of the Century by Congressional decree and a poll of fans by ABC television. Other polls conducted more recently have always placed Thorpe in the top ten, and considering how modern surveys always lean towards more well-known (and more readily recalled) sports figures, Thorpe beats out other athletic greats like Muhammed Ali, Michael Jordan, Wayne Gretzky, Jack Nicklaus and Babe Ruth, Jesse Owens, Willie Mays and Jim Brown, and that is quite a list.

The number of people who are unfamiliar with Jim Thorpe's achievements grows year by year. This is regrettable because Thorpe offers such a positive role model for young people, and the times he lived in provide background and insight to the social, political and economic development which shaped the way North American society is today. This can be overcome by books like this which empower people with information about our shared history. And, of course, authors such as myself benefit from new audiences for fascinating stories which are there for discovery.

No other athlete could have his life story read like a Paul Bunyan tall tale, or maybe a segment of Ripley's *Believe it or Not*. But that is how one feels when Jim Thorpe's achievements are laid end to end. You can print paragraph after paragraph of fascinating, almost unbelievable achievements like "Jim kicked the ball 60 yards in the air and then out-ran four Pitt defenders to catch his own punt and sprint another 20 yards for a touchdown" or "Jim happened by some varsity high jumpers and asked if he could give it a try so they set the bar at 6 feet, which nobody had come close to clearing, and Jim proceeded to jump over that bar in street shoes, suit and even a tie."

So I can fill a normal-sized chapter in a normal-sized book like this with tales about Jim Thorpe that may sound tall but are totally true, even though Jim Thorpe appeared to be, and to look, like any other normal man.

Jim Thorpe was nowhere near normal.

Like most legendary figures, Jim Thorpe was born in a one-room log house on Indian territory before it became Oklahoma. "Wa Tho Huk" (meaning "Bright Path" in Sac and Fox) would go on a journey which truly follows a "path lit by a great flash of lightning" (the long version of his name). Along the way, Thorpe would set world records on a global stage, meet kings, presidents and a pope, before finally flaming out with time, like all meteors must.

The Bunyan-esque exploits began when he made the Carlisle track team in 1907 with that high jump, the start of a track and field career that would see Thorpe win both the pentathlon and decathlon at the 1912 Olympic Games in Sweden. Paul Bunyan himself would have marvelled at a picture taken at those Olympics which revealed Thorpe in the mismatched running shoes that he had to scrounge just before running the 1,500 metre race because his own shoes had disappeared from his gym bag. A teammate provided one shoe, which was too small, but Jim squeezed it on. Jim had to find another shoe in a garbage can, discarded because it was no good any more, but it was also too large for Jim's foot, so he had to stuff an additional four socks in just to keep that shoe on.

Jim had never run a 1,500-metre race before. It was the final event of the decathlon and he needed to win that race to finish with the most total points in the event.

Jim set a new Olympic record while winning the 1,500-metre event, natch.

Jim Thorpe was born on May 28, 1888 in Pottawatomie county, Oklahoma to a couple who were both half-white and half-Native American, approximately, because conflicting research and records list Dutch, Irish, French, Sac and Fox, Potawanomi, Menomini, Kickapoo and other European blood in Jim's family tree, which can be traced back to William Thorpe, who helped found New Haven, Connecticut in 1637.

Basically, Dad Hiram was half Sac and Fox and Mom Charlotte was half-Potawanami, and Jim was raised Sac and Fox. That means he was taught how to hunt by the time he was three, and he built up his stamina on the heels of his hounds tracking squirrels. At the same age, Hiram dropped little Jim into a raging river and made the young boy struggle to safety.

By age six, Hiram had taught his boy to ride, shoot, trap and accompany him on 30-mile hunting treks. Jim quickly became an expert wrangler and he could break wild horses, which he tried to emulate when he ran because of their economy of motion.

Jim grew up with his twin brother Charlie on a family farm. It was if the twins were each half of a whole.

Hiram desperately wanted his boys to benefit from a white man's education, so he made sure that Jim and Charlie attended the schools that were made available for Indians. Charlie didn't have Jim's athletic ability, but he made up for that in smarts and arts, and Charlie was always trying to help Jim with his studies.

The problem was that those studies weren't as much a priority as the work that the Indian schoolchildren were forced to do at the boarding schools. Agency officials maintained it was part of their training to become civilized but it was really little more than a work farm with free labour.

Jim also didn't like how the Indian Agency school belittled his Indian culture, traditions and identity, so he kept running away. Each time, however, Hiram Thorpe would take his son back.

Tragically, a plague of influenza broke out, and Indian boarding schools were an incubator for disease. Charlie died of pneumonia at the age of nine. Jim was spared because he was on the lam at the time but without his twin brother and best friend, and in the deepest of mourning, Jim wanted out of Indian school more than ever.

So when they caught him and returned him to the school, Jim just up and ran the full 23 miles to home.

Many years later, Jim Thorpe would tell his son Richard how deeply and lastingly his brother's death affected him.

Richard states, "I asked my father how he got all his strength and he said he inherited it from his brother when his brother passed away. He just felt Charlie was with him all the time and he carried the strength and spirit of two in whatever he did."

Hiram was adamant Jim get an education, so the boy eventually ended up in the Haskell Institute in Lawrence, Kansas; part of a new assimilation policy the U.S. government was trying, having failed at killing off Indians physically through war, starvation, disease and the forced idleness of reservations. The idea was to discourage all aspects of indigenous identity; language, culture, religion and appearance—basically to "kill the Indian by turning him into a white man."

Jim ran away from that school a couple of times, too, once after his mother died of complications from childbirth (he had requested a leave but school authorities denied him, so 12-year-old Jim set out on the 280-mile trek on foot and completed it in less than two weeks). Jim was sent back and his education was a constant war of wills that was reflected in his marks at times. This has caused some historians to label Jim Thorpe as dumb or lazy but a report card obtained by definitive biographer Robert W. Wheeler reveals some B+ -level grades Jim obtained despite his absences and his instinctive resistance to the philosophy and policies of assimilation that were being followed by the school at the time.

For his high school and university education, Jim was sent to the Carlisle Indian Industrial Institute in Pennsylvania and, after a while, this school stuck because Jim hoped to study electricity and earn himself a living as a tradesman. Jim interrupted his education at Carlisle for a while when he left to grieve the passing of his father. Hiram Thorpe died from a hunting accident during a time when treatment for gangrene wasn't so readily available.

Over 10,000 Indians would pass through the doors of the Carlisle Institute with just over 700 graduating. Over a thousand ran away or "disappeared." Again, they were reacting to the exploitation which the white masters kept justifying as "good for the Indian to learn the white man's way"; such as the "Outing system" which placed students at nearby farms and residences to provide field work and domestic chores. The students were paid half the wages a white employee would receive.

Jim returned to Carlisle to pursue his plans for a career in electricity but those plans got short-circuited as soon as the coaches at Carlisle got a whiff of Thorpe's athletic ability.

It started when infamous coach Glenn Scobey "Pop" Warner heard about that high jump bar Thorpe had cleared in street clothes and he immediately signed Jim up for his Carlisle track team.

Jim wanted to play football but Warner claimed he was too small, obviously not wanting his non-contact sport star to get hurt playing a hitting game like football. That didn't last long and soon, Jim Thorpe was making "Pop" Warner look good at coaching football as well as track and field.

All by himself, as things turned out. The way the Bunyan-esque (but true) story goes is that Carlisle was scheduled for a meet against Lafayette College in Easton, Pennsylvania and the hosts sent out a welcoming committee who were anxious to experience what were becoming known as the "Forgotten Americans." They didn't know whether to be surprised or disappointed when just two Indians got off the train.

"Where's your team?" they asked.

"This is the team," replied Thorpe.

"Only two of you?"

"Well, just one," Jim said with a smile. "This fellow here is the manager."

And if the other teams felt they gained a competitive advantage by ganging up on a single Indian with athletes who specialized in the various disciplines of track and field, Jim's only problem was the schedule, which might hold two events at the same time.

Jim Thorpe could run the 100-yard dash in 10 seconds flat, the 220 in 21.8, the 440 in 50.8, the 880 in 1:57 and the mile in 4:35. He ran and jumped through the 120-yard high hurdles in 15 seconds and the 220-yard low hurdles in 24 seconds flat. Thorpe broad-jumped 23 feet, 6 inches and high jumped 6 foot 5 inches. He could pole vault a height of 11 feet, put the shot 47 feet 9 inches, throw the javelin 163 feet, the hammer 140 feet and the discus 136 feet. All of these times and distances are comparable to the very best that any athlete in the United States could attain when they specialized in just one of the events. Carl Lewis, who took great pride in the fact he competed in the 100- and 200-metre sprints as well as the long jump, and other athletes like Michael Johnson and Usain Bolt who have captured our imagination with their times in the 100-, 200- and 440-metre races would be bedazzled by the one-man tour de force that was Jim Thorpe.

All those numbers Jim could put up make up a decathlon, so it was off to Sweden for the Olympic Games in 1912. Back then, the pentathlon (long jump, javelin, 200 metres, discus, 1,500 metres) and the decathlon (day 1 —100 metres, long jump, shot put, high jump, 400 metres/day 2—110 metres, discus, pole vault, javelin, 1,500 metres) were the premier events at the Games because they required such versatility; the winners of these events were considered the very best of the Olympic athletes. Thorpe won both competitions and there is no doubt that Jim Thorpe was the greatest athlete in the world then and now. Especially when you consider he had never tried events like the pole vault before the Games (there was no way to set it up on the boat deck going over to Europe) and he couldn't practice the pole vault much in Sweden because he was afraid of heights!

No less than the King of Sweden said Jim was the best.

King Gustav, as he honoured Thorpe for his achievements and showered him with gifts, offered this highest praise, "You sir, are the greatest athlete in the world!" King Gustav proclaimed.

To which Jim replied: "Thanks, King!"

Thanks indeed. Thorpe returned from Stockholm with over $50,000 worth of trophies, which included the laurel wreath of victory, a Viking ship presented to him by the Czar of Russia and a replica of King Gustav himself that was carved by the top sculptor in Sweden.

And, of course, two gold medals.

King Gustav was effusive in his praise but nobody could match the accolades bestowed on Thorpe by sports historian Murray Olderman, who called the Native American hero the "greatest all-around athlete in the history of sports, dating back to Coreobus of Elis in the 8th century B.C."

Jim's achievements were even more special to himself and Sac and Fox tribal Elders, who have maintained the sovereignty of their indigenous nations throughout first contact with the newcomers, through all the conflicts which have taken place, to the signing of the Treaties, and on to the relations we share today. In 1912, so-called Indians were not citizens of the United States (they would not gain that status until 1924) so the Olympic victories of Jim Thorpe and all their glory were achieved on behalf of the Sac and Fox nation; the two gold medals placed Sac and Fox ahead of countries like Denmark and Greece.

In order to achieve such magnificent results, Jim was either the product of a rare genetic combination, or he had uncovered training methods which prepared his body and mind much more throughly than other preparations that were known at the time, or both. Today's track and field athletes would obviously benefit from any secrets Thorpe possessed and I would like to pass such knowledge on but there is little known about how he trained (there was that childhood growing up with horses and studying their economy of movement...and just growing up outdoors is conducive to loose movement, which is often mistaken for lassitude...).

"He moved like a breeze," sportswriter Grantland Rice said.

There are many who say that Jim Thorpe was so naturally gifted that he carried around a chiseled physique without much attention to diet and exercise and he attained his times and distances the same way. This raised insinuations that Jim failed to attain the true greatness he was blessed to achieve because he was "a typically lazy Indian." The fact that it is next to impossible to carry a slick, supreme body without a strict regimen didn't stop some people from inferring that Jim didn't put much time into training because of problems with alcohol; another native stereotype.

From available reports, it appears that Jim Thorpe liked to drink and party, but anybody who constantly drinks to excess, and is hungover much of the time, would have difficulty maintaing the kind of low body fat-to-muscle ratio which is apparent from photos of 24-year-old Jim Thorpe (and facts—Thorpe's measurements at the time were a ripped 185 pounds with a 42-inch chest, 32-inch waist and 24-inch thighs).

The problem is that available reports, research and news coverage from 1912 are contradictory and rife with rumours and innuendo and native stereotypes. Jim might be seen drinking, and since nobody ever seemed to see him training, the image of drunken Indian spread.

But here's the thing. Nobody really likes training. But pretty much everybody loves playing the games. Jim was good at 22 different sports, so he was almost always busy competing at one thing or another and this was, in some ways, even better than training all the time. Oh sure, he may not have spent time ironing out the nuances in his broad jump but the cross-training he received from other sports may have offered benefits that were just as effective. And these just weren't the days of specialists and scientifically proven biorhythmicisometricaerobicsynthesis techniques and all that.

Nonetheless, Jim could be his own worst enemy because he often just got tired of what other people thought so consequences be damned. Like one time when a group of athletes were hanging around a hotel lobby, trying to jump up and touch a chandelier that was hanging from the ceiling just out of the reach of their best efforts. Supposedly, Jim staggered in, loaded to the gills, and bet every man $20 he could reach the chandelier. Jim then proceeded to tap the top of the two-foot long crystal tapestry, walking away (in street shoes, natch) tucking a wad of twenties into the vest pocket of the suit he was wearing at the time.

Incidents like this happen because men in their twenties are full of bravado and sometimes booze. But it is hard to separate fact from fiction because native people were subject to so much stereotyping and racism. When the tales go so far as to claim that Thorpe was drunk every day on the boat over to Sweden, refusing to train with the other American athletes, and making a general fool of himself, without proof, it starts to get ludicrous and dangerous, compromising the image of Mr. Thorpe and Native Americans in general. Especially when such stories are only supported by verbal claims (i.e., gossip, rumours and innuendo).

There is concrete evidence that Thorpe actually led the training programs on the ship (which makes sense because he had no experience with most of the events in the pentathlon and decathlon and he wanted/needed to learn/practice). And there is an actual photograph of Thorpe leading the team in a run around the deck.

Besides, wouldn't the u.s. Olympic officials accompanying the team step in and discipline negative behaviour such as drinking and partying and sloth? Star or not, nobody could get away with the kind of behaviour that certain people accused Jim of. Those certain people have shown that they can't believe an indigenous person like Jim could achieve such great heights and accomplish such great things, certain other people were jealous and figured the only way to elevate themselves was by dragging a man like Thorpe down to their level, and certain more other people are simply ignorant racists.

And that is all I am going to say about Jim and alcohol.

Thorpe stole the show in Sweden, finishing first in six of the ten events of the decathlon and dominating the pentathlon just as much.

The feats Jim accomplished are even more remarkable when you consider how unfamiliar he actually was with some of the things he was required to do. For example, the first time he threw the javelin, he had this funny little hop to the side. That's because Thorpe didn't know you could run up to the line before throwing and his first attempt, which covered a comparable distance with the best of the rest, was from basically a standing position. When he was allowed to run and throw, he cleared the rest of the field with ease.

And keep in mind that Thorpe didn't have the decathlon title won until the final event, the 1,500-metre run. The field was tight and Jim needed to win that race, which he did, in those "borrowed" shoes.

After all Jim Thorpe had been through, he summed up his performance this way: "I may have had an aversion for work, but I also had an aversion to getting beat," he said.

And that explains the lack of time Jim put into training.

Thorpe had an ulterior motive for being successful in Stockholm. He wanted to marry his sweetheart back home but her family disapproved of the match and Jim was out to prove that a man could make a living good enough to support a wife through sports.

Point proved. Jim Thorpe and Iva Miller, a girl he met at Carlisle, married in 1913.

And since King Gustav had addressed him as "Sir," Jim said that made him a Lord and therefore, Iva was a Lady.

Thorpe was feted as a hero when he returned from Sweden, including a ticker tape parade in New York. One media report claimed Jim was amazed that one man could have so many "friends" (because so many people in the crowd were calling him by his name) but that sounds like a stretch from a reporter going for the hick angle, or a primitive Indian stereotype.

More important to Thorpe was the fact that now that he had accomplished the most anybody ever could in track and field, he was free to concentrate on his favourite sport, and that was football.

Thorpe's introduction to the gridiron was similar to the first time he tried track. Coach Warner had kept his prized runner under wraps despite repeated requests by Thorpe himself to try running with a ball tucked under his arm. Finally, one day, while strolling past the football field, Warner relented. After all, Thorpe was dressed in (you guessed it) street shoes and casual clothes.

And, you guessed it, Thorpe proceeded to run through all 11 defenders on the field, zig-zagging back and forth to make sure he allowed every single one of the players to have their shot at bringing him down. And in case that wasn't enough to keep up appearances with Paul Bunyan, *"ol' Jimmay Thawp… wudn't ya know it, he done do da exack sam ting agin… leevi' dem po' boys clutchin' at nuttin' bud ayah!"*

"Nobody is going to tackle Jim Thorpe," Jim said to Pop, as he flipped the football back to the stunned group of players strewn across the field.

The accomplishments of Jim Thorpe in college and professional football are well-known and readily available in the library or on the internet, so I will just list the more notable ones.

We need to keep in mind that Carlisle was an all-Indian school, which either provided them with the kind of advantage the Montreal Canadiens used to enjoy when they reaped the rewards of most of the best French-Canadian hockey players, or they were handicapped by being restricted to the talent available from one ethnic group.

And we have to remember that the times were different back in the early 20th century. A school like Carlisle could join in the top level of NCAA competition. Times were so different that Ivy league teams like Harvard and Brown were considered bona fide football powers! The Army-Navy game was a national obsession for more than just two branches of the American military, as it mostly is now.

So it was no small feat when Jim scored all of his team's points to beat Harvard 18-15 in 1911 (Thorpe carried the ball nine straight times for 70 yards for one touchdown, and kicked four field goals, all from greater than 40 yards away, to account for all of the Carlisle scoring). Harvard had been undefeated for a year and a half prior to the game against Carlisle.

People who feel that modern-day college athletes are being exploited because sports like NCAA football are such a huge business with massive revenues which fuel the college administration while maintaining the students as unpaid serfs, will find it interesting to note that Carlisle and Pop Warner received $10,000 each from the revenues generated from the Harvard game, which was a fortune during that time. For all the thrills he provided, Jim Thorpe got nada.

But those thrills just kept multiplying. Like when Thorpe had a 92-yard run for a touchdown called back because of a penalty in Carlisle's 27-6 victory over Army. Thorpe let the referees tack on the 5 yards for the infraction, and then proceeded to rush the ball 97 yards for the touchdown on the very next play. Penn State, Penn, Princeton, Syracuse, all the football powers of the day fell to Thorpe and the Carlisle Indian School team, which captured the national championship in 1912 propelled by Jim Thorpe's 25 touchdowns and 198 points!

Thorpe could run with speed as well as power, he could pass and catch passes with the best, punt for long distances, and kick field goals either by drop-kicking or by placekicking. He showcased this latter talent by preserving a win late in a game by hoofing a punt 95 yards from his own 5-yard line, pinning the opposition down with too far to go and not enough time left to get there.

At halftime during some games, Jim Thorpe would entertain the crowd by drop-kicking field goals starting from the 35-yard line and backing up 5 yards at a time until he reached centre field or the 50-yard line, where he would kick field goals in both directions. Thorpe would repeat the feat on a return to Carlisle in 1941 at 52 years of age, wearing street shoes, of course.

Opponents raved. Crowds went wild and crazy every time.

"He blocked you with his shoulder and it felt like he hit you with 4 x 4," said Jim Wood of the Rochester Jeffersons.

Former president Dwight D. Eisenhower played against Thorpe when Eisenhower was in college at West Point. The future U.S. president was told to "Stop the Indian" by his superiors in the Army.

"I couldn't do it," said President Eisenhower. "As one who played against him more than 40 years ago, I personally feel no other athlete possessed his all-around abilities in games and sports."

Some made something much bigger out of the Carlisle Indian School's victory over West Point Academy because the United States was not too far removed from the so-called "Indian Wars" (the last major armed conflict had taken place at Wounded Knee in 1890, just a couple of decades earlier). Many Indians carried a strong sense of their warrior spirit deep within their hearts and minds, and despite being a vanquished people, they had never given up their sovereignty as nations who made independent treaties with the new country which had developed around them.

Even "Pop" Warner noticed.

"the Indians had a real race pride and a fierce determination," Warner observed. "They believed the armed contests between red man and white had never been waged on equal terms."

In college football, the field was level and the Indians were playing against many of the sons and grandsons of U.S. troops like those that formed the infamous 7th Cavalry under George Armstrong Custer; the controversial Army General who massacred mostly women and children at Washita River before meeting his destiny at the Little Big Horn.

The Indians won both battles.

For his exploits in 1912 and 1913, Thorpe was naturally voted All-American. And because he was such a natural, he rarely practiced, again, not because he was too lazy or partying too much, but because he rarely had time. As we now know, Thorpe was a master at 22 sports in all, including figure skating, billiards and ballroom dancing. Despite winning a national championship in the fox trot, cha cha and the tango, Thorpe preferred football over all other sports, and that is the main reason why he was so much better at it than anybody else.

Thorpe practiced track and field even less. But it was in the Olympic sports where Thorpe gained the most.

And also lost the most.

The rules for amateur status were much different back in Thorpe's day. And the rules for eligibility for the Olympics were strictly (and incredibly unfairly) enforced.

Athletes who received pay for competing in any sport were declared "professionals" and ineligible for the Olympic Games. This restricted the competition to the rich and the elite, who could afford the time off to train. Or to athletes from countries which provided support for their athletes to live in comfort and style while they practiced their skills (Canadians became familiar with this when the Soviet Union played its "Red Army" hockey team against Canadian amateurs during the 1950s, 60s and 70s. The Russian soldiers were paid a salary to practice 11 months of the year while Canadian and American teams tried to fit hockey in with their college schedules. That, or Canada and the U.S. sent part-time, amateur "Senior" league teams to try and compete against the Soviets, who were professional in all but name.

Most of the athletes who represented the United States were college kids, whose room and board were paid out of their tuitions and scholarships. This made Jim Thorpe eligible for the 1912 Olympic Games.

Students could take summer jobs but not any that involved pay for play in any sport. Unfortunately, Jim wasn't aware of this when he played a little bit of what was called semi-professional baseball in North Carolina during the summers of 1909 and 1910.

He was paid badly needed "getting around" money, but Roy Ruggles Johnson, a reporter from the Worcester *Telegram* who was "just doing his job," uncovered the "violation of the rules of the Olympiad" and, without any thought of consequences or fairness, reported the news that would cost Jim Thorpe his gold medals and some of his reputation for a while.

Johnson's story announcing that Thorpe had played "professional baseball" prior to the Olympics was picked up by other U.S. newspapers and the details became well and widely known. Thorpe had indeed played professional baseball in the Eastern Carolina League for Rocky Mount, North Carolina, receiving meagre pay; reportedly as little as two bucks a game and as much as $35 per week. Other college players, in fact, regularly spent summers playing professionally but most used aliases, but not Thorpe, perhaps due to ignorance, naivety or simple honesty.

Johnson never tried to grab his "15 minutes of fame" out of the incident, and the real story would become how the powers-that-be broke their own rules in their blind dash to punish the American Indian star. Even though the public didn't seem to care much about Thorpe's past, the Amateur Athletic Union (AAU), and especially its secretary, James Edward Sullivan, took the case very seriously.

In 1912, strict rules regarding amateurism prohibited athletes who "received money prizes for competitions, were sports teachers or had competed previously against professionals" from participating in the Olympics. Any such athlete was not considered an amateur and was barred from competition.

Most thinking people knew damn well that playing some baseball games had nothing to do with how well Thorpe had outclassed the field in the decathlon. Thorpe didn't argue that point, but he believed he could help his cause by writing a letter to Sullivan, in which he admitted playing professional baseball, but asked for some empathy and understanding:

I hope I will be partly excused by the fact that I was simply an Indian schoolboy and did not know all about such things. In fact, I did not know that I was doing wrong, because I was doing what I knew several other college men had done, except that they did not use their own names...

Thorpe's letter didn't help. On the contrary, it was the worst thing he could do.

While he may have thought he was endearing himself to the IOC by referring to himself as "an Indian schoolboy" who was innocent because of his naivety, he was actually reinforcing his "place" with a category of people who the Olympic organizers just didn't want playing in their Games at the time. The International Olympic Committee was an elitist organization and its rules of eligibility were intended to restrict the Games competition to upper-class white people as much as anything else.

Sadly, this was the way it was in the early 1900s. So much power was concentrated with those who were rich or privileged, the snobs of the day couldn't even see what was wrong with actually putting down in writing "Indians and labourers are excluded from competition" (as it was written in the rule book of the Canadian Amateur Athletic Association at the time). Attitudes like this were more than enough to exclude "an Indian schoolboy" from the Olympic Games, let alone the fact he was paid two bucks a game for playing "professional baseball."

And so the AAU decided to withdraw Thorpe's amateur status retroactively and asked the IOC to do the same. Later that year, the IOC unanimously decided to strip Thorpe of his Olympic titles, medals and awards and declared him a professional.

Even though Thorpe had indeed played for money, the AAU and IOC didn't even follow their own rules for disqualification. The rulebook for the 1912 Olympics stated that protests had to be made within 30 days from the closing ceremonies of the games. The first newspaper reports did not appear until January 1913, about six months after the Stockholm Games had concluded. There is also some evidence that Thorpe's amateur status had been questioned long before the Olympics, but the AAU had ignored the issue until being confronted with it in 1913. In other words, nobody cared until Thorpe rose up and beat the world's best (and favoured) "amateurs".

They say revenge is a meal best served cold and in time, the reputation of the mean-spirited fools, even cowards, who ran the IOC would suffer the most in the historical record, which is the ultimate and permanent judge of character. Thorpe's good name was eventually restored and his legacy lives on.

Several years later, in 1951, when Johnson was introduced to Thorpe at a dinner, the reporter, who had gone on to edit the news with his same strict adherence to the basic rules of journalism at the *Boston Globe*, let Thorpe know he considered him the greatest athlete in the world. Thorpe let Johnson know that he understood the reporter was only doing his job.

The only positive element of this whole affair for Thorpe at the time was that, as soon as the news was reported that he had been declared a professional, he received numerous offers from professional football and baseball teams. Thorpe would become a crossover star long before Bo Jackson and Deion Sanders, and attracting "Breakfast of Champions" endorsements like decathlete Bruce Jenner received (although Thorpe's breakfast would more likely have been chased down on the heel of those hounds and consist of squirrel stew and gravy instead of grown in a field like traditional Wheaties).

Thorpe's career also included top-level performances in lacrosse, boxing, rough-and-tumble, hockey, archery, rifle shooting, canoeing, handball, swimming, skating and ballroom dancing (he won the U.S. Intercollegiate pairs competition in 1912). He was good, and tough, and no matter what sport he played, he rarely had to leave the field of play because of an injury throughout his long and varied career.

But we will focus on the major sports.

Thorpe continued to dabble in track and field after his victories at the Olympic Games. He broke the record for the decathlon later in 1912, formerly held by Martin Sheridan. Sheridan, a five-time Olympic gold medalist, was present to watch his record broken. He approached

Thorpe after the event, shook his hand and said, "Jim, my boy, you're a great man. I never expect to look upon a finer athlete." Sheridan told a reporter from the *New York World*, "Thorpe is the greatest athlete that ever lived. He has me beaten fifty ways. Even when I was in my prime, I could not do what he did today."

Thorpe followed up his college football career with an outstanding decade in professional football. But this was a time when pro ball was fledgling and attendance at professional games dwarfed in comparison with long-established college rivalries which had faithful followings.

Thorpe first played professional football in 1913 as a member of the Indiana-based Pine Village Pros team which had a several-season winning streak against local teams during the 1910s. He then signed with the Canton Bulldogs in 1915. They paid him $250 ($5,769 today) a game, a tremendous wage at the time. Before signing Thorpe, Canton was averaging 1,200 fans a game, but 8,000 showed up for his debut against the Massillon Tigers. The team won titles in 1916, 1917, and 1919. He ended the 1919 championship game by kicking that wind-assisted 95-yard punt from his team's own 5-yard line, effectively putting the game out of reach.

In 1920, the Bulldogs were one of 14 teams to form the American Professional Football Association (APFA), which would become the National Football League (NFL) two years later. Thorpe was nominally the APFA's first president, but spent most of the year playing for Canton and a year later was replaced as president by Joseph Carr. He continued to play for Canton, coaching the team as well.

And then there was the period between 1921 1923, which just might be the most fascinating, and certainly most intriguing time, in Jim Thorpe's life. It was a time when his Indian background, his sports pedigree, and the complexities and contrasts that were involved in the development of professional football, met up with some good old American-style hucksterism and marketing. And behind the scenes was one of the most colourful and offbeat of the many friends and acquaintances a superstar sports figure like Jim Thorpe would make in the ever-expanding and evolving world of show business.

Wealthy and eccentric businessman Walter Lingo was one of those hangers-on who had sufficient resources to cross paths with sports celebrities, and he had this great idea to form a unique football team. He wanted Jim Thorpe to coach, play for and manage this venture (or adventure, as things turned out). And so, during a hunting trip, which had been arranged between the Indian superstar and the eccentric entrepreneur, the "Oorang Indians," the first, last and only all-Indian football team that ever played professional sports, was born. An all-Indian team that played for two full seasons in the National Football League, the most popular, well-respected and richest sports league in the world today!

The team was hastily assembled from a colourful cast of personalities who had come from all over the country to try out. Big Bear, Napoleon Barrel, Joe Little Twig, Ted Buffalo, War Eagle and Long-time Sleep made up some of the roster. An "all-nations squad," there were Cherokee, Mohawk, Chippewa, Blackfoot, Ho Chunk (Winnebago), Mission, Caddo, Sac and Fox, Seneca and Penobscot nations all represented on this barnstorming (but all within one league) team.

Unfortunately, many of the Indian players spent as much time living life in the fast lane as running fast on a football field.

"White people had this misconception about Indians. They thought that we were all wild men, even though almost all of us had been to college and were generally more civilized than they were. Well, it was a dandy excuse to raise hell and get away with it when the mood struck us. Since we were Indians we could get away with things the whites couldn't. And don't think we didn't take advantage of it," said Leon Boutwell, Oorang's quarterback.

By their record, the Oorang Indians were not a very good team. In two full seasons, 1922 and 1923, they didn't score a touchdown in more than half their games despite the presence of two future football Hall of Famers, several All-Americans and the greatest athlete in the world in their lineup (which gives us a pretty good idea of how much they cared and how much effort they made to compete). The Thorpe-led Oorang Indians only managed a handful of victories, missing out on the kind of opportunity the Carlisle Indians took advantage of to gain some measure of revenge for Indian nations against the Army at

West Point. The Oorang Indians were relegated to a quirky footnote in NFL history after only two seasons.

The team was, however, a cultural touchstone that matched the times they were in. The Oorang Indians fit right in with the spirit that was the "roaring twenties."

Ultimately, their dismal record in the face of enormous potential didn't turn out to be the main talking point of the Oorang Indians. It's not even the unique achievement of coming into existence as an all-Indian team that keeps tongues wagging about this obscure phenomenon. It is the how and why behind the real reason the all-Indian Oorang football team came to be created that is the stuff of bizarre legend.

You see, Lingo had an obsession with breeding and selling Airedale Retrievers. He declared his prize Airedale dog named King Oorang "the greatest utility dog in the history of the world." Walter also happened to love Native American culture because of romantic tales he heard around the campfire during his childhood.

Lingo believed that a supernatural bond existed between Indians and Airedales. So when Lingo got together with Thorpe on that hunting trip, the two came up with the scheme to create an all-Indian football team, but the primary purpose was not to showcase Indian talent, and neither was success on the scoreboard really necessary. The primary goal was, wait for it, to travel the country and promote Airedale Retrievers!

And so a team that was based in LaRue, Ohio, a town of less than 1,000 population, was born. Lingo bought an NFL franchise for an astonishing $100, less than the cost of one of his Airedales. The average value of an NFL franchise today is $1.2 billion.

Thorpe, who was always open to ideas to cash in on his celebrity, agreed to run the football operation and manage the kennels. Thorpe would use his massive celebrity to attract sports fans where they would not only see a football game but be exposed to half time entertainment showcasing the dogs. And based on the team's on-field record, it was obvious what the priority was. Lingo was merely using the Oorang Indians as an advertising vehicle for his business of breeding Airedale Retrievers.

Thorpe must have been aware of the potential harm the team could do to the image of Native Americans, but what harm can there be in fielding a team of all Indians who would at least be competitive with hand-picked teams of professionals? And Thorpe was entrepreneur enough himself to laugh all the way to the bank by collecting a salary of $500 per week, a small fortune at the time.

It was their half-time entertainment that made the Oorang Indians such a huge attraction anyways. There were shooting demonstrations by team members with the dogs retrieving the targets. There were ceremonial dances and tomahawk and knife-throwing demonstrations. Thorpe drop-kicked footballs through the uprights from midfield. Long Time Sleep even wrestled a bear on occasion. Those aren't bad images for Indians. Or Airedales (but for the fact that so-called "Oorang Airedales," which are supposed to be a larger breed of the dog, have been criticized as genetically defective due to inbreeding, which certainly fits with the kind of logic that the illogical Lingo might adopt).

Although the Oorang team's record was 3–6 in 1922, and 1–10 in 1923, Thorpe played well and was selected for the *Green Bay Press-Gazette*'s first All-NFL team in 1923, which would later be formally recognized by the NFL as the league's official All-NFL team in 1931.

But Thorpe never played for an NFL championship team. He retired from professional football at age 41, having played 52 NFL games for six teams from 1920 to 1928.

There is no doubt that Thorpe's greatest fame was achieved in track, his greatest achievements were split between track and football, and his absolutely favourite sport was football.

But it was baseball where most of the action and attention was focused during the 1910s and 20s.

Baseball was all the rage in the early 20th century as the sport truly became "America's favourite pastime." Thorpe had dabbled in baseball in high school and college, and played in those summer leagues, but most players who truly excel in baseball play the sport almost exclusively, developing their skills through childhood followed by college or long stints in the minor leagues. Thorpe was good, but certainly not as dominant as he was in track and football, mostly because he hadn't spent much time playing ball. But Thorpe had to wait while professional football incubated and grew, so the first professional team sport he tried his hand at was major league baseball.

Thorpe's professional career began when he signed with the New York Giants in 1913. He played sporadically with them as an outfielder for three seasons. But after missing a call from tough gruff manager John J. McGraw, and being called a "dumb Indian," Jim picked up the baseball icon whom everybody else feared and just about shook all the tough out of him. After playing in the minor leagues with the Milwaukee Brewers in 1916, he returned to the Giants in 1917 but was sold to the Cincinnati Reds early in the season.

Certainly those are not "Thorpe-like" achievements. You could say that baseball simply wasn't Jim's game but he was also very busy being vastly superior in those other sports like football and track and field, and those other sports which made up that total of 22 in all that he was proficient in. Like, Thorpe regularly golf scores in the 70s and that was from "squeezing in a game" whenever he could.

And we must keep in mind that just playing in the major leagues was a major, major achievement! Almost every young boy in the United States dreamed of becoming a major league baseball player during the early 1900s, yet so many of the best little league and PONY players never made it past the minor leagues during the glory days of Babe Ruth. Yet Jim Thorpe was able to compete with such men at the top level during baseball's glorious beginnings.

But the numbers indicate that baseball managed to bring Jim down to the level of mortal men and made him appear rather normal for once. Some people noted that baseball is full of prospects and players whose careers were compromised by that old, but all too common bugaboo; they couldn't hit the curve ball. And neither could Jim Thorpe, or so they said. It is worthy of note that Thorpe's batting average was .327 during his last major league season with Boston. Considering the man's abilities and track record, it could be he was just on his way to mastering the curve.

Bottom line, Thorpe had little time to practice pitching and batting and catching and throwing because a) he was too busy participating in all those other sports and b) Jim just didn't like to practice.

But, naturally it seems by now, Thorpe's most notable achievement in baseball would be those things that get talked about around the water cooler, and then the lunch counter, and then the diner, for decades down the road.

It was a classic pitcher's duel between James Lesley "Hippo" Vaughn of the Cincinnati Reds and the Chicago Cubs' Fred Toney in 1918. Both of these fireballers had their best stuff going and they had that rarest of rareties going; a double no-hitter. With runs so absent, onlookers just knew it would take a single score to end this game, and it would take a special athlete to rise to the occasion.

You guessed it. It was Jim Thorpe who drove in the winning run in the 10th inning to break the 0-0 tie.

Tip O'Neill, Speaker of the House of Representatives, relates the tale of how his dad took him to his first professional ball game in the Old Polo Grounds in New York.

"Jim was at bat and the third base coach put on the bunt sign," O'Neill recalls. "Thorpe squared around into his bunting stance and then, through the corner of his eye, he saw the third baseman rushing in. Jim just pulled the bat back and with his hands still spread two feet apart for that bunt, whacked a line drive into left field."

In his major league baseball career, Jim Thorpe amassed 91 runs scored, 82 runs batted in and a .252 batting average over 289 games.

In the major leagues!

Most folks were unaware that Jim Thorpe also had a career of note in basketball but by 1926, Jim Thorpe was the main feature of the "World Famous Indians" of LaRue, which sponsored travelling football, baseball and basketball teams. "Jim Thorpe and His World-Famous Indians" barnstormed for at least two years (1927–28) in parts of New York and Pennsylvania, as well as Marion, Ohio. Although pictures of Thorpe in his WFI basketball uniform were printed on postcards and published in newspapers, this period of his life was not well documented. They weren't the Harlem Globetrotters, but these bronze-skinned representatives of the First Nations of North America "put on a great show wherever they go," according to promotional materials.

———————————

While Thorpe was involved in a career in sports that was overloaded to say the least, he did have a personal life, even though maintaining any sense of family with all of the travel and obligations a 5-sport, 5-star athlete had to endure certainly doesn't leave much time to raise a family in the traditional sense. Whenever he was around, however, he was considered a good father who passed on positive qualities that his children cherished and carried through to future generations. Thorpe married three times and had eight children (seven of whom survived to adulthood).

In 1913, following the Olympic Games, Thorpe married Iva Miller, his love from his days at Carlisle. They had four children: Jim Jr. died at age two, and the loss was especially hard on Jim, who absolutely doted on his first heir, when he was able to be around. Jim's constant travel was especially hard on Iva. The couple would have three more children, Gale, Charlotte and Grace, but Miller filed for divorce from Thorpe in 1925, claiming desertion.

In 1926 Thorpe married Freeda V. Kirkpatrick (September 19, 1905 – March 2, 2007). She was working for the manager of the baseball team for which he was playing at the time. They had four sons: Carl, a lieutenant colonel in the U.S. Army, William, Richard and John ("Jack"). Kirkpatrick divorced Thorpe in 1941 after 15 years of marriage.

Jim's last wife was Patricia (Gladys Askew), who would play just as prominent a role in his death as in his life.

Thorpe always struggled to provide for his family after his athletic career ended. He found it difficult to work at a non-sports-related occupation and various jobs, like working as a construction worker, a bouncer (doorman), a security guard and a ditch digger led nowhere. Although past the age for acceptance by the Army or Navy in World War II, Thorpe joined the merchant marine in 1945 and served on an ammunition ship before the war ended.

Life insurance salesmen and teachers can have long careers and then retire gracefully but that is not so for athletes. Thorpe struggled after his body inevitably gave out and he couldn't perform at a level that provided him with a living (still, he managed to pull off that field goal feat from the 35-yard line to the 50 and then boot both ways until the age of 58). His efforts as an Indian activist and lecturer met with limited success. He spoke passionately and eloquently for stolen lands to be returned to rightful tribal owners and for Native Americans to be given their fair share of revenues from resources taken from Indian lands. His very presence and story were an inspiration, providing motivation for all Native Americans to aspire to greater physical and mental perfection and safeguarding their health.

It must be noted that Jim's notoriety provided him with numerous opportunities to cash in on his fame but most of the books and films that were made about him only provided him with what might be called a fair shake. Jim Thorpe didn't have the business acumen and/or that sense of promotion and PR to exploit his own career like many others have been able to do.

The most well-known film about Thorpe is the 1951 Warner Brothers biographical drama *Jim Thorpe—All American*, starring Burt Lancaster. Although there were rumours that Thorpe received no money, he was paid $15,000 by Warner Bros. plus a $2,500 donation toward an annuity for him by the studio head of publicity, which is pretty good money in today's values.

Burt Lancaster was very gracious about the honour of playing Jim Thorpe, and always spoke of "the man" with the highest regard. An interview with Lancaster that was conducted by historian Robert Wheeler provides the best rationale for disputing the disparaging stories about Jim's problems with alcohol. Lancaster, a model of physical fitness, explains how impossible it would be to maintain a physique like Jim's without constant training and staying away from time-wasting body destroyers like alcohol. Burt should know, he had to look like the superman Thorpe on screen.

In the 1930s, Thorpe himself appeared in several short films and features. Usually, his roles were cameo appearances as an Indian, although in the 1932 comedy, *Always Kickin'*, Thorpe was prominently cast in a speaking part as himself, a kicking coach teaching young football players to drop-kick.

The tragedy that is a fading athlete and a forgotten people is dramatically illustrated in one film where Jim plays an Indian in a headdress who sells some furs to a little white man who isn't happy with the amount of the payment. The little white guy knocks Thorpe down with a single punch and when the Indian gets up, he is shot and killed by another cowboy. Neither of the white characters shows any remorse or even notice for that matter.

The light that was "Bright Path" (Wa Ho Huk) would go out at the age of 65 while living in a trailer park in Lometa, California. His third wife, Pat, disputes reports they were living in poverty, claiming the trailer provided the mobility Thorpe needed.

Perhaps the greatest controversy of this great man's legacy has come after his death.

Jim Thorpe was such a legendary figure that only his life could be a four-act play.

Birth, Life, Death and Afterlife. Because Thorpe's death set off the strangest sequence of events anywhere, anytime (Walt Disney and Ted Williams got nothing on what you are about to read!).

To put it mildly, Thorpe's death, but mostly the commemoration of his remains, has created an in-house Hatfield-McCoy feud which has lasted over 60 years. The situation is very complicated, and I do not want to take sides in the matter, so I have cobbled together this summary from available research, including video presentations from the Thorpe family on YouTube, which is as objective a version as I can provide.

Memorial services had begun in a traditional Native American way. Immediately after Jim died, his children held a traditional Indian burial ceremony on the Sac and Fox Reservation in Oklahoma. Mourners shared a meal as the great athlete's body lay in full view inside a lodge.

But the scheduled three-day ceremony came to an abrupt halt when Thorpe's widow, Pat, barged in. Accompanied by state troopers and a funeral hearse, she seized the body and drove away.

———————

It was widow Pat who had first transported her dead husband's body to his native Oklahoma for internment. But it was also Pat who suddenly barged in with the cops, declared that Thorpe's body was "too cold," and had him carted away in a hearse.

Pat had frequently clashed with her seven Native American stepchildren, and wanted to make certain that her husband received what she considered a proper and fitting memorial. She also believed she should be financially compensated for providing the famed athlete's body for interment. But Oklahoma governor Johnston Murray broke a promise to Thorpe's Sac and Fox relatives and Pat not to veto state funding for a proposed memorial, and the $25,000 he had promised fell through.

So Pat started to look elsewhere to bury her husband. Thorpe's body criss-crossed Oklahoma to six different locations as his widow sought what she believed would be a suitable burial place.

As things turned out, related matters took Pat to Philadelphia to visit the National Football League offices in September 1953, where she saw a television report about two neighbouring Pennsylvania towns—Mauch Chunk and East Mauch Chunk, that were contemplating a merger and seeking a new venture to spark a badly needed economic revival. Something clicked, and the next thing you knew the widow Pat was making a proposal to the two towns. They could have her dead husband's bones if they rebranded themselves with his name and built a suitable shrine.

Envisioning the presence of the century's greatest athlete as a tourist draw, the towns, which had no prior connection to Thorpe, agreed. On February 8, 1954, nearly a year after Thorpe's death, bells pealed, schoolchildren lined the streets, and businesses closed down for the day as the great, but late, Jim Thorpe arrived in the town of East Mauch

Chunk for the very first time. He was placed in a crypt until a tomb could be erected.

And thus, the town of Jim Thorpe, Pennsylvania began to appear on our maps. The new community of 6,000 people built a memorial park that includes a pair of statues, historical markers, and an above-ground red marble tomb, which depicts various scenes from his athletic career and is emblazoned with the quote from King Gustav. The casket rests on soil that includes dirt from Stockholm's Olympic Stadium, as well as from Oklahoma.

Although Thorpe's three daughters eventually made peace with his Pennsylvania burial, Thorpe's sons, all in their 20s at the time of his death, weren't happy with the arrangement. In 1953, shortly after Pat had gained control of Thorpe's body, the sons had asked Governor Murray to prevent its removal from the state, but Murray refused to intercede, setting off a family battle that would last more than 60 years.

In 2010, Thorpe's son Jack filed a federal lawsuit seeking to return his father's body to his native Oklahoma and re-inter the athlete's remains a mile away from his birthplace and near those of his father, sisters, and brother, on Sac and Fox land. He argued the agreement between his stepmother and the borough of Jim Thorpe was contrary to the wishes of other family members. After Jack's death in 2011, the lawsuit continued to be pressed by Thorpe's other two surviving sons, William and Richard, although a number of Thorpe's grandchildren have expressed their desire for their grandfather to rest in peace in the Pennsylvania foothills.

In April 2013, a federal judge ruled in the sons' favour. The town of Jim Thorpe, Pennsylvania, filed an appeal, and a final resolution of the case could take years.

Meanwhile, the annual graveside celebration of the superstar's birthday has taken on a bittersweet tone as the town of Jim Thorpe, Pennsylvania, contemplates life without Jim Thorpe.

Some of the townsfolk have adopted a defensive crouch.

"People in this town are determined to keep our memorial, and keep the body here," said Jim Thorpe's mayor, Michael Sofranko. "We've done nothing wrong. We've done nothing but honour Jim Thorpe all these years."

James Francis Thorpe is buried in his favourite white buckskin jacket along with a rosary. The memorial overlooks a grassy slope featuring statues saluting his varied athletic career. Tributes are inscribed on the monuments and mausoleum, including that famous comment to Thorpe from King Gustav V of Sweden at the medal ceremony: "Sir, you are the world's greatest athlete." (But not Thorpe's reply, "Thanks, King.")

At Anne Marie Fitzpatrick's gift shop downtown, a sign on a glass jar stuffed with cash read "Keep Jim Thorpe In Jim Thorpe." Fitzpatrick set up several donation jars around town to raise money for the legal appeal. Interesting to note that prior to becoming Jim Thorpe, PA, the towns used to put out jars asking for a nickel a week from each citizen to spur a badly needed economic revival at the time.

Fitzpatrick was in grade school when Mauch Chunk and East Mauch Chunk merged in 1954 to form Jim Thorpe, PA. For years, she helped organize an annual Jim Thorpe birthday ceremony in May at the memorial. Events included an Olympic torch run by local high school athletes, known as the Olympians.

"He's been here over 50 years, and we're not about to give him up," Fitzpatrick said as she stood sentinel over the jar next to the cash register.

Then there was the Jim Thorpe, PA civic official who complained about the deal saying, "All we got was a dead Indian."

The Thorpe family is divided on the matter.

It is difficult for outsiders to comprehend the adoration for Thorpe from townspeople whose only connection to him is his name (and the fact the Carlisle Indian School is also located in Pennsylvania). Residents and private groups have raised money over the years, with a small contribution from the borough council, to erect a $60,000 statue of Thorpe throwing a discus and a $50,000 one of him running with a football. Fundraising is underway to add a baseball statue.

"The town was built around my grandpa—people revere him," said John Thorpe, 56, who lives in South Lake Tahoe, California. He has joined with another Thorpe grandson to fight their uncles and their tribe in an effort to keep Jim Thorpe in Jim Thorpe. Mike Koehler, 75, another descendant, has said the town honoured his grandfather's legacy. "For God's sakes, leave him alone," he said.

John Thorpe and Koehler have travelled to the town of Jim Thorpe, PA for years to take part in Jim Thorpe celebrations. They point out that Oklahoma could have kept Thorpe in 1953 but passed on the chance.

But some members of the family persist in their fight to have Jim's remains return home to Sac and Fox territory for a proper traditional burial, and they make a valid argument point, as well. Indigenous people throughout the world have been exploited, their sacred artifacts have been stolen, and both have been put on display in museums and galleries (the extreme example might be Truganini, the last of the aboriginal people of Tasmania, whose remains were placed on display; a human being!).

And, of course, there are the profits to be made from souvenirs and trinkets of Jim Thorpe's likeness.

Some of Thorpe's surviving children insist that "Without a complete Indian burial ceremony, their father's spirit is a restless traveller from one dimension to another, at home in none of them."

And they are supported by noted and highly respected historian Robert Wheeler.

Grandson John Thorpe offers this: "The town has done nothing but honour and respect and love my grandpa. The state of Oklahoma did not want to erect a mausoleum or do anything to honour him. They weren't willing to do what the town of Jim Thorpe did."

John speaks of taking part in a sacred sweat lodge ceremony in Texas where a medicine man told him that his grandfather had made contact saying, "I am at peace and I want no more pain created in my name."

Nothing but truth can be spoken in a sweat lodge.

I hope they can sort things out.

Jim Thorpe deserves nothing but the best, just as he was.

One final thing.

Over the years, Thorpe's supporters attempted to have his Olympic titles and gold medals returned and his status reinstated, but IOC head honcho Avery Brundage rebuffed several attempts, once saying, "Ignorance is no excuse." Brundage was a well-known supporter of Adolf Hitler, who celebrated and encouraged the Nazi salute at the 1936 Olympic Games in Berlin.

In 1982, author Robert Wheeler and his wife, Forence Ridlon, established the Jim Thorpe Foundation. Armed with support from the U.S. Congress and evidence from 1912 proving that Thorpe's disqualification had occurred after the 30-day time period allowed by Olympics rules, they succeeded in making the case for reinstatement to the IOC. In October 1982, the IOC Executive Committee approved Thorpe's reinstatement. In an unusual ruling, they declared that Thorpe was a co-champion even though all the other athletes have always said they considered Thorpe to be the only champion. In a ceremony on January 18, 1983, the IOC presented two of Thorpe's children, Gale and Bill, with commemorative medals. Thorpe's original medals had been held in museums, but they were stolen and have never been recovered.

Thorpe's family maintains that Thorpe wouldn't care all that much for the medals and the lines in the records books or any of the other material things that simply acknowledge what he already knows, and what everybody else knows, and that is what he achieved in 1912.

And that should be the bottom line.

Jim Thorpe out ran, out-jumped, out-threw and out did pretty much everybody at everything at those Olympic Games and we all know it. Taking away the medals was unfair and childish and it only reflects badly on the Olympic organizers and the other people who controlled athletic competition at the time. We all know the truth and that's good enough for Jim and it's good enough for us.

But it's still nice to set the official record straight and a tremendous amount of gratitude and appreciation should be extended to the folks who went up against those small-minded, selfish idiot elitists and exposed them for what they are, and revealed Jim for what he was.

"A gentle person, intelligent and funny, with many flaws. Jim Thorpe was not a complicated man. But what happened to him was."—KATHY BUFORD, AUTHOR, *NATIVE AMERICAN SON*

Jim Thorpe made his own unique stamp on the world of sports (and the U.S. government issued a stamp commemorating Thorpe). He is in every notable Hall of Fame that football and track and field have ever built and the NCAA honours the top defensive back in the country every year with the Jim Thorpe Award. An over-sized statue of Thorpe greets visitors at the Pro Football Hall of Fame in Canton. He is constantly referred to as Jim Thorpe, All-American.

Ol' King Gus got it right: "You Sir, are the greatest athlete in the world!"

Ed "Wahoo" McDaniel

2

"Waaahoooooooooo!"

At first glance, Wahoo McDaniel conjures up images of a Hollywood B movie stereotype Indian, complete with headdress, stomping around in time to music from some mysterious orchestra hidden in the hills behind an Indian village.

"Bum…bum bum bum bum!"

In reality, Wahoo McDaniel is one of the most accomplished athletes, Native American or otherwise in professional sports. Wahoo starred in the biggest and most popular sports league in the world for six years, yet he was able to turn his back on the National Football League to pursue an even more lucrative career in the wild and wacky world of professional wrestling. There aren't many people from the 1960s who don't know who Wahoo McDaniel is but there is a lot about this nice, proud man that people don't know.

For one, "nice" is the most appropriate adjective to apply to this huge, aggressive athlete and seemingly fierce Indian warrior.

And wearing that headdress was a most sincere expression of pride in his Indian heritage.

It wasn't always this way.

McDaniel hated being an Indian as a young child.

"How come I always have to be tied up and killed?"

Little Ed tried to say he was white but, despite some German on his grandmother's side, there was no mistaking the brown skin and high cheekbones and that noble, native nose.

There was nobody else like him in the Texas and Oklahoma towns Ed grew up in as the family followed his father, an oil patch welder, to various jobs. It makes things easier if there is somebody like you around to share your experiences and feelings with.

But sometimes, a role model can substitute for any real-life images to emulate. Eventually, Ed "Wahoo" McDaniel would overcome his isolation to become one of North America's most famous and beloved sports heroes. And that's because his father, Hugh McDaniel, was familiar with the greatest athlete in North American history and Hugh used the sterling example of Jim Thorpe to point the way to his son.

By the time Ed McDaniel was growing up, Jim Thorpe had been declared Athlete of the Half-Century by *Time* magazine, so Jim stood atop Knute Rockne and Lou Gehrig and Jesse Owens and even Babe Ruth. Thorpe's achievements in football, track and baseball are well-covered in the first chapter of this book, but one of the by-products of his success was to pass on hope to those who would follow by being a positive role model. And little Ed McDaniel could certainly use a "you can do it, too" from someone who looked like he did.

Hugh McDaniel could see the confusion and frustration his young son was going through and he knew it would take more than just providing an example of some bygone glory to bring the kid out of his funk. Fortunately, Dad knew the secret to Thorpe's success wasn't just the physical.

"The Great Spirit runs with him."

It took some time and teachings, but gradually Little Ed McDaniel stopped wanting to be the Lone Ranger because the Tonto character began to have more appeal. A sense of identity and a spirit is important to a young boy and Eddie embraced his Native American background. He would run with the spirits for the rest of his life.

That didn't stop the misconceptions about "Wahoo" McDaniel, and it was mostly because that name "Wahoo" conjures up images of wild

Indians and war whoops and other stereotypes. Coupled with the fact McDaniel appeared in full headdress and moccasins had people wondering if he wasn't just cashing in on an image or (shudder) stereotype.

But the actual name "Wahoo" had nothing to do with the family's native background.

Hugh McDaniel was widely known for putting up a good fight mano a mano ever since he was a child, and he was also very adept at big game fishing. His prowess with the rod and reel and that "never say die" stamina for battle reminded people of a Wahoo, a fish known for fighting ferociously for its life. Somebody got to calling the old man Big Wahoo and the name stuck.

Little Ed simply took that nickname from his father (dropping the "Big," of course).

And that head dress was a sacred symbol of leadership and lifestyle, culture and history, to Wahoo McDaniel. If just one of the many feathers on that bonnet was harmed in even the slightest way, Ed was known to be moved to tears and he was quick with a sacred ceremony to heal his most precious belonging.

Then he would beat the livin' snot out of whomever had harmed his headdress.

Far from being a comical or misleading stereotype of Native American people, Ed "Wahoo" McDaniel was a proud and positive representative of a people whose culture and spirituality is often misunderstood, misrepresented, maligned and diminished.

But mostly, Wahoo's story is simply one of the most fascinating sports yarns ever spun.

Ed McDaniel was born in Bernice, Oklahoma on June 19, 1938. His father was an oil patch welder and so the family followed the "Texas tea" to Midland, Texas when Ed was 11. It was a humble beginning, made harder for the part-Chickasaw, part-Chocktaw child because Indians were so widely portrayed as losers; in his textbooks at school, at the Saturday movie matinees and on the town's television set, wherever it might be. Despite the fact Ed's grandfather had been one of the first

Indians to become a u.s. marshall in the Oklahoma territories, little Ed always had to be the "bad guy" when the neighbourhood kids played cowboys and Indians. Ed hated being an "Injun" but it toughened him up by bringing home as many black eyes and cut lips as left out in the neighbourhood.

It didn't help that the only other Indians Ed heard about were stuck on reservations in despair and desperation. So some father-son fishing trips on nearby Lake Amistad started to have a new purpose. Not so much to show young Ed how to keep up the good fight and land the big one as to Dad started to spinn larger-than-life tales about this Jim Thorpe fella.

"It was like the Great Spirit was cheering him on."

By the time Ed's head was full of the feats performed by the one they called "Jim Thorpe—All-American," Big Wahoo didn't even have to en-hance his message by stressing things like how Thorpe, like themselves, was a mixed blood. Little Ed McDaniel was more proud to be Native American than All-American. He really believed that if you listened to the wind closely back in those days, you could hear the Great Spirit chanting "Wa-Tho-Huk" (which means "Bright Path"—Jim Thorpe's Indian name).

Big Wahoo was wise in his way and he knew enough to keep the dreams realistic. The simple message, father to son, was not to listen to the people who said he can't win because he is an Indian.

"Any challenge you set your mind to you can achieve. And the Great Spirit will always cheer you on."

It helped that the Great Spirit laid more than a few pounds and inches on the little boy and he grew into a strapping lad who soon dis-covered he was superior at sports; almost any kind, just like Jim Thorpe.

Midland, Texas has gained some notoriety for its high school football team, playing in the same conference as football powers like Odessa (Permian High) and other small-town Texas high school teams that at-tract thousands of fans to sit under their stadium lights on fall Friday nights. On one of those nights, they watched Ed Wahoo McDaniel score five touchdowns!

On ye Bulldogs, on ye bulldogs, Fight right through that line
Ever onward ever forward, We will win or die!

One of Wahoo's biggest fans was his sister, Margaret, who was 18 months younger.

"I was a cheerleader at Midland," Margaret White, now 77, recalls with utmost lucidity, "and it was definitely a thrill to cheer for my older brother."

Oddly, being Indian in this wealthy, mostly Republican town was rarely a problem once the McDaniel kids became school-aged. Mostly, because they could prove what they could do and much of that was better than most.

"Ed and I ran with the 'in crowd,' or most popular kids, because he was a sports star and I got very good grades and we just fit in as equals. Midland is a very wealthy town, very Republican, but we were included in everything at school."

Margaret recalls with regret that women weren't allowed to play those games the boys played because her little sister, Dana (Erdmann) once beat the entire Midland High football team, including Ed, in a foot race.

"They had to do a lot of laps after that," Margaret says with a hearty laugh.

But if there was one drawback to being immediate family to a "he-man" like Ed, it was the over-protective nature big brothers often have towards little sisters.

"He watched who I could date right up until the day of my wedding," Margaret says with another boisterous laugh. This strong bond between the siblings would last a lifetime.

"We were able to attend all of Ed's football games, college and pro, but when he started wrestling, we could only enjoy his visits during holidays and breaks because he would be off to Japan for four months one time, then living in New York, the west coast, all over the world."

But those high school games on the gridiron—with Ed running roughshod through the other team's line and Margaret doing cartwheels on the sidelines, were the best. There was always plenty to cheer about, while the players and fans on the other side could only speak in awe. Former Abilene High football player David Bourland played against McDaniel: "He was tough as a boot, and he played both ways; fullback and linebacker. He weighed about 240 pounds in high school and that was bigger than most people in those days. He could do anything. He ran over me a bunch of times."

Rah rah rah! On ye Bulldogs, on ye Bulldogs, Fight for victory.
Fight Bulldogs, fight, fight, fight, and win this game!

McDaniel led the Bulldogs to a 15-5 combined record in his two seasons as a two-way star for Midland High in 1954 and 1955. He was a two-time all-state player and led the state in rushing in 1954. The bruising fullback and crushing linebacker made his Bulldog team one of the few squads to mount a proper challenge against the famous Abilene High "streak" teams of that era.

Yeah Purple, Yeah Gold, Yeah Bulldogs
Go, Go, Go!

Teams schemed to stop McDaniel but most didn't. He even found a way to gain over 100 yards against Abilene but the Bulldogs ultimately lost to the state powerhouse.

"We knew we had to stop him to win the game," former Abilene High quarterback and defensive back Bourland once said. "I'm not sure that our coach didn't just tell our linebackers to tackle Wahoo on every play whether he had the ball or not. A lot of times they didn't tackle him, they'd hit him and get dragged five yards before they could bring him down."

Wahoo grabbed headlines nearly every time he played and other players swore he came through the line with a "war whoop."

Midland fight, Midland fight, Yeah Midland fight!
Midland fight, Midland fight, Yeah Midland fight!

Of course, because he could run fast, he joined the track club, and started outrunning everybody in town between football and baseball seasons.

Ed wanted to excel at every sport that Thorpe did and because Bright Path won the gold medal in the decathlon at the 1912 Olympic

Games in Sweden, Wahoo would have to learn a smorgasbord of track and field events.

Except for the pole vault. Like his role model, Wahoo was afraid of heights.

"It's just the way those Plains Indians are," a Chiricahua Apache might say.

But in almost all of the other events which make up the gruelling decathlon (100 metres, long jump, shot put, high jump, 400 metres, 110 metre hurdles, discus, javelin and 1,500 metres), Wahoo's times and distances and heights were almost equal to the world record Thorpe had set. This is amazing when you consider that Wahoo was a high school kid at the time while Thorpe had reached full manhood by the time he went to Sweden.

Meanwhile, in the Midland spring, the kids in the bleachers would chase the balls Wahoo would smash into the stratosphere. The super-athletic McDaniel wanted to do everything his idol Thorpe did and he could hit, catch and run so well he led his PONY League baseball team to the Texas state championship finals.

Baseball provided Wahoo with his first brush with fame. People who follow politics might know that George H. W. Bush Sr. made his fortune in the oil business and the Bush family spent considerable time in Midland. They had a passion for baseball and it started with George Sr. coaching the local PONY team in town. His All-Star catcher was an Indian who went by the name Wahoo.

"He was a wonderful kid who captured the imagination of West Texas in the 1950s," Bush proclaimed. "He was idolized and worshipped by everybody who knew him."

It was a mutual admiration society for the folks in Midland. Margaret still lives there and she has fond memories of all the Bushes.

"We got along great with them," Margaret recalls. "They were all nice people and we are all proud to know that two American presidents have come from our little town." Yes, George Sr. went on to become President Bush, George Jr. would end up owning the Texas Rangers (and also become President Bush) and Ed would go on to become Chief Wahoo.

Hugh McDaniel was proud of everything his son was achieving in sports but nothing made him happier than when Wahoo Jr. (or Little Wahoo) picked up wrestling.

"Every Indian has to know how to rassle," Big Wahoo proclaimed.

Most of Ed's major achievements on the mat and then in the ring came later on in life because football overshadowed everything in West Texas. And it was football that got Ed into the prestigious powerhouse that was the University of Oklahoma.

Ironically, this came at the expense of the American Armed Forces, who had drafted Wahoo when he turned 18. By this time, Wahoo was almost 6 feet tall and weighed 280 pounds; a weight-to-height ratio which told the army bureaucracy he was "obese." Despite Wahoo's incredible achievements in most every athletic pursuit, the u.s. military rejected him. Imagine the irony and frustration all those Vietnam War-era draft dodgers felt after wasting their time shooting themselves in the foot during a hunting trip or carrying a purse to their appearance before the draft board only to be accepted for duty while this incredibly accomplished athlete wasn't called when his number came up.

And so it was time to return to his birthplace and join legendary Oklahoma coach Bud Wilkinson's powerhouse Sooner squads. Wahoo wanted to be with the best and the Sooners were number one in the nation, enjoying a 47-game winning streak.

Like many other elite athletes, Wahoo wasn't an academic overachiever but he was smart enough that if he went to his classes and studied as much as most other students, he would have no problem earning high enough grades to continue playing football without any problems. But Wilkinson knew there are plenty of distractions that come a manly man's way and Wahoo, with his dark features and he-manly build and heroic exploits every Saturday afternoon in front of 80,000 adoring fans, would face plenty of temptation that would interfere with his studies, if not his dedication to football on the field. Besides threatening to kick Wahoo off the team if he didn't follow the rules and get good grades, Wilkinson ingeniously figured out how to decrease the amount of trouble Wahoo could get into away from the stadium by using its stands as a form of both negative and positive reinforcement.

Every time Wahoo missed a class, he had to run up and down the bleachers 25 times. By the end of his first season, Wahoo had run those bleachers 700 times, which didn't do that much for Wahoo's grades but certainly built up his endurance.

Which came in handy one time when somebody bet Wahoo he couldn't run from college town Norman to Chickesaw, Oklahoma, a distance of 36 miles, or about 10 miles longer than a standard marathon. Wahoo had never run "long distance" before, so when he covered that jog in under six hours, he immediately joined the company of most every well-trained marathoner in the world.

Wahoo was constantly breaking new ground. You had to look far and wide to find an Indian who was a full pledge in a fraternity but there was the name "Wahoo Ed McDaniel" in the members book of Sigma Chi at Okie U. Like other pledges, and his football teammates, Wahoo enjoyed a few beers after games but you're not going to find his name on a "Dean Wormer's bad list" like in *Animal House*.

But Wahoo did perform one feat of drinking and eating that was the talk of campus in the '60s and still is.

Wahoo would do most anything on a dare (as well as to loosen a few bucks from his frat bros). And so he once performed the incredible edible feat of downing a gallon of hot, hot jalapeno peppers, then washing them down with a quart of motor oil! Wahoo wasn't fazed in the least, except for the fact he says that for about a month every time he sweat he smelled like an old pickup truck.

And what would college be like without a confrontation with a soda machine? Believe it or not, far too many Americans die under a drink machine when they try to shake a stuck coin loose. But Wahoo McDaniel topped them all by hauling a soda machine on his back up onto the top of a two-story building and heaving the huge, overgrown refrigerator off the roof. Quarters and Cokes for everybody!

Wahoo was disciplined enough to maintain an academic standing which kept him on the Sooners roster for three years. He learned to listen and learn mostly because he respected winners and Wilkinson had already won a national championship.

Wahoo got smarter on the football field, too. A two-way player in high school, he knew it was much more pleasurable to hit than to be hit, so he switched from the offensive backfield to defensive end, which was, at the time, a position more suited to his size (then again, could you imagine how invaluable a 6-foot-tall, 280-pound running back with near Olympic sprinter speed would be in today's NFL?). The Sooners won two more national championships and Wahoo lettered three times!

Oh yeah, Wahoo also set the Sooners record for longest punt at 91 yards; a mark that still stands!

Indians have enjoyed a special relationship with the University of Oklahoma. As you will know from other chapters in this book, the only Sooners quarterback who ever played in the National Football League during the 20th century was "Indian" Jack Jacobs (Creek). The quarterback from Oklahoma U who finally equalled Jacobs' achievement would be another Indian, Sam Bradford (Cherokee). The only two QBs from Oklahoma University to play in the NFL are Native Americans.

But easily the most famous Indian to ever graduate from Oklahoma is Wahoo McDaniel. And he completed his college degree at just the right time because the American Football League (AFL) was just starting up, ramping up salaries for players who now had two major professional leagues competing for their services. The 5-foot-11 McDaniel was chosen by Los Angeles in the second round of the 1960 AFL draft but despite the good money that was being tossed around, McDaniel would bounce around the AFL from Houston to Denver to New York and Miami because he was bouncing in and out of a wrestling ring just as much as he was romping around a football field. In the end, the wide world of wrestling would win out but not before Wahoo provided some unique moments on the gridiron.

It is a testament to Wahoo's ability to attract attention that it would be in The Big Apple, where 12 million people compete for their 15 minutes of fame, that Wahoo started to become a household word. In his very first game with the Jets, after he made his first tackle in the game, the stadium announcer merrily proclaimed "tackle made by Wahoo McDaniel" over the P.A. and the sold-out crowd of 45,000 hardened New Yorkers all started to laugh. Loudly.

Well, that made Wahoo mad. Always driven to make fans love him and opponents fear him, Wahoo became practically unstoppable in this game, flying all over the field like a banshee in heat. Wahoo wouldn't be stopped until he had made 23 tackles in that game, and when Wahoo became unstoppable, that stadium announcer and the crowd would not be stopped.

"Who made that last tackle?" the P.A. announcer would shout.

And the crowd would roar back, "Waaa-hooooo!"

And so the legend began. Wahoo McDaniel soon became one of the most popular players in the AFL, so popular that he was the only player in league history who was allowed to put just a single name, his first name, on the back of his jersey.

"Wahoo" was the only thing the fans could see over McDaniel's number 54.

Former NFL superstars Joe Namath (Jets) and Larry Csonka (Miami), who played with Wahoo early in their careers, both included stories about the skillful Indian in their autobiographies. Kansas City Chiefs quarterback Len Dawson has been quoted as saying, "The hardest hit I ever received on a football field was by Wahoo McDaniel."

It all started to come together for McDaniel in New York City, even moreso off the field. He had already been sidelining in smaller, minor-league wrestling circuits around the country during the off-season from football but the Big Apple was the the home of Madison Square Garden! And the owner of MSG just happened to be Sonny Werblin, a prominent owner of the Jets. Far from trying to prevent one of his biggest football assets to be drawn off by another sport and another venue, Werblin welcomed splitting (doubling) his investment by having Wahoo McDaniel become a feature attraction in the wrestling ring in the Garden.

"I'll rassle in Madison Square Garden and make me a fortune!" is how Wahoo put it.

McDaniel had learned collegiate-style wrestling from the Sooners' nationally number-one ranked wrestling team but he needed to learn the highs and pitfalls of the professional circus...er, circuit. Wahoo's good fortune continued because celebrated wrestling champ Dory Funk Sr. was available to show Wahoo the secrets of the ring, like how to come up with "signature moves" to help sell his image. Wahoo had never exploited his Indian heritage, but he was going to wrestle as a proud product of North America's First Nations, so developing holds like the "Indian deathlock" and attacks such as the "tomahawk chop," which could be heard in the nosebleed seats whenever it landed, were essential. Coupled with football-style tackles and standard dropkicks, Wahoo became the total package.

The string of good fortune continued when promoter Jim Barnett came along looking specifically for an Indian wrestler. The final touch leading to a long career in professional wrestling was to dress like a proud indigenous warrior and announce that he was now Chief Wahoo.

Back in those days, wrestling promoters often created ethnic characters to battle each other. After all, this was entertainment (like all sports are) and despite the fact the fighting is very real to the wrestlers walking around with concussions and stitches and broken bones and bruises, the bottom line was show business and that was most certainly so on the biggest stage there was, Madison Square Garden in New York.

Ethnic rivalries were immensely popular. So you had masked Mexicans facing mad sheiks and raging Russians running after wild Indians. Certainly this created room for misleading stereotypes, but sometimes life is a trade-off and Wahoo was righting a few wrongs which were being perpetrated about his people and his culture.

First of all, wrestling would finally feature a real Indian playing an Indian, not some white guy in an Indian costume adorned with a cardboard ring of chicken feathers for a headdress. Most important, Wahoo maintained that his "character" would fight as a "good guy"; that he would only play the "hero" (the wrestling term for good guy, the bad guy is known as the "heel"). Up to this point, the wrestlers posing as Indians displayed mostly negative characteristics like cheating and sneaking around behind their opponents' (and the referees') backs.

Wahoo carried that positive image inside and outside the ring. He wanted to balance the negative, misleading images portrayed by the likes of Chief Wahoo of the Cleveland Indians (for obvious reasons), the Washington Redskins (a name that celebrates the genocide of paying bounty for murdered Indians) and other stereotypes. Wahoo wore an authentic tribal headdress, and if the feathers were damaged by an opponent, he wept for his lost honour and then prepared a sacred healing ceremony, before beating his opponent senseless (such as when Ivan Koloff and the super Destroyer ripped apart Wahoo's headdress—suffice to say that the Destroyer got destroyed and Koloff was cooled off).

Wahoo slept on a bear rug and got in touch with his relatives, and through them, his heritage and culture.

Even so, Wahoo still had his critics who claimed he was being used by the white man. All he could do is tell them that he was a Native American who was finally standing up to the "cowboys."

"We Indians have been pushed around for years but now the pushing is over."

And Wahoo often used his name and fame to open doors for generations of Native Americans to follow.

Wahoo also took advantage of his football stardom. His name on the marquis filled arenas and he quickly became one of the most popular wrestlers in North America during the 1960s. And there is big money in wrestling; bigger than professional football at the time. And, for a while, McDaniel was cashing cheques from both sports, which made him one of the highest-paid athletes in North America.

Wahoo's drawing power as a football player-cum-wrestler in New York was more than evident in his MSG debut; a sell-out crowd showed up to see Wahoo beat on a no-name at the time, Boris Malenko. And media coverage was enormous. Even when Malenko began to make a name for himself, one of his main claims to fame came from submitting a $3,000 dental bill to Wahoo for breaking his teeth.

Most important, Wahoo was becoming a hero to young Native Americans, who rarely saw their personalities and image appear anywhere in popular culture, let alone depicted as winners proud of who they were and where they came from. There were other Indian sports figures like Jim Thorpe and Billy Mills, and plenty of Indians starring in the National Hockey League.

But Wahoo McDaniel was starring in the National Football League! The most popular professional sports league in North America by far!

As well, Wahoo was a rising star in professional wrestling, which brought in a whole new audience. Wrestling attracts plenty of regular sports fans but it is also well-known for bringing Grandma and Grandpa and drunk Uncle Jeb ringside to join everybody else who has a flair for the dramatic and loves the basic elements of a soap opera.

We often hear people say "It's all fake" when they talk about wrestling, but that is often not true, and Wahoo McDaniels has over 3,000 stitches on his face to prove it. Wrestling is one of the original Olympic Games sports, and it doesn't need the inclusion of ballroom dancing and curling Olympiads to justify its presence now.

Wahoo battled the biggest stars in the wrestling world—Andre the Giant, Sgt. Slaughter and Jesse Ventura. His feud with Superstar Billy Graham set box office records and his battles in Texas against the son of his mentor, Dory Funk Jr., had to be moved from the Houston Coliseum Arena to the giant Astrodome stadium to accommodate the crowds.

Fans loved him. Opponents feared him. A standing offer of $15,000 to TV star Hulk Hogan was never collected. Wahoo began to win every wrestling championship available, and trust me, there are many, many, many wrestling championships around to be won.

The internet has a listing of Wahoo's wrestling titles that covers a couple of printed pages using eight-point type. The way wrestling worked during the 1960s (before the advent of WWF pay-per-view extravaganzas) was that a grappler would go into a geographical area about the size of a state or two, introduce his act or character, and build a following until he was popular (or reviled) enough to challenge for the local title belt. Wahoo won titles in Texas, Florida, and Georgia, and the hugely popular mid-Atlantic championship (which he won five times!). Ed McDaniel was often the very first "person of colour" to win these championships.

Nonetheless, to rise to the top and to win at that level, and maintain your supremacy at that level, required incredible athleticism, physical and mental stamina, and perseverance. The most coveted crown is the United States Heavyweight title and Wahoo McDaniel won that in 1981 by beating "Rowdy" Roddy Piper. It is the highlight of those pages and pages of titles.

A particular claim to fame for Chief Wahoo was the "Indian strap match"—a unique show of skill, stamina and strength that nobody ever won against the Chief.

The Indian strap match tied two wrestlers together with a 20-foot-long leather strap wrapped around their wrist. They battled until one of them dropped and then the winner had to drag the loser to each corner of the ring, tagging the turnbuckle (corner post) as they went. Pinning a 300-pound opponent was an enormous feat all by itself, but dragging the vanquished beast to all four corners without him getting up is a whole other thing. An awesome feat, and Chief Wahoo McDaniel was the Grand Master.

One of Wahoo's fiercest rivals was Johnny Valentine—a handsome, blond grappler of Polish descent (real last name: Wisniski) who alternated between hero and heel. They are famous for a fight that tumbled out of the ring and into the stands, then down to the dressing rooms and all the way into the parking lot!

A plane crash ended Valentine's career (broken back) but not before he lost the mid-Atlantic heavyweight championship to Wahoo on July 26, 1975, in what witnesses say was the most brutally intense battle ever fought.

This rivalry even extended through the generations as Johnny's son, Greg Valentine, attacked Wahoo and broke his leg. Wahoo traded the title back and forth with young Greg but then, teaming up with Ric "Nature Boy" Flair in a TV interview, Greg taunted Chief Wahoo by throwing change at him and asking him if he needed a wheel chair for his "fat body," All too often, amateur behaviour crept into professional wrestling.

Ultimately, Wahoo's fiercest rival turned out to be Nature Boy, and not because Flair was making a claim to be more in harmony with Mother Earth than some Indian. Wahoo and Nature Boy squared off in the ring 180 times in a single year and although they developed much mutual respect, there was the odd gouged eye and knee in the nuts that created lots of room for revenge.

Their most famous battle became known as the "table leg and forty stitches" fight, and that title says it all. Flair had just returned to wrestling after recovering from injuries he sustained in the same plane crash that took out Valentine (wrestlers have a schedule similar to other entertainers' like musicians, so they rely on small charter planes to hop from venue to venue).

It was a dramatic return to the ring for Flair but Wahoo wanted the heavyweight title that Flair held. As they battled, both fell out of the ring on to a timekeeper's table, which was smashed to smithereens. Desperate and dazed, Flair grabbed one of the table legs and swung wildly, ripping a gash around Wahoo's eye that took 40 stitches to close. Flair apologized later on. He hadn't noticed there was a nail still sticking out of the table leg, and ripping the gash in Wahoo's face was an unintended faux pas (as if bashing your opponent over the head with a wooden club was OK).

"Wahoo was the toughest man I ever fought," Flair said. "He's the kind of guy who, if you let up for one minute, it's all over."

No kidding.

Flair pinned the wounded Wahoo and kept his crown. Wahoo was whisked off to Mercy Hospital in Charlotte where that massive gash to his head was closed and stitched up, but also opened up a mindset that was hell-bent on revenge.

And Wahoo avenged that forty-to-the-face by taking the mid-Atlantic heavyweight belt Flair was wearing on December 27, 1976, and that late calendar victory carried Wahoo to Wrestler of the Year honours.

Even though athletes such as wrestlers and boxers face each other mano a mano constantly, each trying to take the other's guy's head off by any means necessary, the combatants don't generally dislike or hate each other because of things that happen through the physical combat that takes place in the ring. They develop hate for another guy because they think he is a jerk or because one guy screws another guy professionally or socially. Bad-mouthing in the media is rarely taken seriously; it's usually just part of hyping the show.

The public only sees the bad blood that is spilled in the ring and most folks think guys like McDaniel and Flair really hate each other.

This set up a comical, confusing incident after Flair's plane crash, which happened right at the height of their highly publicized feud.

Wahoo was one of the first to hear about the accident, and he rushed to the hospital to try and help out, but hospital staff thought he was there to finish ol' Nature Boy off. McDaniel had to fight off restraints from hospital attendants and security guards when actually he was only there to provide "comfort and aid to the enemy."

In fact, Flair and McDaniel were good friends, and Flair considered Chief Wahoo to be his mentor. Many young wrestlers discovered that after they had been beaten by the Native American legend, he would provide them with pointers about what they could do better next time around and they would always come a lot closer to beating the old champ in their next matchup (but never close enough to win).

Inevitably, "Old Champ" is what all the great ones eventually become, and there came the time when Chief Wahoo had to hang up the headdress. As I wrote earlier, the list of titles Wahoo won can be scrolled on the internet. The miles he travelled can never be remembered exactly and he estimates he added 3,000 stitches to the 40 he received from Ric Flair and that timekeeper's table leg.

"What I experienced in the ring was tougher than any football game I ever played," Wahoo McDaniel often said.

And truly the toughest part of wrestling was keeping in step with the widely held belief it was all fake, because much of wrestling was scripted and you had to follow the arc of the storyline. There was no other way to maintain the intensity and style on display for the time that was needed to put on a lasting show. But there were also moments when one guy went too far and tempers flared and there was some serious damage done.

The semi-quasi script sometimes went against Wahoo's best instincts and desires. Like when Flair was scripted as a hero against Indian Chief Wahoo and Wahoo had to fight as a "heel" against a hero for the first time.

Then there were some natural promotions that didn't need any of the Madison Avenue fakery.

Like when Wahoo fought Angelo Mosca, who likewise had turned from football to wrestling. Mosca is famous for knocking Wille "the

Wisp" Fleming out of the 1963 Grey Cup game with an out-of-bounds piling-on penalty which insured the Hamilton Tiger-Cats victory over the BC Lions. Mosca's matches against Wahoo McDaniel pitted the Canadian Football League against the National Football League and fans absolutely went nuts over it!

And, of course, there would be the inevitable matchup between the "tomahawk chop" and the "karate chop." Wahoo's battles with Kim Duk ("the Korean Assassin") forsook wrestling for whacks back and forth until red Wahoo chopped his opponent into submission.

Yes, it could truly be called a circus atmosphere, but an element of realism that kept creeping into the goings-on that betrayed the phoniness. Like when Sgt. Slaughter took Wahoo's title after an elimination tournament that was held because Wahoo wasn't available due to an injury inflicted by Abdullah the Butcher, who almost gouged out Wahoo's eye with a coat hanger. This created a classic drama, as Wahoo maintained Slaughter had never really won the title mano a mano and set up an epic struggle between the two which Wahoo eventually won. And it goes on and on like this with news in rapid fire succession; the kind of BS that just does not exist in other "true" professional sports, so you just have to take some bad with the good.

But you will never convince me that professional wrestlers aren't true athletes. They are indeed some of the most athletic sportsmen around.

The hardest part of professional wrestling is life on the road. Not even baseball or hockey players, with their gruelling schedule of games, have to spend as much time away from home as professional wrestlers did during Wahoo's time. Throughout his career, Wahoo had to pick a territory, become a star there, then move on to the next territory to start again. There was no national TV coverage back then, so he had to become a brand new celebrity everywhere he went. Wahoo moved from New York to Florida to Minnesota to Texas to the mid-Atlantic. He travelled the world, seeing Russia, Europe, Mexico and Japan, where he was invited 32 times. Wahoo wrestled well into his fifties. He fought for over 30 years, battling in over 11,000 matches, sometimes eight to ten fights a week.

As an example of just how busy the world of pro rasslin' is, I offer an "edit, select, copy and paste" of one paragraph from Wahoo's Wikipedia entry; one of many similar paragraphs in the wiki account:

> Wahoo returned to Mid-Atlantic in 1981 and feuded with Roddy Piper over the United States title which ended when Piper brought in Abdullah the Butcher and Abby put Wahoo out on injury. Wahoo returned and had another bloody feud with Sgt. Slaughter for the U.S. title when Slaughter won the title while Wahoo was injured. In 1984, he turned on Ricky Steamboat, taking the U.S. title for the fourth time when Tully Blanchard came to Wahoo's assistance with a steel chair. He was stripped of the title but regained it in a tournament later that year. Wahoo successfully defended it at Starrcade of that year against Billy Graham but lost it to Magnum T.A. in early 1985 in a steel cage match. Wahoo feuded again with the now babyface Ric Flair for the NWA World Heavyweight title at various times before Flair turned heel again. After losing the U.S. title, he booked and wrestled mostly for Championship Wrestling from Florida. He made a tag team with Billy Jack Haynes which won the promotion's version of the NWA United States Tag Team title from Rick Rude and Jesse Barr (aka Jimmy Jack Funk). Wahoo wrestled some high profile matches in Florida like an unsuccessful world title bid against Ric Flair and a draw against Bruiser Brody at the Florida promotion's nationally syndicated big show, Battle of the Belts. In 1986, he returned as a face to Mid-Atlantic wrestling in some of his famous Indian Strap Matches with Jimmy Garvin and Rick Rude. He won the NWA National Heavyweight Championship from Tully Blanchard in front of a packed house of 11,000 fans in Los Angeles at The Forum (Inglewood, California) on August 28, 1986 during a wild and bloody match, but lost a unification match against NWA U.S. champion Nikita Koloff.

The years of hard-fought clashes and endless travel took their toll on Wahoo. They resulted in failed marriages and some children who only knew their father as a TV star. McDaniel was married five times to four different women. With his first wife, Monta Rae, he had two daughters: Nikki, born in June 1963 and living in Houston, Texas, and Cindi (Black) born in October 1965, living in Rowlett, Texas. He has four grandchildren: Dustin and Brittany from Nikki, and twins, Morgan and Taylor, from Cindi.

Although Wahoo McDaniel had countless fans and all the money he needed, he had never experienced being a good family man. It wasn't until his dad, Big Ed Wahoo McDaniel, passed on, that little Chief Wahoo remembered how much Big Wahoo had done for him and realized it was time for him to do the same.

He started by paving the way for some extended family. Wahoo advised other Native American wrestlers like Ricky Steamboat and Chris "Tatanka" Chavis, who were on their way up. Because of the example set by Wahoo, only real Native Americans portrayed Indians in the ring by now. And because of Wahoo, young fans could see the Indian as the good guy. Wahoo even launched a wrestling school called The Chop Shop so that underprivileged kids could have a shot at the big time, too. And he worked behind the scenes as a promoter to help newcomers get their start. And, of course, he tag-teamed with some of the up and comers, like Mark Youngblood, brother of Jay Youngblood, Indian fighters all.

In an official World Wrestling Federation ceremony, Wahoo passed the torch to Chris Tatanka, a 100% Native American who vowed to represent Indians with honor. Wahoo was now being called the greatest Indian wrestler of all time and one of the great wrestlers of the 20th century. Tatanka credited Wahoo for being his biggest influence.

It is refreshing to note that Wahoo didn't resort to being the bitter, curmudgeon-like veteran who does nothing but bitch and moan about "how hard it was in the old days and how easy the kids have it now" because of the huge salaries being paid to modern-day wrestlers who have risen to superstar status through Vince McMahon's World Wrestling Federation using more glitz and glamour and soap opera than real toughness and skill. As far as Wahoo was concerned, it was "more power to them and you deserve whatever you get so take it with both hands." Whenever he was near a show, Wahoo would be there seeing his old friends backstage and talking to the new generation of wrestling stars.

"We talk. They treat me very nice," he said of the youngsters. "They all come up, shake my hand. Very polite."

The final scene in the 1962 film *Requiem for a Heavyweight* is one of the most tragic in sports film history. "Big Mountain" Rivera (played by Anthony Quinn) is a punch drunk boxer whose career has ended, in a memorable scene that opens the film featuring a young Cassius Clay on his way up dispatching a "tomato can"/Rivera on his way down. Mountain's manager, played by Jackie Gleason, wants to continue exploiting Rivera by turning him into a wrestler on the "win one lose one" sideshow circuit. It is a deeply damning and shameful end to a once proud man's career and it appears Rivera isn't going to go along with it, walking away from the ring with his good guy trainer played by Mickey Rooney.

But then Big Mountain stops, bends down and raises up a head dress, clutching a rattle in one arm. He takes a deep breath, and then starts to dance around the ring "Indian-style", whacking himself in the mouth, chanting "Woo woo woo woo woo!"

Unfortunately, there were a few wrestlers on sideshow circuits who did the schtick portrayed by Quinn; some of them had native blood, others just had dark enough skin to pass. You really can't condemn a man for making a living, but it's too bad the story of Wahoo McDaniel isn't more widely known because the image of an Indian wrestler like the one in *Requiem* is often too well known and believed.

The true story of an Indian wrestler in the ring is the one told by Wahoo McDaniel. And Wahoo went out with pride and dignity, just like he came in, and just like he did throughout his life.

After the birth of his only son Zac, Wahoo finally retired for good. He became an avid golfer and some say that may have been his best sport, except that he always lost because the partner he matched 70s with just happened to be Lee Trevino, one of the greatest golfers of all time.

Once described as "unique as a snowflake and unpredictable as the weather who rained bloody murder down on football fields and in the wrestling ring," Wahoo made a lot of money, friends and fame inside the wrestling rings of the world, but it was his life outside the ring which ended up defining his life.

In retirement, McDaniel drove a pickup truck with a feather arrangement dangling from the rearview mirror, a symbol of his Native American heritage, and a sticker on the bumper that read "Sure you can trust the U.S. government. Just ask an Indian!"

Wahoo found trust and love within his family in the end. He settled down in Texas where his mother lived, and spent time with his young son, sharing custody with Karen, the boy's mom, in Florida, in a friendly, supportive relationship that had Zac bouncing back and forth between their two homes in a good way.

Spending time with son Zac became the most important thing in the world to Wahoo McDaniel. He wove many incredible but true tales for young Zac, who became fascinated with all the amazing characters in his father's adventures. As Zac grew older, Wahoo taught him how to wrestle, passing on the secrets of the ring.

"Any challenge you set your mind to, you can win. People may say you can't be a champion because you're an Indian. But the Great Spirit will always cheer you on," he told his son.

On April 19, 2002, Ed "Wahoo" McDaniel lost his life to a common foe that Native Americans have been fighting a losing battle with ever since, due to the high carbohydrate diet of white flour, lard and sugar that was introduced to their communities, along with smallpox-infected blankets and alcohol. The rate of diabetes amongst First Nations people is far higher than for mainstream society.

———————

Zac's devotion to his father was absolute.

"We spent a lot of time together. I started mat wrestling when I was six and we would travel to meets, spend a couple of days in one state for one of my tournaments and then move on to the next state where Dad would be wrestling," says Zac.

"I will never forget the time when one of his opponents took Dad's headdress off and threw it on the floor and Dad...well, mopped up the floor with the guy. I never saw my dad fight like that before. That was the time I saw my dad turn from a wrestler into a fighter, a really fierce fighter.

"Because of my dad, I always did well at history in school, because we would be assigned a lot of projects and I had a natural interest in Native Americans because of the pride my dad instilled in me," Zac explains. "My dad would tell me what he knew about our Chocktaw and Chickesaw background but we also went by the book, going down to the library together to look things up. He was just as much a student as I was and we went on a journey of self-discovery together."

Zac trained hard at wrestling for four years between the ages of 16 and 20, which mostly taught him just how difficult it is to develop the skills and stamina needed for "the show." Zac had a lot of motivation to carry on the positive image of native people that his father cultivated but as he travelled around, it became apparent it would be an even greater achievement if he could just become the kind of man Wahoo McDaniel was.

"Everybody spoke highly of my dad," says Zac. "Everybody liked him and they automatically embraced me and wanted to help me simply because I was Wahoo McDaniel's son."

But there were complications and conflicts with management and his trainer and in the end, Zac was getting dragged down by the people who were closest to him more than they were giving him a boost. Zac has mostly moved on to other things.

But it was good for Zac to learn that in an ultra-competitive sport like pro wrestling, where there is a lot of money and prestige at stake, where it is extremely rare for anybody to be universally well thought of, his father, Wahoo, was the epitome of what you would call a nice guy, and there is nothing nicer you can say about a guy.

There is a widely-carried story about how Zac and his dad used to fish together on Lake Amistad:

Today, Little Wahoo fishes alone on the lake where his father's ashes are scattered. Under the endless blue skies of Lake Amistad, he listens closely to the wind, where the Great Spirit chants the name of heaven's newest hero:

Waaahhooooooooo!

Great story. Unfortunately, there's not a speck of truth in it.

"Those stories about fishing on Lake Amistad are about my dad and his father and that writer just took liberties with it," Zac says today.

The truth is more meaningful than fiction.

"Near the end, my dad was getting real sick so my mom came and packed us both up and moved us all back together in Florida so she could take care of both of us," says Zac. "Then one day I woke up and Dad had his pickup packed with stuff and he was heading back to Texas. He told me he had to finish up some business back home but it turned out he was going to say good-bye to his family and friends there.

"About a month later, I was in class at school and I got that dreaded call to come to the principal's office. I had acted out on the bus that morning and I was expecting some trouble, so when they told me that my father had passed away, I was really caught by surprise and I guess I acted out even more than I normally would, demolishing every stick of furniture around me.

"I was a boy becoming a man and I just lost the only man I ever knew.

"That night I had trouble sleeping and I don't know if I was dreaming or I had just woke up from a dream or I was hallucinating or what, but there was my dad in the corner of my bedroom," Zac recalls with the vivid memory one doesn't usually possess following a dream.

"He told me he loved me and that everything was OK.

"My mom told me that was my dad's way of saying 'goodbye for now,' and I'm sure it was.

"There isn't a day that goes by when I don't think about my dad. He is my guiding light and he sets an example for me and my own son about how to live and how to carry ourselves.

"One of the stories my dad told me was about how he wanted to name me 'Crazy Horse' after the legendary warrior, or at least have

'Crazy Horse' be part of my name, like 'Zachary Kalen Crazy Horse McDaniel.' But my mom didn't agree.

"We had decided to name our son 'Kalen Kai McDaniel,' but when my partner saw me holding my son in my arms for the first time and I mentioned that story, we agreed to add 'Crazy Horse' to my son's name."

When Zac found out later that the real name of this great warrior is "He Has the Spirit of His Horses" but it was misinterpreted by white settlers and historians, Zac beams with pride because he knows that the spirit of wild and free horses of the western plains flow through the veins of his son.

"I think if my dad would have known that, he would have won the argument with my mom and my middle name would be 'Crazy Horse' or 'He has the Spirit of His Horses' or something like that," Zac says with some regret.

But he is still "Little Wahoo."

Waaahoooooooooooo!"

Billy Mills

3

A Formula for Success

The fact that Billy Mills pulled off a monumental upset in the 10,000-metre race at the 1964 Olympic Games in Tokyo was obvious by the sheer surprise in NBC Race Analyst Dick Bank's voice:

"Look at Mills! Look at Mills! Woo hoo hoo hoo hoo hoo! Look at Mills!"

The more sedate race announcer, Galen Rupp, was focused on the leaders and didn't even notice the unlikely, but thrilling charge coming up from behind.

"Look at Mills! Look at Mills!"

Billy Mills was such a long shot in this race that only he and his wife, Pat, thought he had even a remote chance to win. Mills had never run close to the time he needed to be competitive with the elite field he was up against, yet he somehow made up 45 seconds on his own previous best time and more to put on the greatest performance of his life and win a gold medal in the 10,000 metre race at the 1964 Olympic Games in Tokyo, Japan.

Wow!

Billy Mills is a product of the Pine Ridge Indian Reservation in South Dakota; the poorest of the poverty-stricken Native American reservation system in the United States. Pine Ridge has the highest unemployment rate, lowest high school graduation rate, highest suicide rate, lowest income and generally just leads the country in pretty much every negative socioeconomic statistic you can think of by a country 10,000 metres.

And yet the people who live at Pine Ridge have a proud history of fierce independence, a strong sense of identity and spirituality, and a culture and history marked by victory as much as loss alongside some of the horror which has been inflicted on First Nations since 1492.

Residents joke about the "crab mentality" that has afflicted the tribe ever since the white man, or "Wasicu," arrived:

> A Pine Ridge Indian and a white man are fishing. Both are using a pail of crabs for bait.
>
> Every time the white man loses a crab off his line, he lifts the lid off his pail and grabs a fresh crab to put on his hook, then quickly slams the lid on his pail back down shut.
>
> The Indian doesn't even have a lid to cover his pail of crabs with.
>
> So the white man asks the Indian, "Hey, how come your crabs don't escape from the pail?"
>
> And the Indian replies, "Oh, these are Indian crabs. They don't even try because by the time one of the crabs makes it up the side to the top of the pail, another crab reaches up and pulls it back down.

Billy Mills overcame the poverty, dysfunction and crab mentality of the Pine Ridge Indian Reservation by applying a "Formula for Success." Mills has spent his life teaching others how to rise from the crowd by using the same formula.

———

It has always been about identity for Billy Mills. Finding out who you truly are so that you can serve the destiny that is ordained for you—about finding the human connection, how you fit in, and how we all fit together.

The process began for Billy Mills when he discovered how running made him feel, how he was most relaxed and most comfortable in his own skin whenever he was "pickin' them up and layin' 'em down." From a very early age, Billy loved to run as much as eating and breathing, partly because it was an escape from the poverty of Pine

Ridge, partly as flight from the racism he experienced from the only two worlds he knew at the time (Billy was "half from the white and half from the red").

But mostly, it was about gaining the only source of identity that was given to the young child, which came from running. And instead of running away from things, he would be running with a passion to succeed; running would become the catalyst to pursue his dreams.

William Mervin "Billy" Mills, traditional name Makata Taka Hela or Makoce Te' Hila, was born on June 30, 1938 on the Pine Ridge Indian Reservation in South Dakota.

"I loved my father completely," Mills says. "He always said, 'It's the pursuit of a dream that heals you and fulfills you.

"He'd get me out of class and we'd go to the fishing hole. He knew that he could never be alone when he fished because he'd had a stroke, and if he had another one, somebody had to run for help."

Billy's father, Sidney Thomas Mills, was Catholic, but also found peace in taking Native American spiritual ways and parallelling them with the tenets of Catholicism. It would take a lot of time for the same peace and reconciliation to find its way to his son.

The introduction of "white man's religion" to the indigenous peoples of the Americas has not gone smoothly. The horrors of Indian residential schools run by the churches of various denominations are well-documented. While the intentions may have been good but ill-considered, and the message of peace, love and forgiveness Jesus carried was certainly acceptable, certain emissaries have compromised the effort by acting wrongly. In Billy's case, the acts weren't criminal, but he was hurt by the hypocrisy he witnessed at times.

Like the time he was in second grade. Above all, Billy wanted to please his father, so he attended catechism class and prepared to make his First Communion. Billy learned his prayers better than most in his class, and was hoping to be first in line on the day of his communion. For the ceremony, "I needed a clean white shirt," Mills recalls.

"So, Billy's father made plans to take him to the town by the reservation where they could buy a clean, white shirt. But that morning Sidney had a stroke.

Billy and his father had to walk about a mile to the hospital and after Sidney got settled, Billy asked him what he should do about the shirt.

"Jesus Christ doesn't care if you take Holy Communion stark nekkid!" Sidney bellowed. "Wear your sister's blouse."

So my sister ironed a blouse for me and I wore it. A nun noticed and she complained to the priest about it. I explained to her, 'Jesus Christ doesn't care if I take Holy Communion stark nekkid!'

"The nuns made me go *last*."

Mills grew up with the loving support of his parents but tragically, not nearly long enough. His mother, Grace, died just before his eighth birthday and Sidney died with a rosary in his hands when Billy was 12.

"Two weeks before he died, my father took me fishing," Billy recalls. "Seeing his expression as I reeled in a catfish remains a golden vision for me. For years I would never fish for catfish, to keep the memory of Dad special."

Excerpt from Billy Mills live presentation:

I remember my dad...shortly after my mother died... We were fishing... He hugged me...

"Son, you have broken wings," he said. And I started to cry...

"Then my dad said, 'son, I am going to share something with you, and if you follow it, some day, you may have wings of an eagle... He took a stick. He drew a circle.

"Step inside of the circle, son..."

I remember stepping inside... I'm nine years old.

"Look inside of your heart," Dad said.

He closed my eyes and he put his hand on my chest...

"Look inside of your heart... your body, your mind, your spirit... What do you find?"

I'm too young to understand...

BOOM! He clapped his hands!

"I'll tell you what you find. Anger...because you lost your mother. You have anger, son...and you have a whole lot of self-pity. You have jealousy, son, and that jealousy blinds you. You don't see the beauty in our own culture, in our own family, in other cultures...in other people... And you have a whole lot of self-pity...

"All of these emotions, son, will destroy you...

"Look deeper, son, way down deep... to where the dreams lie, son. "Find your dream...it is the pursuit of the dream that will heal you."

I was nine years old at the time...couldn't make much sense out of what I was hearing...but I have pieced it together over the years so that it is what I share with you today...

My dad died when I was 12. His last words to me were, "Find your dream, son"...

He knew I like athletics...

"I hope you try sports, son," he said...

From then on, Billy was raised by his older brother and sister. But without his father's guidance, the conflict between the white world and the red man's ways began to grow.

There is a lot of similarity between Lakota teachings and the message carried intThe Bible, Quran, Torah and other religious gospels and texts. There can be a lot of difference between theory and practice, however, and Billy was caught between two worlds. He often experienced rejection because he was half-white or a "half-breed."

He found that running was a way out. A way of physically getting out, getting away, running through the canyons and washes, and crossing the stark badlands. Almost subliminally he became a tireless runner.

The father had always told the son that running would make him more fit. But Billy also had learned that when he ran, he drew strength from Mother Earth and from Heaven, which better prepared him to meet challenges. Such as racing.

Before he died, Sidney could see the connection between his son and sports and he encouraged it.

Excerpt from Billy Mills live presentation:

I was nine years old when I read my first Olympic book. It said that "the athletes are chosen by the Gods." I liked that, I wanted to be chosen by the Gods, not because of the Olympic Games but simply because my mother had just died and I thought if I was chosen by the Gods, even if they were just the Olympic Gods, I would be able to see my mother again...

The books also quoted Socrates and a few other Greek philosophers from which came... "with achievement comes honour, and with honour comes responsibility"...

My Dad started taking me to Native American storytelling circles. Culture, tradition and spirituality... and he told me "we don't tell stories just to tell stories. We tell stories to teach lessons depending on the level of responsibility and accountability we have reached in our lives. There is a different lesson, different consequences"...

So as a youngster, I'm taking Greek mythology...Native American storytelling, culture, tradition and spirituality, blending them and I found Olympic idealism...global unity through the dignity, character and beauty of global diversity; the future of humankind.

It's the journey, not the destination, that empowers us...the daily decisions we make in life, not the talent that choreographs our destiny.

But there are always obstacles on the road. Various perceptions that we face...fragmented perceptions...that many of our people don't want to listen to one another...don't want to work together...

I was blessed by strong brothers and sisters... my seven siblings raised me until I went off to high school at the Haskill Institute in Kansas.

My sophomore year, I worked building grain elevators over the summer months, slept in the back of my car, bathing in the creek, but I found an hour each day so I could train...

Because I wanted to be an Olympian...

Billy also excelled in the classroom. He had that great work ethic that all runners must have and he got good grades. When he was 15, Billy's teachers sent him away to the Haskell Institute, which was, in one way, an elite boarding school for Native Americans, but also a central plank in a nationwide effort to recreate Indians "in the white man's image."

At Haskill, Billy took up cross-country and track, running excellent times in the two-mile race (9:08) and the indoor mile (4:23) during his senior year in 1957. He was also an excellent boxer and his proficiency in sports gave him a choice of colleges.

Mills chose to run away from people rather than trade blows with them so he accepted an athletic scholarship to the University of Kansas in Lawrence because it was a track powerhouse. Despite a clash of style and wills with Coach Bill Easton, Mills was part of the 1959 and 1960 outdoor national championship teams and was named an NCAA All-America in cross-country three times. In 1960, he won the individual title in the Big Eight cross-country championship.

Mills had chosen Kansas because of its track record and the reputation of the coach there, Bill Easton. But instead of the "folksy sage" and "ladler of lore with a twinkle in his eye" that Billy expected, Easton had a "tough love" approach that created a constant test of wills and a clash of spirits with Billy.

The very first thing Easton did was shoot down Billy's Olympic dreams, preferring to keep things real and reachable. But can you learn from someone who sets out to destroy the dreams you've had since you were nine years old? Billy, who lost both parents at an early age, needed guidance and support, not distance and discipline. Athletes need to know that their coaches share and believe in their dreams, Mills more so than most.

Easton pulled stunts, like discouraging the speed work that Billy thought he needed because "Negroes are sprinters, Indians run forever." Easton would taunt Billy from the side of the track with insults and useless advice like "Get out in front or get off the track." Billy actually dropped out of one race because he couldn't run with Easton's yelling in his head. And later, when Mills went on to run for the Marine Corps, Mills had to ask Easton not to even watch his race.

"Coach, I can't run when I hear your voice," Mills said to Easton.

But they say what doesn't kill you makes you stronger, and Mills speaks favourably of Easton in retrospect. Maybe Mills needed to suck it up at this time in his life and learn how to take it, and never quit. The relationship between Mills and Easton climaxed at the Olympics after Mills conquered the world by winning the 10,000-metre Olympic race and Easton smothered Billy with praise.

"You are the greatest Kansas Jawhawk of them all," said Easton.

Billy was gracious in accepting the praise and Easton was either sincere or making a selfish attempt to draw credit back to his coaching.

Neither man has ever said. Mills learned later in his life that his submission to Easton was influenced by low blood sugar he was experiencing due to hypoglycemia which wasn't diagnosed at the time. The hypoglycemia made him dizzy and weak which was exacerbated by Easton's bleating from the sidelines of the track.

In sharp contract to Easton was Tommy Thompson, Billy's coach in the Marines.

After graduating with a degree in physical education, Mills entered a three year commission with the United States Marine Corps in 1962. He was a first lieutenant in the Marine Corps Reserves when he won the gold medal at the Tokyo Olympics in 1964.

Mills blossomed under Thompson's tutelage, the first white person since high school who didn't tell him not to dream too big.

For example, when Thompson asked Billy what his goals were, Mills replied, "An Olympic medal and a time of 28:50."

Thompson let Billy know that his time of 28:50 wasn't good enough, he would need 28:25, and that was what Billy wrote down in his track journal.

Then Thompson asked Mills, "And why a medal?"

Mills responded, "Why, don't you believe I can?"

"I do, dammit, but if you run just to medal, you could end up third; after all, there are three medals, bronze, silver and gold," Thompson pointed out.

Point taken. Billy wrote down "gold" in his journal.

"Now, where do you see yourself when you think about that race?" Thompson continued relentlessly.

"Being on Clarke's shoulder," Billy responded, beginning to like the trim, fit, white-haired gentleman in front of him more with each passing comment.

"Why Clarke?" Thompson asked with a somewhat sly grin.

"He's the world record holder," said Billy, wondering what could possibly be wrong with that answer.

And Thompson pointed out the obvious.

"Clarke might be fifth. The thing you have to visualize is being on the *leader's* shoulder."

It was with this kind of common sense, knowledgeable and experienced coaching, and simple belief in his runners, that Thompson was able to get athletes like Mills believing in himself like thet should. Mills got to visualizing his time, and gold medal, and place in the race in the way Thompson pointed out so incessantly that the process became a sort of self-hypnosis.

Away from the track, but crucial to Billy Mills' success, was his family. Not the seven siblings he left behind in Pine Ridge, although they sent their love as often as they could, but the family Billy would build for himself with his lifelong partner Pat.

They met at the University of Kansas in 1961, when Billy was given the task of showing off the campus to potential recruits and he wanted to make the outing a bit more "festive." A prospective girl Billy knew in a dormitory had already gone home for the weekend, so Billy kept trying others who might make the Kansas campus more attractive for the potential Jawhawk. After a while, the girl on the switchboard realized it was the same guy trying girl after girl and she asked what was going on. When Billy explained and mentioned the recruit was from Coffeyville, the switchboard operator indicated she might know the guy because she was from the same town. The next step was obvious but Patricia Harris "didn't do blind dates." So Billy asked her to join him for a Coke (after all, they were hardly strangers, having talked on the phone about ten times).

It was kind of "curiosity at first sight" and it took a while for the attraction to grow. Pat's first serious words to Billy turned out to be a question he had often asked himself.

"What are you?"

"I am a Sioux Indian from the Pine Ridge Reservation in South Dakota."

"I knew you were something but I didn't know what."

Pat was petite, bright and assured, and she wanted to be an artist. But she was willing to put her career aside when her initial curiosity about Billy turned to fascination that drew the young man out.

"When I opened up to her, she believed! There was not a doubt in her mind that I could conquer the world. She was the first white person I completely trusted," Billy says.

They married on February 27, 1962 and, of course, helpful, loving old coach curmudgeon Easton asked Billy, "Why do something so stupid? Why not somebody rich? She's poorer than you are."

The voice of ignorant authority. I think Mills was always too gracious towards Easton but that is my opinion, not Billy's.

Pat became Billy's best friend and partner in life. As an interracial couple, both would have to weather confused glances and discrimination and downright racism. Pat stood up to it as well as, if not better than, Billy.

Like, at a party, when some dolt threw bongo drums over to Billy and said, "Here, you guys are good at beating on the ol' tom toms!"

Billy always seemed to get more hurt than angry at racial taunts and when you look at it, that dolt was really just trying to be funny. He was more ignorant and insensitive than mean.

Pat simply diffused the situation by grabbing the drums and saying, "I know how to play these things," and pounding out the percussion that beat that beast back into the box.

Racism is always best handled by staying on the high road and letting others learn through your example. Confrontation, lectures, speeches and the like often just increase the divisions between people.

And so when Billy was being rejected by motel managers at every stop that he and Pat made on a journey across the southern u.s. when he got transferred to Camp Pendleton, CA, Pat just revisited one of the motels and handled the registration her own sweet, white self. Pick your fights wisely, save your energy for the important stuff and don't go down to the low road.

Pat became, and is, Billy's rock. In June 1962, Mills got his degree and was free to shape his future with Pat. She would be therapist, helpmate, wife, and mother.

They were living in the age of austere amateurism, so Billy's training for the Olympics had to be done while he somehow supported Pat, who was pregnant with their first daughter. Mils realized that if he wanted to achieve his goal of a gold medal, his best option was to join the u.s. Marines, which had a track team and a coach.

"Pat liked the Marine Corps approach," says Billy. "I could take a three-year commission in late 1962. That would give me just over a year and a half to make the 1964 Olympics, and the year afterward to run for the Marine Corps. Then I'd be out and we could start a business."

He enlisted and Pat got a room near the base in Quantico, Virginia and a job in a bank.

Pat became indispensable.

"She did my massages; she prepared the meals that I planned out," Mills says. "I had just been diagnosed as pre-diabetic and hypoglycemic."

Billy's volatile blood sugar caused periods of sweaty faintness and weakness if he didn't get something sweet into his system fast.

"Because Pat was with me, I was able to ramp up and get the best out of myself very quickly when we moved to Camp Pendleton."

"Having given up my art career to assist Billy and raise our family," Pat says, "our life revolved around Billy's training, marine requirements, and his travel schedule. I would take Christy to the track to have an outing, when other mothers were taking their children to the park."

Mills' training was so voluminous, it was preparing him for the marathon as well as the 10,000.

"I could run my long runs farther there than ever before, in part because there were orange trees all over the place, and I'd be peeling them as I ran. That kept my blood sugar from going low."

Mills made the American Olympic team by placing second in the 10,000-metre race at the u.s. trials. There was just one problem remaining. Billy wanted, no needed, Pat to be in the stands.

"We took out a loan from the bank to pay for Pat's ticket to Tokyo," says Mills. "I lay awake nights worrying about how to pay it back. I took a long run just to ponder. 'Do I need her there to win? Yes, of course I do. I could not possibly win without her."

So Pat the partner, wife, best friend, office manager, mother and housekeeper came to Tokyo. Pat's mom took care of baby Christy.

Excerpt from Billy Mills live presentation:

"There were two seats left open when I got on the bus from the dormitory to the stadium. One was beside Randy Matson, a 285-pound shot-putter from Texas A & M, and off over here was a vacant seat by a very beautiful young lady from Poland…"

It appeared to be a no-brainer, which it was, but not in the way Mills would prefer to use the word.

"I ignored Randy and it turned out to be a big mistake. The Polish girl spoke perfect English and she asked me what event I was in and I told her I was running in the 10,000-metre run."

"Today's the final," she said…and I said yes.

"Who do you think is gonna win?"

Billy laughs.

"You don't ask somebody (who is in the race) that! I could not respond.

"Then she taps me on the shoulder and asks me, 'Who do you think is gonna win? Clarke, the world record holder, or Petr Bolytnikov, the defending champion from Russia?"

"Now she's giving me a choice…that did not include me!

"I dug down as deeply as I could, and I quietly came up with… 'I am going to win'…

"What's your name?" she asked.

"Billy Mills."

"Oh."

"No more dialogue the rest of the way."

No matter how many times you watch the film of Mills' victory, the thrill of the race keeps coming back again and again because it is such an exciting, come-from-behind upset.

Prior to those 1964 Olympics, Mills was a virtual unknown in the running world, especially globally. His time in the preliminaries was a full minute slower than the favourite for the gold medal, Ron Clarke of Australia, who held the world record for the 10,000-metres. Mills' best time was 45 seconds slower than Clarke's.

All you have to do to realize the difference is to imagine a runner crossing a finish line and then waiting almost a full minute for the next guy to cross the line. Nobody could imagine anybody making up such a huge deficit, especially in the field of elite-level long-distance running, where gains are made in small increments, year by year, race by race, mile by mile and second by second and micro-second.

There were only two other runners in the field who were expected to provide any kind of challenge to Clarke: Murray Halberg of New Zealand, who had won the 5,000-metre race at the 1960 Olympics, and defending champion Pyotr Bolytnikov of the Soviet Union. But Clarke, just as sharp of mind as he is fit of body, had come up with a new racing strategy which threw everybody else off; some out of the race, and some for just a while.

Clarke decided to surge every second lap and by the time the race was half over, there were only four runners who had kept Clarke in sight and supposedly within reach. Then, with two laps to go, there were just two runners remaining to give Clarke a go. One was Mohammed Gammoudi of Tunisia, who was running a very close second to Clarke, and the other was Mills, who was battling for the lead as they entered the final lap.

Excerpt from Billy Mills live presentation:

We get to the track and the race got underway... lap after lap runners fall behind and we cross the 3-mile mark... the time was 13 minutes, 29 seconds...

Two problems...I'm in 4th place...that's the small problem...the big problem...I'm within one second of my fastest 3-mile ever but the race is not 3 miles...it is 6.2 miles...

I can't continue... I'm going to quit...

When you quit a distance race, you look into the infield... you want to quit where nobody recognizes you... I looked into the infield and all the people were local Japanese people from Tokyo, I'm an Oglala Lakota from Pine Ridge... anywhere there was an ideal place to quit...

But you also look into the stadium... I'm running... 80,000 people cheering and screaming and I'm on the verge of quitting...

Far faster than I had ever run before...

But who do I focus on?

I focus on my wife, Patricia...

She's crying...

Not because I'm going to quit...

But we made a commitment...she came into my world...and I was learning her world...

We made a commitment based on Native American virtues and values... stumbling many times along the way, but a commitment was made...

She was crying because of the first world record in my family... set by my adopted sister... who had 24 children... No, that's not the world record... Of the 24 children, she had 8 sets of twins!

Crying because I couldn't join a fraternity in college... It was not the University of Kansas...it was America! "You can't join because you're Indian. There is absolutely nothing you can contribute."

Not being able to room with two dear friends of mine because one man's white, one man's black, and I'm Indian...the three of us not allowed to expand upon the love, the diversity, the compassion we can empower one another with...

She's crying for another reason. After my younger brother Chick was born, our mom and dad divorced. Our mother remarried... my dad's younger brother. So my uncle became my stepfather. My mom died of cancer, tuberculosis, diabetic at the age of 42. So my uncle, or my step-father, remarried...my mom's younger sister... I've never counted the multitudes of perceptions that go along with that... And, as First Nations people, indigenous people throughout the world, as Native Americans, there are multitudes of perceptions that people have of us...

There's no way I can quit...

I had to choreograph my journey into this vast universe of opportunity that awaits me...just like we have to help our young people choreograph their journey...

Because so many of our indigenous young people have broken wings... broken families, broken promises, broken hearts... devastating levels of suicide...diabetes...

I continued lap after lap after lap...

By now, they were lapping runners and as they ran down the backstretch, Clarke got boxed in. In desperation, he pushed Mills, knocking him off stride and into the outer lanes. Mills recovered and starting charging once more but then Gammoudi pushed by both Clarke and Mills, knocking Billy off stride again, and surging into the lead as they rounded the final curve. Clarke began chasing Gammoudi but it looked like Mills had lost too much ground from all the pushing and being knocked off stride to recover (it takes a lot of energy to regain the natural rhythm of your stride). Mills had fallen 12 metres off the lead, seemingly much too far to get back into contention with just 400 metres to go.

Excerpt from Billy Mills live presentation:

I made the All-American team in my freshman season...

There is an official photograph the American Athletic Union takes every year at the end of the NCAA track and field season...but when it came time to take the official picture...

I remember the words, "You! Yeah, you the dark-skinned one. We want you out of the photo, so step aside."

I broke...

I stepped out.

And nobody seemed to wonder why Billy Mills, the All-American from the University of Kansas, wasn't included in the picture, not even officials from U. Kansas.

The next year, I made All-American again. And I heard the words, "You, the Indian guy. I want to take two photos, one without you, and one with you."

And a little bit more of me broke.

I stepped out of the picture...

Next year, the words were "Congratulations, Mills...three times All-American...I want to take two photos...the first one without you and the next one I'll take with you.'"

Faced with racism all his life, shunned by the white world because he was an Indian, teased and taunted by Indians on Pine Ridge because he was half-white, discriminated against whenever he tried to find a place to stay, or to work. Billy realized that he had been coping with all of it by running, and it just seemed to be getting him nowhere.

"I was running to escape, I was running to find an identity. I had been running all of my life."

More tragically, Bill seemed to have forgotten everything his father had told him. About the obstacles, the fragmented perspectives.

"So I went back to my hotel room, which was on the sixth floor, and I placed a chair in front of the window," Mills says. "And I was going to jump...

"I want to tell you why I didn't jump...

"I didn't hear through my ears. I heard it underneath my skin...

"Don't.

"Don't...

"That loving, soothing...

"Don't.

"I thought it was my dad's voice. I remembered I needed a dream to heal a broken soul...

"I got off the chair...

"That compelling, compassionate, firm, soothing, loving voice that said, "Don't."

"Don't."

"And so I got down off that chair..."

Mills was too great a fighter to go meekly into that nothingness. Not without a fight. Death was too easy.

"I grabbed my notebook and I wrote down, 'Gold Medal, 10,000-metre run'...

"Believe. Believe. Believe. Believe!"

NBC race announcer Galen Rupp focused on the frontrunners but race analyst Dick Bank could see that Mills, despite being bounced all the way out to the fourth lane, creating even more distance between him and the finish line, was making up ground like "Mine that Bird" at the 2009 Kentucky Derby. As Bank screamed with delight, Mills, with mighty, literally bouncing strides that carried him past both Clarke and Gammoudi, won in an Olympic record time of 28:24.4; almost 50 seconds faster than he had ever run the 10,000-metre distance before.

I deliberately chose the verb "bounced" to describe Mills' gait as he flashed/sprinted/sped by his two opponents because Mills might have caught a break by being forced out to that fourth lane. Call it destiny or fate, the cinder track in Sweden was rather well-worn by the time the 1964 Olympics were held. Lane one, because it provided the shortest distance around the track, was severely beaten down and flat. The lanes on the outside had experienced much less traffic and provided a lot of spring, or bounce, to a runner's stride. You can see this in Mills stride to the finish line.

But there can be no doubt that Mills' victory was deserved. I mean, he was pushed by Clarke and knocked sideways into the fourth lane and a distant third place, interrupting his stride numerous times. Stride is so important to the speed, pace and psyche of a runner that for Mills to recover from all of this is a tremendous achievement. Perhaps that destiny which Mills was trying so long to find decided to play a role in that fourth lane, it is also interesting to note this would be the last time a cinder rack was used for the Olympic Games, but Mills earned his gold medal fair and square on this day.

The Olympic spirit also played a role. Gammoudi had beaten Mills with a late sprint at the 1963 world military championships in Belgium, and the Tunisian advised Mills to build more speed into his 10,000 metre strategy. So Mills, finally rejecting Easton's "old school" advice, started adding sprints to his training regimen, and it paid off by catching and passing his "mentor" with that late sprint in 1964. Kind of like the 1936 Olympics when Jesse Owens kept fouling his attempts in the long jump trials. His main competitor, Lutz Long of Germany, advised him to move his mark back a foot and Owens qualified. Owens would end up beating Lutz in the long jump final to provide a classic example of the brotherhood of sport.

Both Clarke and Mills ran the marathon after the 10,000-metre event. Clarke finished in 9th place, and Mills finished in 14th, in a respectable 2:22:55.4, approximately two-and-a-half minutes behind Clarke.

Mills later set U.S. records for 10,000 metres (28:17.6) and the three-mile run, and had a 5,000-metre best of 13:41.4. In 1965, he and Gerry Lindgren both broke the world record for the six-mile run when they finished in a tie at the AAU National Championships, running 27:11.6.

The honours that Mills accumulated as a long-distance runner are readily available on the internet. A brief summary: Mills has been inducted into the U.S. National Track and Field Hall of Fame (1976), U.S. Olympic Hall of Fame (1984), and the National Distance Running Hall of Fame, the Kansas Hall of Fame, the South Dakota Hall of Fame, the San Diego Hall of Fame and the National High School Hall of Fame.

By the way, NBC fired colour commentator Dick Bank for being too exuberant during the call of the race (the last lap is available on the internet and the excitement in Bank's voice is a priceless delight all by itself). Rival networks quickly scooped Bank up and he went on to a long and satisfying career in TV sports announcing, which might just be an indication of how far the benefits of this moment in Olympic history would extend.

Mills was honourably discharged from the marines with he rank of first lieutenant in 1965. Eventually, the Mills family (Christy would be joined by three sisters) settled down and Billy started an insurance business. Later they moved to Fair Oaks, a quiet, modest town northeast of Sacramento.

Life with the Mills became a balancing act between business and family, the PTA and kids and kids' sports and other extracurricular activities, but the schedule of speaking engagements kept expanding as more and more requests to hear Billy's special story were received. It took a while, but finally Billy and Pat were able to find enough time to begin working towards his true destiny.

Billy and Pat both knew that his mission in life had been established by his father a minute after he crossed the finish line in the 10,000-metre race at the Olympics. To harness the transient appeal of a single gold medal to do service for his Oglala Lakota people.

His experiences had provided Billy Mills with a special message which he knew had to be shared with future generations, as well as people who were searching for answers to the questions in their lives.

This included answers to improve their own lives, and all the way to building a world based on unity and brotherhood and peace.

So Billy and Pat set up a speaker's forum and after a lengthy period of hard work, with the living room of the Mills household serving as head office while Pat organized Billy's speaking schedule and all of the administration and logistics which are an integral part of such a business, and continued to juggle the PTA and supervising or driving the children to all of their school and extra-curricular activities, Pat got a handle on the organization that was needed to accommodate the fact that Billy was in huge demand as a speaker throughout the world.

"One of my greatest honours," Mills says, "was the Lakota nation declaring that I had counted coup against all the other runners in the world. They declared me a warrior of my nation.

"But I still owed a giveaway.

"In the Lakota tradition, a giveaway is a bestowing of thanks and gifts to people who helped empower you. It would not be easy because a few of our tribal leaders were saying I had a white wife, I was half-white myself, and I lived in the white world, so I probably wasn't going to fulfill my giveaway."

Anybody who has seen Billy Mills' live presentation knows why he is in such high demand. For those of you who have never been blessed by this experience, I have been incorporating a condensed version of his talk which includes some repetition of information at times but is necessary to maintain the flow of Billy's story. I have strived to be accurate but the printed word can never match the compassion and eloquence which Billy maintains throughout his live presentations.

By giving readers a sample and a sense of the message Billy Mills has carried around the world a half a dozen time times to 106 countries,

I hope to help readers make more sense out of Billy's story, and to provide as many benefits as possible from his inspiring message.

To hear (or read) this story mostly in Mills' own words is the best way anyway.

Excerpts from Mills presentation:

> I truly felt that I had wings on my feet... I was told that moment was magical, that the world had just witnessed the "greatest upset in Olympic history unfold," I was told that it was "electrifying"...
>
> However, that is not what I took from sport...
>
> What I took was that it was the journey, not the destination, that empowered me... those daily decisions I made during 15 years of training... those 60,000 miles I ran to prepare for that moment that empowered me as an athlete...not breaking the tape...
>
> It's the daily decisions we make in life, not just the talent we possess, that choreograph our destiny...
>
> I carry a true sense of global unity through the dignity, through the character, through the beauty of global diversity... unity through diversity... which is not only the theme of the Olympic Games... far, far more significant... it is the future of humankind..."

Every part of Billy Mills' life from birth to the present can be found in the events that took place on one day, October 14, 1964. Everything that had happened in Billy's life and everything that would take place for the rest of his life would be connected in some way to this day.

Excerpt from Mills live presentation:

> I graduated from college...Patricia and I went off to the Olympic Games and it's time for my race...
>
> I get on the bus to go to the track... I'm being paged. I go back inside the Olympic Village where we were living...I pick up the phone... it's my sister from the Reservation...

"I hope we're not bothering you, Billy... We love you... We've been praying for you... Regardless what happens, we..."

And then we were disconnected...

But just the simple thought somebody back home is thinking about me, somebody cares, somebody loves me... my confidence went way up!

But this would be a day when emotions went from sky high to lowest of the low and back and forth up and down.

The numbers were scary. This citizen of the Oglala Lakota Nation, who had grown up on the poverty-stricken Pine Ridge Indian Reservation, was 24 years and 6,000 miles removed from his birthplace, was just one statistic in a world of sports which is completely dominated by numbers.

The most important statistic was that Billy's best time for covering the 10,000-metre distance was a full 50 seconds slower than of the world record holder and race favourite Ron Clarke of Australia. And there were three or four other runners who could stay close to Clarke. This made Mills not only an "unknown factor" but a huge underdog, and he had to draw on everything and anything he could find in his heart and mind to convince himself that he had an even remote chance of winning the race.

But Billy Mills carried the love of a father, the dreams of a child, the faith of a good woman and the spirituality of a proud nation into the race and it was a combination that would create a vision that would be fulfilled.

By this time, memories of how the United States Olympic Committee had refused to supply him with running shoes had become irrelevant, just as they should have been when he went out and found some good people who borrowed him a pair (this is the second native athlete who had to scrounge a good pair of running shoes and it doesn't end here).

Mills managed to stay with the lead runners and by the final lap, Billy was running in second place, just off Ron Clarke's shoulder. Mills actually took the lead at one point and then the crowded field made it so they would have to lap the slower runners.

Excerpt from Mills presentation:

Clarke pushed me all the way out to lane 4 so that he would have room to get by the runner but Muhammed Gammadi surprised us both by squirting through the opening and bursting into the lead. I stumbled and fell about ten yards back of Ghammadi and Clarke.

And then I quit again...

I was going to quit in the most cowardly way of all...

I took off after Clarke, and for pushing me, I was going to catch him, and hit him!

The most cowardly way of quitting...

But the virtues and values I trained on...the Native American virtues and values I was trying to implement in my life...kept me going...

Just one more try...one more try...one more try...

I started to go low blood sugar... One year before the Olympic Games I was diagnosed hypoglycemic...you get clammy sweat, shaky, blurred vision...I didn't know if I could go with the runners...

I decided to let them get maybe 10 metres ahead of me and I would make one more try coming off the curve...

They're now 12-15 metres ahead of me. 200 metres to go...80,000 people screaming, all I could hear was the throbbing of my heart... the tingling sensation going up and down my arm...my vision coming and going...

Now! I've got to try and catch them now! Lifting my knees and pumping my arms...100 metres to go 8 metres behind...that's a lot of distance to make up...

Now! Now!

Lapping runners, Clarke and me. A lapped runner, Lutz Phillip from Germany was in front of me in lane 4...I would have to go 4 or 5 more yards to get around him... What do I do?

Lutz saw me and moved over to lane 5 and opened up the lane for me...

Now! Now!

As I go by Lutz Phillip, I glanced to make sure our legs weren't going to get tangled and trip me... and I see in the centre of his jersey, was an eagle... an eagle!

Back to my dad…"Son, if you do these things, you can have wings of an eagle…"

I can win, I can win!

Thirty yards to go I saw the tape stretched out over the finish line… my thoughts became, "I won, I won, I won," and then I felt the tape break across my chest…

I remember a Japanese race official coming up to me and yelling, "Who are you? Who are you?"

At first I responded, "Oh my God! Did I miscount the laps, do I have another lap to go?"

The Japanese official said, "Finish! Finish! You are the new Olympic champion!"

I went to find Lutz Phillip to thank him for that eagle that helped me win the gold medal…

I found him…there was no eagle…

It was simply a perception…

But always, there was his dad's voice. The voice that spoke of wings of an eagle on his feet. That gentle, soothing voice that said "Don't" when he needed to hear that certain word the most at that certain time.

We have many of our young people today going to accomplish great things because of perceptions…and how they have dealt with perceptions…

But we have many who have signed a note…and they've taken their life…

And the notes simply said…

Nobody cares…

I don't feel I belong…

It's my last attempt to show a badge of courage…

Billy pauses to reflect and collect himself.

I'm taken to the awards ceremony and I'm on the victory stand…

There's no more beautiful music to hear than our national anthem when you're representing our country and you're in the number one position with a gold medal hanging around your neck…

But I want to tell you what I felt, which overpowered all emotions...

I felt my Dad's words again...

"Son, you can step out of the circle now..."

Billy refers to a painting Pat has mastered that depicts Billy well past the finish line.

Perhaps that is why the painting my wife painted of me has me half in the circle and half out...

"Son, you can step out of the circle now...

"Look beyond the hurt, the hate, the jealousy, the self-pity...all those emotions will destroy you, son...

"Look deeper, way down deeper where the dreams lie...

"You can bicker and complain and you can quit... or you can go back into the competition and prove what you can do.

"Find your dreams, son... it is the pursuit of the dream that heals you..."

Years later, Mills would learn that his subconscious cannot separate dreams from reality and therefore, his dreams can become reality.

I felt my dad saying to me, through feeling, "Take the foremost, powerful virtues of our people...bravery, fortitude, wisdom, generosity, and here is how you use them...

"You take bravery and fortitude and you go on a journey to the centre of your soul. And that's where you find the virtue of wisdom. You use the virtue of wisdom to make the right choices for yourself... The right choices will empower you and lead you to generosity and that generosity will allow you to empower others. When you do that, son, you become an emerging elite warrior...responsibility with accountability, humility...the power of giving...centred around a core of spirituality.

"And there are four spiritual steps a warrior seeks to fulfill...

"To be unique, to belong, to make a difference to society and to understand."

And I say through understanding, promote global unity through the dignity, the character, and the beauty of global diversity; the future of humankind.

The same as the Olympic ideal...the pursuit of peace and inter-cultural connection through international sport.

The stated goal of the Olympic movement is "to contribute to building a peaceful and better world by educating youth through sport without discrimination of any kind."

Many, many of our young indigenous people, First Nations people in Canada, Native Americans in the u.s., aboriginals globally, are pursuing their dream, for the betterment of themselves, for the betterment of their families, for the betterment of their nation, for the betterment of the world.

I felt that I had a simple obligation in my life... I felt that winning that gold medal was a gift to me from a higher power... and I wanted to take that one moment in time and give back..."

The giveaway.

Billy readily admits that the understanding he has of those words his father spoke are his interpretation after thinking for many years about those times with his dad. The words were comforting and made sense when he was 9 and 12 years old but their meaning has grown over the years to fit in with the many cultures and experiences that Billy's journey through life has provided.

———————————

As with Jim Thorpe, a movie was made about the life of Billy Mills. Financed by the oil-rich Ermineskin First Nation of Alberta, *Running Brave* was an earnest attempt to capture the spirit and the surprising story that was Billy Mills, and the film was quite well-received. But without a big budget and major stars, it wasn't a major box office success.

Some controversy was raised by the fact the actor who played Mills, Robby Benson, is white, but Mills is half-white himself and the resemblance between Mills and Benson was quite remarkable. Mills had no objections.

Bill Easton is given a positive portrayal in the movie as a kindly old coach who is largely responsible for Billy's success. Portrayed by the veteran character actor who specializes in kindly old curmudgeons, Pat Hingle, Easton comes off as a positive mentor in Mills life when the opposite could be just as close to the truth.

Roger Ebert gave *Running Brave* a favourable review. It was a nice film, kind of "Disney-style," before it became Touchstone.

Mills is much more renowned for his work away from sport following his retirement as he remained obsessed with fulfilling his giveaway. The notoriety he gained from *Running Brave* allowed him to spread the word, and it reached Gene Krizek, a global philanthropist whose credentials included a presidential commendation. Krizek knew the ins and outs of setting up an ambitious charitable organization. Running Strong for American Indian Youth was established in 1986 with Billy Mills as its principal (and tireless) spokesman.

The scope of Running Strong can only be described as vast and unique in that it serves youth by creating a healthy environment in which to grow. Projects include building 20 log homes in one year so that a kid has a positive immediate environment to be surrounded by, and wells, to provide badly needed clean, fresh, healthy drinking water in Pine Ridge and other reservations. They extend to establishing dialysis clinics in Indian country (three so far) in response to the epidemic of diabetes that plagues Native Americans, along with education about healthy diets in the schools to counteract the devastating effects of switching from an active, hunting lifestyle with a diet of wild meat and healthy plants to the sedentary lifestyle of the reservation with its white flour, lard and sugar.

Running Strong has even ventured into unique projects such as a heat matching program, which provides propane, electricity or firewood to families in need.

And, of course, because education is always key to positive youth development, there is academic support; the Billy Mills Scholarship for education students at the University of Kansas.

Mills is eternally grateful for the donations that make the work of Running Strong possible. And for the opportunity to turn that one moment of single victory into a giveaway that is lasting for generations.

Wherever Mills goes, he is sure to pass on the value and virtues of Lakota teachings.

It has been great work, but the problems of Native American youth seem to keep getting bigger. Especially the number of suicides. Mills can relate to that from his own personal experience but he can only reach so many people directly. And this led to another project.

In 1990, Mills and an old friend, novelist Nicholas Sparks (of *Message in a Bottle* fame) wrote *Lesson of a Lakota,* a book that gently addresses depression and the emotional factors that can lead to suicide, and alcohol and drug abuse. It is the story of a young boy who, filled with grief from the loss of his mother, is guided to the habits of mind which lead to contentment and happiness by a knowing Elder (an obvious connection to Billy Mills and his father, Sidney).

Billy has also served as a role model and inspiration for the Native American youth who strive to fly like he did. While nobody has ever matched his success in track, Billy has fostered achievement by serving as an original board member of the Wings of America's Indian youth development program. The real success is in the effort, not the perfection.

"It is the journey, not the destination."

It is from this that Billy Mills has moved ever forward: the lessons he learned on that day when he overcame all of the obstacles in his life and achieved the success that allowed him to step out of the circle.

To form Running Strong for American Indian Youth. To travel the world with his message of the warrior spirit.

If things don't appear to be getting better on the surface, Mills refers to books like *The New Jim Crow* by Michelle Alexander, which points out the massive socioeconomic forces that are impacting impoverished communities such as ghettos and reservations—backed by resources that small, sincere community-based organizations cannot match.

And so Running Strong for American Youth achieves what it can—significant, positive change in that corner of the world in which it strives to provide its benefits.

Always, Billy Mills has been in search of the answer to that question, "Who am I? What am I?" His father being a Catholic, Billy grew up with those teachings, but some hypocrisy he witnessed called him to question white man's religion.

Then there were the acceptance issues he encountered, being half-white on an Indian reservation.

The spiritual conflict only grew as Billy travelled the world and was introduced to the multitude of faiths of Islam and Hindu and Judaism and all the rest. How could he reconcile all this with his Oglala Lakota teachings and spirituality?

What was the truth?

Is there one truth?

The seven sacred teachings of love, goodness, truth, respect, knowledge and humility are well and good but nobody can be expected to live by these traditional First Nations teachings every second of every minute of every day of every year. But they are universal truths to strive for and they find commonality in most all of the world's religions.

If there can be one truth, it can only be found through the tolerance which accepts the beliefs of others as valid as your own. And Billy found his way to this truth through the teachings of Joseph Campbell.

Campbell is a renowned mythologist and philosopher who has authored some best-selling books, most notably *The Power of Myth* and Bill's favourite, *The Hero with a Thousand Faces*. Campbell, who was a fine collegiate half-miler in his own right, believed that all religions are cultural masks over the same fundamental truths.

Mills, a mystery to himself, felt liberated. His Lakota traditions were just as compelling, and just as powerful, as any other. And if all religions are searching for the same answers, he didn't have to reject one or another, Catholic or Lakota.

"It allowed me to take my Native American culture, tradition and spirituality," Mills says, "and blend them with Christianity."

Like the commonly called Golden Rule—"Do unto other as you would have others do unto you" is universally accepted.

The Oglala Lakota Nation gave Billy Mills his name, "Matata Tak Halo," which means "He respects the Earth" or "He loves his country." Billy's

Lakota name certainly matches his respect for the land he has travelled and the nations he has represented.

Addendum from the author:

I first met Billy Mills over 30 years ago when I was part of a group in Winnipeg that invited Billy to give his presentation and inspire people. The experience revealed how the Billy Mills presentation can benefit local organizations in a practical way by bringing people together to work cooperatively for the common good.

I had been working with the first Indian woman to be called to the bar in Canada, Marion Ironquil Meadmore, on a small economic development program that was designed to create wealth and employment for native people in Winnipeg's inner city. We were tired of all the emphasis on social services and make-work programs that didn't seem to be working, so we decided that the answer to much of the dysfunction, which is mostly caused by poverty, was to create a way for people to have long-term jobs, sustainable through profits from successful businesses.

The Indian Business Development Group (IBDG) of Winnipeg did just that by, for example, lending $15,000 to a couple of native hairdressers who were working for somebody else downtown to set up their own business. After a couple of years, this hair dressing salon had repaid the loan with interest and the two original women had hired two other native women to do hair at their new successful salon.

We realized that our new businesses could benefit from "networking" with other businesses in the city, kind of like "I cut logs and you build homes so why don't we get together and do business?" So we decided to hold a gala dinner at one of the top hotels in downtown Winnipeg to bring white businesspeople and native entrepreneurs together to network and raise some money at the same time. We charged $100 a plate and we called the event "Formula for Success."

Prior to this, fundraising dinners for First Nations organizations had consisted of potluck dinners at the St. John's Bosco Centre in our rundown downtown. Many of our colleagues were apprehensive about our move downtown and told us we were doomed to fail.

"Nobody is going to come to a high-class honkey dinner like you're planning. What native businesses there are won't be able to afford the hundred bucks for the dinner and the white business crowd doesn't want to socialize with a bunch of Indians no matter how much you dress them up," they said.

Well, lo and behold, with a lot of good organizing, hard work and cajoling, our gala dinner was a huge success. It completely sold out and, by the business cards we collected to enter our draw for a door prize (but actually to develop a database), we could see the matches we were making made sense, and we received reports of quite a few viable business connections that were made as a result. Even if two small business owners didn't form some sort of formal partnership, a lot of mentorship relationships formed and everybody had a good time (especially moi, because the only door prize I could get donated for our draw from the fish bowl where we collected the biz cards of all attendees was a chainsaw and I had a helluva a lot of fun revving it up at the most surprising, exciting, simply fulfilling times...

R-r-r-r-r-ooom-m-m-m-ding-ding-ding-ding!

Holding a roaring chainsaw is right up there with sex for most guys.

The surprise hit of the evening was the guest speaker we had brought in; an Indian long-distance runner from the United States who was largely unknown in Canada but who had a reputation for giving a good after dinner presentation about how to succeed in business that he called, coincidently, "Formula for Success."

Nobody in Winnipeg had heard very much about Billy Mills before our event but we needed a native entrepreneur, a small business-type, to fill the role of speaker, and Billy fit the bill. So I can't say that his name was a big draw for ticket sales, but his fees were reasonable and we ended up selling 500 tickets using a large volunteer phone bank, a huge database and plenty of hard work and sweat and we made some decent coin on the event.

Most rewarding was the fact that businesspeople on both sides of the line could see the merit in this idea and it was the start of some beautiful new friendships through which Indians crossed the tracks to the other side, where lucrative partnerships lie.

And still, the presentation by Billy Mills outdid everything. Mills' passionate and eloquent address was the best we could ever imagine for our first try at this kind of function, and anything we could envision for the future...

Billy Mills is registered with the prestigious *Sports Illustrated* speakers bureau so we kind of expected he was going to be a well-seasoned professional. It was a huge bonus that Billy Mills retains his down-home enthusiasm and immensely personable style while recreating the excitement of his huge Olympic victory and relating it to his success, and his audience's success, in business.

Billy starts his presentation with a film of the actual 10,000-metre race from 1964. The closeness of the race, Billy's comeback in the last lap, the near miraculous win by an underdog, really got the 500 people in attendance excited. The wild exuberance of the announcer taking place at the same time as the crowd of 80,000 in Tokyo is cheering so loudly gets the live dinner audience screaming at the screen at the top of their lungs, too. All of a sudden, you are swept up in the excitement as if you were back in 1964 and seeing the race for the first time yourself! It's a lot of fun and it always bring the dinner guests to their feet, wildly applauding in a standing ovation.

"Mills wins! Mills wins!"

"Oh my God! What an upset!"

As the murmurs die down, Billy Mills begins his presentation. Handsome, fit, articulate, eloquent and charming, Mills reviews events leading up to the race, what he went through during and after, and then goes on to tie the values of dedication, perseverance, discipline and hard work to the development of his successful insurance business and life as a family man. The major theme of his presentation is how the teachings of the Oglala Lakota Nation fit with the Olympic ideal to change self and the world around you. By the end of his presentation, Billy Mills' audience is armed to the teeth (heart and mind) with the philosophical and practical ways that make up his "Formula for Success."

Everybody at the fundraising dinner in Winnipeg went away knowing their C-note had been well-spent, and most highly motivated to incorporate this new formula for success with the successes and struggles they were going through in their own life and business.

Notah Begay III

4

"Almost There"

Notah Begay is one of the original "code talkers"—Navajo Indians who used their language to send messages for the American military which the Japanese and Nazis could not decipher during World War II. It was an invaluable role that saved thousands of lives and played a huge part in making VE and VJ days happen. The role of code talkers became widely known through Clint Eastwood's movie *Wind Talkers*.

Grandson Notah Begay III is an original; the only Native American to qualify and play on the Professional Golf Association (PGA) tour.

Notah Begay III's great-great-grandmother was one of 8,000 Navajo Indians who endured a forced march—300 miles from their home in Arizona to a barren reservation in New Mexico. Before their journey, the ancestors had been forced to sign a treaty that was one-sided in favour of newcomers to their lands on matters such as territory, ownership, resource sharing, human rights and so on.

Notah Begay III has walked 300 miles every year since he began to play golf; across manicured lawns called fairways, and grass carpets called greens, first as an amateur and then as a professional golfer, and now, for recreation and leisure, as well as in his role as a consultant course designer. Notah III is often asked to sign autographs at the end of each stretch of his golf trek.

Notah III knows the difference between the two journeys isn't measured by distance but by generations.

"We're not there yet. Things are better but they are not perfect. But we are getting closer," Notah III says.

Notah means "Almost There" in his Navajo language. His business and charitable work is getting his people "notah" to the social and economic justice and quality they seek.

Hitler and Hirohito didn't know their defeat was "notah."

One of Begay III's first forays into sports was the Pueblo seed ball game called "shinny," which is a popular game amongst his mother's people. Young Notah III excelled at manoeuvering the leather-covered ball of seeds with a curved, hook-style stick (not unlike a golf club) and led his teams by getting that ball through the opposition territory to their end of the village, which was the way the game ended. That, or when the ball split open, and the Pueblo men would plant the seeds in a ceremony to bless next year's crop.

Notah III learned that, contrary to popular belief in golf, "You *can* make a ball do what you want it to do."

One of the unique ways that Notah III got a golf ball to obey was to become the first true "switch-hitter" in golf. Like a baseball player, who tries to make a curve ball break his way from a left-handed pitcher or a right-handed pitcher by switching sides of the plate, golfers theorized that you can handle a breaking putt on a curved green more effectively by switching from a left-handed to a right-handed putting stance and vice versa. Notah III was the only one who went so far as to create a two-faced putter, smooth on either side.

Begay III is also one of just a handful of professional golfers to shoot 59 at a pro tour event. Notah III thought he could have shot 57 and he set his sights on that.

And so Notah Begay III is different. And not just because he is the first and only Native American to play on the PGA tour.

You can credit the grandfather for starting more than just the string of Notah names.

Back in the early 1940s, a group of about 375 Navajo Indians were recruited to help win World War II as code talkers. Notah Begay was one of the very first to sign up.

The U.S. government, after decades of trying to suppress the Navajo language, but just four months removed from the Japanese attack on Pearl Harbour, had discovered that this Native American dialect could be used as a code that was so different in structure and form and style that the Japanese could not decipher or "break" or otherwise understand what two Navajos were saying to each other. And so an indigenous people and a language that had been almost wiped out became the secret weapon that could save the flag, freedom, apple pie, mom and Chevrolet.

The American way.

The code talkers could pass secret information throughout the Pacific and Europe (Hitler's Gestapo, SS and Wehrmacht weren't any more successful than the Japanese at deciphering Navajo). The code talkers could scout enemy troops on secret missions and report on enemy positions.

There were adaptations to be made, of course. Just like guns and bullets were foreign (and deadly) to the bow and arrow-shooting native peoples when Europeans first arrived here, there were many military terms that did not exist in the Navajo language, so they formed rather creative analogies: a spy plane became an "owl" and "chicken hawk" meant dive bomber, just as "fire stick" had come to mean rifle in the local dialect.

Notah Begay was a true Navajo and his nation was an American ally. Despite all of the suppression and hardships that he grew up with, the true Indian warrior has an obligation to protect, and to provide, and to keep the peace. Notah respected the fact that the Navajo Nation had sacred treaties with the United States, living side by side here in North America.

As a boy, Notah had been taken from his home near Gallup, New Mexico, and placed in a boarding school in Arizona where bureaucrats anglicized his name, ordered him not to speak his native language, and cut off the traditional Navajo knot in his hair. Defiant as he could be, Notah ran away, but they caught him every time and he finally quit the Albuquerque Indian School in grade nine.

But he served his nation when called upon.

That fighting spirit has been passed on to his grandson.

Things have been easier for Notah Begay III, but he certainly wasn't born with a silver club in his crib. He worked hard for everything he achieved and a lot of credit can go to those good genes that flow from a Navajo legend.

———————

The way the stories go, Notah Begay III was at an age when he was just starting school and his father was about to embark on his daily three-mile run. Father told son to wait on a mound outside his house. The boy started to cry because he wanted to do everything he could with his father. So Dad said, "Okay, but I am not stopping for you."

"I'll be darned if that little guy didn't keep up with me the whole way," the father states proudly. "That showed me the heart of a champion right there."

And to make his sons even tougher, Notah Begay II wrapped boxing gloves around their hands and told them, "Have at each other." Notah III went without headgear to level the matches with his brother Clint, who was two years younger.

Notah II got into horse racing at one stage of his career, wanting to become the first Navajo to train a horse in the Kentucky Derby. He settled for being sire of the first Native American to play in the Masters.

"The son is on a different track than the father," says Notah Begay II, "but he is still a pioneer."

———————

"A pioneer for the Pueblo!" proud mom Laura Ansera likes to point out. "

Laura believes that her son is a victory of her tribes, the San Felipe and Isleta. It was in these Pueblo cultures that Notah Begay III spent much of his childhood, on 3,000-strong reservations where the boy learned to pray toward the sun in the San Felipe tradition and respect the world he was given—a form of spirituality that helps him become "one with the moment," a term he has used to describe when his golf game is really on. In this state, the ball is not an object trying to negotiate a hostile set of circumstances, and the club is not a weapon against danger. They are connected to their natural surroundings and work together—along with the energies of other human beings.

"Probably the easiest way to understand it is that it's a small world," Begay said. "We are continually reminded of that when we run into somebody who knows somebody who knows somebody who is close to you. We're all tied to each other, and we're all dependent on the earth and its resources, the sunlight, the water—for survival."

Said Laura, "We always tell him that he's not out there alone, that the spirits are with him."

The spirit of the Navajo code talkers are carried in the boy's genes. Notah III also carried his culture on his face when, at the age of 14, after watching some Pueblo runners, he started placing red clay under his eyes before golf tournaments as a sign of respect for the challenge ahead.

Having respect for a challenge is spiritual and proper and good form. It is bound to make you concentrate more, prepare better, try harder and all those good things a warrior keeps in mind when he responds to a challenge ("the true warrior does not judge his greatness by the goals that he sets for himself but by the obstacles which he overcomes"—First Nations philosophy).

Which would be very handy in golf, with all of its obstacles like sand traps and water hazards, although some golfers might say the Indians are stretching it when they say "The true warrior welcomes these obstacles, for they provide the challenge with which to prove one's greatness." (You can just imagine someone like Notah III reciting that chant like a mantra as he stands behind one of those six-feet high bunker walls that block the way from a sand trap back to the grass on a links course in Britain.)

The face paint had an unexpected impact on some of the young Navajo's foes. Notah III remembers how it "scared the daylights" out of one teenage opponent, who thought it was some kind of war paint and got psyched out in the late stages of a junior tournament. Despite the fact Notah III might be clad in dockers and a golf shirt, with nary a loincloth, bone choker or quiver of arrows in sight, the poor kid who was paired up with this "fierce-looking" Indian squandered a four-shot lead when the battle got heavy in the final round.

Begay kept painting his cheeks with clay right through his college years at Stanford, telling people it was to draw the bright rays of the sun away from his eyes like the football players do.

Notah stopped using the paint when he turned pro in 1995. As he became a young man, and began to develop a strong social conscience, he was worried about perpetuating a hostile Indian stereotype.

It is always difficult for First Nations people who achieve a level of notoriety and fame to make this kind of choice because there are those in the crowd who would accuse them of "selling out" or "going apple" ("red" on the outside but "white" on the inside). They say that if you take the time to explain that the clay paint is a sign of respect, a symbol of the everlasting spirituality of the Pueblo people, then you are doing good by creating awareness and understanding.

Which is all well and good, if you have the time to explain all this to huge crowds of live audiences and television viewers in an accurate and comprehensive manner. Sometimes, the subject doesn't come up until somebody makes a wisecrack, and/or media coverage relies on speculation and rumours and stereotypes instead of solid research and facts. And then the guy wearing the face paint ends up dealing with misconceptions and controversy when all he was trying to do was show some respect for his culture.

Even when given the chance to explain the significance of certain cultural traits or beliefs, sports writers often get it wrong or have their own agenda and will serve their own stereotypes no matter what you tell them. And despite the fact that many athletes from ethnic backgrounds know their history and heritage well, and are quite comfortable talking about it, it is not their job to teach the public about such things. They are athletes, the best way for people to learn about Native American culture and teachings is through oral and written history, and from the Elders and the experts.

Bottom line, if you are going to write about the paint Notah Begay III puts under his eyes, please get it right.

In any case, Notah Begay III handles issues such as this with typical grace and humour.

"Last time I checked, I hadn't killed anybody on a golf course," he says with a wistful grin.

Much has been made about Notah Begay III's Native American background, partly because the folks who write about him recognize that it is interesting and an integral part of who he is, and partly because Notah III carries his heritage up front—he is proud of where he comes from and the role it plays in all aspects of his life.

———————————

Navajo people generally live far from each other. Even today, their homes are scattered throughout their territory like golf balls on Tin Cup's driving range.

The Pueblos, on the other hand, know about negotiating tight spaces. The Pueblo have lived wall-to-wall in small communities along the Rio Grande valley where they have farmed for centuries.

On the Navajo side of his family, Notah III is of the Folded Arm people and his name means "Almost There." On the Pueblo side, Notah III descends from the Fox Clan (matrilineal), his name means "Morning Star" and he still participates in the dances and feast days of his Pueblo nation.

Notah Begay III is a registered member of the Navajo Nation and a son of Mother Earth.

Exactly how any of all this relates to his play on a golf course is best known to Notah III, his relations and his ancestors.

I have offered the information because it tells us more about who Notah Begay III is. I hope and pray that I have been accurate and that I have not misrepresented the strength and beauty of either the Navajo or Pueblo history and cultures.

Ultimately, it doesn't matter if his heart "soars like a hawk" or "thumps like a bunny rabbit," Notah Begay III still had to learn how to move a small, white, dimpled ball as much as 500 yards from an inch-high tee into a three-inch-wide hole by hitting it with a bunch of weird-shaped clubs as few times as possible.

And then he had to get on the right side of that infinitesimal "inch" that separates the superstars from the stars.

The difference between shooting in the 90s and the 80s and the 70s for club golfers is basically the athletic ability you bring to the course and the amount of time you put in practicing. On the PGA tour, the difference between regularly shooting 72 and posting a 68 once or twice every four rounds, and firing 69, 64, 71, 63 on a quasi-regular basis involves athletic skill, sound thinking, emotional control, techniques, intricacies, detail and a whole gamut of other things which separate Jack Nicklaus and Tiger Woods and Phil Mickelson from Jim Furyk, Steve Stricker and Angel Cabrera. The ones who win the most on a consistent basis are the ones who always end up on the "right inch of the hole."

Notah Begay III had everything that would put him on the right side of the inch heading into his career.

First of all, he loved the game.

"Golf is a good walk spoiled." (Mark Twain)

Mark Twain was wrong.

But to enjoy any kind of success in golf (and avoid spoiling your walk), you must enjoy the game. To be an overachiever, like the guys on the PGA tour, you must love the game.

Notah Begay III fell in love with golf at a very early age. His childhood did not begin like that of many Native American children who had gone before him, like his grandfather. Instead of being sent off to an Indian residential school where his culture and identity would be suppressed, young Notah III was enrolled in one of the best of the best schools, the Albuquerque Academy, not because his parents were enormously wealthy, but simply because they wanted the best for their child and they worked hard to get it for him.

And Notah III repaid them by excelling academically. The only thing that interfered with his education was the fact that his father lived across from the Ladera Golf Course in Albuquerque, NM. Notah III was able to access the golf course through a hole in the fence near the 14th green.

Discipline, study, ethnic pride, the love of a mother and father, a commitment to the spiritual, even good genes—those are all good things, but they don't produce a PGA golfer with Begay III's velvet touch on the greens, nor the array of things he can do with the irons and drivers and the rest of the 14 clubs the U.S. Golf Association allows a player to carry in his bag.

You get to the Masters the same way you get to Carnegie Hall. Practice, practice, practice. However, violin lessons and practice time for golf are both expensive.

"I would never say I was poor, because I know people who were a lot worse off than I was," Begay III says. "We just didn't have the luxury to do some things."

And Notah III's family was already paying substantial tuition costs.

Fortunately, Notah III's dad's new house was across from the golf course. Notah III could sneak on to the course but he would also sit outside his father's house and watch some very good, but mostly very bad, approach shots. You can learn a lot from other people's mistakes.

The Begays were the kind of lower-middle class family in which hand-me-down clothes were a given and so was sports equipment. So the early days of Notah III's development included enough character-building work to provide him with a desire to make all the effort and sacrifices worthwhile.

"At the age of six, I started collecting and recycling aluminum cans to raise enough money to buy a bucket of balls. By age nine, still a skinny little Indian kid, I introduced myself to the club pro and told him I'd work for nothing if I could practice on off-hours. From then until I went to college, I'd show up at 5:30 every morning and put in a couple of hours performing tasks like emptying trash, sweeping floors and parking golf carts. Then I'd get to practice from 8 a.m. till 6 p.m.

every day—at no charge. I thought it was the greatest job in the world because I got to hit as many golf balls as I wanted."

Waking at 5 a.m. to move carts, wash range balls and generally serve as an all-purpose gopher until sunset, Notah III got good enough to play in national junior tournaments, and again, he did whatever he needed to get there. Often, a bus ticket was all his family could afford. But by age 17, he was the No. 1 junior golfer in the country (with friend and later Stanford college roommate Tiger Woods in second place).

"There weren't a lot of brown guys out there at the time, just me and Tiger," he says.

At the top, no less! How rare is that?

There had been other brown faces on his high school basketball team, which, led by Notah III, won back-to-back state championships.

NBA basketball stars can start out on public playgrounds and high schools, but Notah III knew that golf was his passion and his proficiency, and he shot his way out of the public courses, excelled at the national junior level and soon it was off to college.

Stanford University changed its sports nickname from the Indians to the Cardinal in the early 1970s in order to comply with the effort by Native Americans to stop the use of their image and culture as mascots. That is a complicated issue we deal with in another chapter of this book.

Stanford University was quick to show respect, but it's not like they had much direct experience with Native Americans. When Notah Begay III arrived on campus in 1990, he quickly noticed he was one of very few native students there.

Which is, in a way, fortunate, because there were no special advantages handed out to ethnic minorities at Stanford. You had to be an excellent student to get in and success at the prestigious 14,000-student California school was strictly based on ambition, effort and results. Notah III wouldn't have it any other way.

Of course, Tiger Woods was a rather BMOC (Big Man On Campus). But there were a plethora of future business and political leaders at

Stanford, some of the world's next high-tech pioneers, and more than a few Sheldon Cooper prodigies.

Many of the students were from well-to-do, conservative families and one such student was Mark Freeland—a member of Stanford's golf team whom Notah III became best friends with.

On the golf course, it was kind of like *Tin Cup* meeting David Simms, but the matchup was also reminiscent of an old western pairing between an Indian who relies on instinct and skills and a rather straight-laced frontiersman who charts a cautious, well-worn path through the wilderness. This would help both golfers shape their games for the better.

"We were so different," said Freeland, who described himself as a normal white guy from a conservative, upper-middle-class community outside St. Louis. "We grew up in different environments and we were able to learn from each other."

Freeland's game derived the benefits of Begay III's more freestyle approach; Begay III constantly encouraged Freeland to check any Type A urges at the first tee and play more "from the heart." Freeland had learned the game on a difficult, private course, which taught him caution and such notions as scoring 2 to 3 strokes under par is enough to win. Begay III, who was used to improvising his way around the Ladera course to a 67 without that being considered a special kind of day, reminded Freeland that the lowest score wins.

Begay III, in turn, began to incorporate some of the elite grooming Freeland grew up with, including that all-important component: course management. Notah III began to think twice before he automatically pulled out a driver on that 325-yard hole after noticing that Freeland often got to the green more safely with a five-iron and a sand wedge, even if that approach seemed horribly stifling and (shudder) programmed.

Using the best formula golf while improvising and freelstyling at the right times was an enormous success. As a sophomore, Notah teamed up with Casey Martin to lead Stanford to the NCAA championship in 1994. Begay III shot a 62 in the second round of that tournament, a record at the time.

But there were more important lessons to be shared between Notah III and Casey Martin that helped both golfers on and off the course.

One was the notion they would putt better if they became switch-putters, based on the popular idea that a left-to-right putt is easier for a left-hander and a right-to-left putt is easier for a right-hander. Martin eventually gave up on it, but not Begay, who believed it would make him better in the long run. Begay would develop that putter that was smooth on both sides.

Ironically, Notah III was perhaps more blessed by having Martin as his teammate than the other way around. In Martin, Begay III saw firsthand an example of heroism and perseverance in contrast with misleading stereotypes of rich, white people who are spoiled by all of their advantages. Notah III found himself a genuine hero of a different complexion who offered an invaluable life lesson.

"One of the biggest images that sticks in my head was when we first got to school and we were on our first road trip and he (Casey) and I roomed together," Begay III said of Martin, who has a medical condition that has gradually shrivelled his leg (and would eventually create the controversy over whether golfers should be allowed to use carts on the pro tour). Despite having a definite physical handicap, PGA players objected to Martin using a cart even though it was painfully (and I mean painfully) obvious that Martin's leg could not stand the rigours of walking 18 holes on today's extra-long courses.

"We were winding down after a long day, and he was going to hop in the shower and he took his stocking off."

Hearing about Martin's leg was one thing; seeing it was another.

And so Notah III was reminded of how little he had to overcome and how advantaged he was, no matter how much farther he had to go.

"That is just as much testament to Notah's character that he so easily dismissed the financial hardships, being the only Native American player in 'a white man's game' and so on," says Martin. "But Notah was able to turn a kind of cocky, arrogant attitude into an asset without making enemies because we all understood how his 'it's me against the world' helped him overcome obstacles and achieve success.

"It was a powerful place to be for Notah," Martin says. "Which was great for the team, of course."

It is not widely known, but it was Begay III and Martin who built Stanford into a golf powerhouse, not Tiger Woods. A tale that has grown too tall has Woods making them worse when he arrived in 1995, because the Cardinals failed to repeat as champions with Woods on the team. But in reality, Martin is quick to point out, Woods was dominating competitions, and failing to win the NCAA with Woods certainly wasn't his fault.

"We weren't that quick to needle Woods the freshman because he was such a great player," says Martin. "Except for Notah, but that was just Notah's way."

Notah III made Woods, the celebrated freshman, carry his bags, the polite form of hazing that golf allows, and always made sure to show up at fraternity parties where he could poke fun at Woods's notoriously bad dancing. (Complexion confusion seemed to rule the day at Stanford, I mean, a black guy who can't dance?)

As with Freeland, Notah III and Casey Martin were polar opposites coming from vastly different backgrounds; which turned out to be a positive rather than a negative.

"We enjoyed our differences and learned from each other. I still consider Notah one of my very best friends to this very day; he is one of those guys you would take a bullet for."

Notah III was also one of those overachieving Stanford grads. He got a degree at Stanford in economics and has consistently maintained that achieving that degree is the greatest accomplishment of his life, surpassing anything he has done on a golf course.

Notah III also continued to build his self-awareness, immersing himself in the affairs of the Native American cultural centre on campus.

Yet, "Whenever anyone writes an article about Notah III, he is called Tiger's teammate," Freeland says.

The question was, "Would it always be that way?"

It certainly appeared that way when Notah III's professional career got off to a slow start. Notah III got bit by the bugaboo that plagues most every golfer, even Tiger, when Begay III lost control of his driver after trying to change the fundamentals of his swing. After a lot of frustration, Begay III eventually reconciled with his original swing and he surged, finishing 10th on the Nike Tour in 1998, qualifying him for the PGA Tour.

Notah Begay III's PGA tour start was almost Tiger-esque. He made more than $1 million in his first year with victories at the Reno-Tahoe Open in August, 1999 and the Michelob Championship in September.

Soon President Bill Clinton wanted to play with Notah Begay III. The call came after his first tour victory, asking Notah III if he could play a round with the commander-in-chief.

"Schedule's too tight," Notah III told Clinton's people.

But could Begay III dominate like Woods would?

"There are all these mental walls on the PGA Tour," Freeland says. "A single-round score of 58 is one barrier. No one shoots 30 under for a tournament is another. These numbers scare a lot of people if they're playing well and get close to them. Notah III doesn't have that. He doesn't play by the same rules. Right after he shot his 59 (at the Nike Tour Dominion Open in 1998), he was telling me he was sure he could have had a 57."

Notah III, like Tiger, was the type who could envision new heights and he was seen that way by others after some incredible early success on the PGA tour.

There were some early rough patches. Sometimes his worlds collided. At a Nike Tour stop in South Dakota, a group of American Indians new to golf followed Begay III around the course, piercing the requisite quiet of the golf course, and golf etiquette, with a series of traditional, high-pitched tribal cheers. Freeland, his caddie that day, recalls that Begay III's pride was tempered by his concern for any disruption that was caused to his playing partners. He failed to make the cut at that tournament. But that was only part of that top ten finish on the Nike Tour in '98 that got him his PGA tour card.

Begay III got off to that terrific start (a rookie rarely wins two tournaments in his first go around the PGA tour), and he repeated the feat the next year (FedEx St Jude Classic and Canon Greater Hartford Open—2000). People started saying he would be the major competition his former college golf teammate Tiger would face in the new millennium.

But while Woods soared to inconceivable heights, Notah Begay III fell back steadily from those dizzying early highs to the level fairways of the ordinary and then less than ordinary lows of the fallen PGA pro.

And it had nothing to do with his natural ability, his effort, his attitude, his native background or any other number of factors which can befall an athlete. Notah Begay III's career was effectively ended by a physical catastrophe.

It happens to a lot of golfers, who must twist and turn their backs in the most unnatural ways to get out of trouble on the course. Something slipped between Notah III's fourth and fifth vertebrae one day and soon he was fighting trouble with his back. His game steadily levelled off until it got so bad he played under a Major Medical Exemption by 2005. He put in a stint on the European and Nationwide Tours and even got his PGA card back for the 2008 season through Q-school (Qualifying), but the writing was on the scorecard.

And so, while Tiger Woods would dominate the golf tour, college teammate Notay Begay III fell into the rough. Like every other thoroughbred athlete, Begay III tried to play through the pain but it just got worse and worse year by year until he finally just couldn't go on in the way that he should and the way that would make him proud.

Fortunately that drive to give one's best effort that professional athletes and code talkers have would smooth the way for Notah Begay III away from the golf course.

"Obtaining an economics degree at Stanford University is the proudest achievement of my life," Notah Begay III has always said. Begay III has also been very proud to carry the culture and heritage of his Native

American background. It was natural that he would combine the two to fulfill his vast unspent energy and ambition when injury forced him to look for greener fairways away from the fields of golf.

And so NB3, a consulting and golf course design company, was formed along with the Notah Begay III Foundation, which raises funds for native youth leadership and sports programs.

Both organizations fit so naturally.

Tourism has become an important industry to many Native American tribes after gaming was legalized on Indian reservations. Prior to federal legislation, which was called "the modern white buffalo" by some, gaming was legal only in the state of Nevada. Facing longstanding and widespread poverty and unemployment on Indian reservations, the federal government passed legislation which could benefit Native Americans in a similar way cities like Las Vegas and Reno have grown and generated enormous wealth and jobs. Huge casinos such as Foxwoods and Mohegan Sun in the east and California casinos such as Pechanga and San Manuel would soon be adding "resort and country club" to their operations and yes, there was a need for a professional golf course design company with experience, expertise, and a heart, a mind and a spirit geared to the history and culture of First Nations, like the Pascua Yaqui tribe's 18-hole course set in Tucson. It has all been a natural fit for NB3.

In 2005, Notah III established the non-profit Notah Begay III Foundation. The immediate goal of the foundation was to provide health and wellness education to Native American youth in the form of soccer and golf programs. The broader purpose of the foundation was to stand as a catalyst for change in the Native American community.

On August 26, 2008 the foundation hosted the first Notah Begay III Foundation Challenge at the Turning Stone Resort & Casino, a skins golf match to raise money for the foundation. The five players for the tournament were Begay III, Stewart Cink, Vijay Singh, Camilo Villegas and Mike Weir. On August 24, 2009 the foundation hosted its second annual Notah Begay III Foundation Challenge at the Turning Stone Resort & Casino. Turning Stone is an economic enterprise of the Oneida Indian Nation.

And, of course, college buddy and teammate Tiger Woods supports Begay III's charitable efforts whenever he can, as does Rickey Fowler, who is one-quarter Navajo.

According to outreach materials, the core of NB3F's mission is to reduce the incidences of obesity and diabetes and advance the lives of Native American children through evidence-based sports, health and wellness programming. NB3F has established itself as a leader in research, advocacy and strategic grant-making in Native American communities, beyond its proven record of developing sustainable, replicable, evidence-based programs. More than 15,000 native youth have benefitted from NB3F programs, including soccer, golf, health and wellness and programs.

That's not to say there weren't any rough patches in Notah Begay III's career path after he stopped playing competitive golf. Like anybody else, there were pot holes in Notah Begay III's road, and one bigsink hole Notah III will always be climbing out of.

It happens to a lot of professional athletes, just like it does to a lot of regular folks. There is no excuse for impaired driving. It is a stupid, selfish act which all too often has tragic consequences.

So you can't say professional athletes should know better because they know their actions will affect more people, especially young kids seeking role models, or because of the increased publicity they know their actions will attract, or simply because they can afford limo drivers. Impaired driving is the stupidest thing you can do and it can hurt other people beyond all measure while it hurts yourself and everything you value. With all the information out there about the consequences of impaired driving, it should not happen. No matter who you are.

But impaired driving does take place and what is most important is what can be done to prevent it from happening in the future. It is a credit to many people who have committed the crime of impaired driving that they have gone beyond saying they are sorry and that they will not do it again.

A good friend of mine, Elijah Harper, a First Nations leader who also served in the cabinet of the provincial government of Manitoba and as a Member of Parliament, was once convicted of impaired driving. Elijah was devastated at what he had done, and eternally grateful that his actions had not harmed anybody else at the time. He knew that his actions had fed into misleading and unfair stereotypes that would set his people back, even moreso because of his stature.

I ran into Elijah about four years after the incident and he asked me for a ride home. I knew that his driver's licence had been suspended for six months, which was standard punishment for impaired driving at the time, and that Elijah had stopped drinking cold turkey immediately after the incident.

Elijah needed a ride because he had suspended his own driver's licence for five years and he still had a year to go.

And he never touched a drop of alcohol again before his passing in 2013.

Notah Begay III behaved in a similar manner by taking full responsibility and facing the consequences following a late-night parking lot collision which happened while he was impaired by alcohol. Notah III admitted that it was actually his second DUI incident. This time he drove into a parked car while leaving a bar in Albuquerque and was subsequently arrested and charged with DUI and failure to look out. Begay III was sentenced to 364 days in jail, with all but seven days suspended.

"It's a negative impact, but I would expect nothing less," he said. "If you do something wrong, it shouldn't help you. You do something wrong, you pay the price. It's going to take some time to regain the confidence and support of some of my fans, and I'm going to lose some of them. That's just the nature of the beast.

"It's a cut-and-dried case of bad judgment," Begay III said, "It will not happen again."

Begay III also said he doesn't expect to be treated differently because he is a well-known sports figure in New Mexico.

"I'm not backing down from anything," he said. "I want to be held accountable for what's gone on. Everybody makes mistakes. I'm not trying to ever tell anyone to try to get away with anything because that's not the way it's supposed to be done. I'm just not very happy with myself."

The seven days in jail were humbling enough, but talk about being caught between a sand trap and a water hazard. Begay III had already started a program lecturing youth on the dangers of drugs and alcohol and now, facing the students was hard, "knowing that they look up to me," he said.

And so it was doubly difficult when one of the first things he did following the incident was to speak to kids at the San Felipe elementary school on a Pueblo reservation north of Albuquerque, where the children were unaware of the charges.

"My mind was preoccupied with what had gone on, and I felt like I didn't really belong up there," he said. "It really hurts me inside to know that I made a mistake that big, and I don't want to perpetuate that sort of image to anybody, especially to the young kids."

Notah III's sincere contrition convinced the people around him that he had truly learned his lesson and he would spend the rest of his life steering away from the wheel of a vehicle and steering others towards a sober path.

And he certainly has, up to the point in time this book was published.

And so, with his playing career over, Notah III has moved on to the other stages of what has become a multi-faceted career. In addition to the demands on his time running NB3 and overseeing his Foundation, Notah III has found time to remain in the public eye as an expert commentator on TV.

The handsome, fit Native American made his TV debut in 2010 during Golf Channel's "Live from the Masters" news coverage, and along with being a walking reporter, he contributes to Golf Channel news programs and coverage of the majors (e.g. the Masters).

The circle is sacred to native peoples and everything is connected. And so goes the life of Notah Begay III.

The buffalo is connected to Native American life on the plains. Revered by the Lakota for the teachings provided by White Buffalo Calf Woman, the buffalo provided food, shelter, clothing, tools and weapons. Perhaps most importantly, the buffalo was associated with an industrious, roaming lifestyle, instead of the sedentary life of white flour, lard and sugar on a reservation which resulted when the buffalo almost became extinct from over-hunting by new arrivals to this continent.

So Begay III began KivaSun foods, which sells bison meat. KivaSun became successful by sourcing bison from the 57-tribe InterTribal Buffalo Council. Profits from KivaSun support the non-profit work of the NB3 Foundation, which encourages health through sports and education to address childhood obesity and diabetes, which is the result of a lifestyle which changed from buffalo hunting to reservation lifestyles.

And so a circle which was weakened is becoming strong once again. And larger.

"If we don't start making changes in our lifestyle choices, our people's lifespans will continue to get shorter. Native American lifespans are the shortest of any U.S. minority group, and it doesn't have to be that way."

The man-who-made-it offers a message to Indian children trying for their own successes: "Don't limit your dreams. Educate yourself, take care of yourself, push yourself to fulfill your goals."

A child of loving parents, product of the public links, graduate of Stanford University, registered member of the Navajo Nation, son of the Navajo and Pueblo people, and creation of Mother Earth.

Notah Begay III.

Author's Note: In the spring of 2014, Notah Begay III, at the age of 41, overcame a huge, personal challenge when he suffered a heart attack, brought on by a blocked artery and a history of heart trouble in his family. Notah and his medical team came through the trauma with flying colours and Notah was back in front of the cameras covering NCAA golf a month or treatment and rest. All who know Notah or know of him and his work wish him the very best as he resumes his career as a broadcaster and as a tireless philanthropist working on behalf of American Indian youth. At last word, Notah was hoping to add diseases of the heart and treatments as another area of work for the NB3 Foundation.

Jack Jacobs

5

"The House that Jack Built"

It was Sunday, September 28, 1947. The defending world champion Chicago Bears were in Green Bay, Wisconsin to take on the legendary Packers in the season-opening National Football League game for both teams. Wealthy and wily Packer owner Curly Lambeau (who also served as coach and general manager, as was the custom of the day), knew that he needed more scoring from his Green Bay offence, which had only managed 148 points in 11 games in 1946—a paltry average of 13.4 points per game, to stand any chance of defeating the mighty Bears.

Lambeau hoped he had made the correct, crucial step towards lighting up NFL scoreboards by turning a "redskin" into a "packer." More literally, Lambeau had obtained Washington Redskins quarterback "Indian" Jack Jacobs for Bears halfback Bob Nussbaumer in a straight-up one-for-one trade during the 1946-47 off-season, because Lambeau had decided to abandon his treasured "Notre Dame Box" attack for the more modern "t-formation," which puts the quarterback directly behind the centre to take the snap and opens up a lot more offensive options and opportunities. Jacobs, who had starred at quarterback for the Oklahoma Sooners in major American College football (which was more prestigious than the fledgling professional game at this time), would prove to be equal to the task.

And much more.

You see, just like those other amazing Native American footballers Thorpe and McDaniel, Jacobs not only played quarterback, he played

both offence and defence and he didn't take punting downs off! A ferocious defensive back who made receivers pay a mighty price with vicious
tackles if they happened to catch the ball, those same receivers faced
major competition hauling the ball down from a DB who routinely led
his team in interceptions. Jacobs was a true "60-minute man" because
he was an outstanding punter and field goal kicker who regularly led
his teams in average distance and scoring.

And so the play-by-play of that game between the Packers and the
Bears went like this:

Jacobs drops back to pass. It's into the Bears end zone, and it's complete! That is the second touchdown pass of the day thrown by Jacobs.

Now later on in the game, the new Packer quarterback decides to
run. Twisting and turning, Jacobs rambles for 17 yards to set the Packers
up on the Chicago one-yard line. On the very next play, Jacobs calls his
own number again and crashes through for the touchdown! The Packers
line up for the convert and Jacobs splits the uprights for the extra point.

Now the Packers need to punt and the versatile Jacobs boots one
with enough hang time for fans to grab a beer and a hot dog before
this one comes down... It's a towering 59-yard boot that negates the
poor field position Green Bay was in—one of four punts on the day
by Jacobs, and now we see why this versatile athlete is ranked third
in the league in that category.

The Bears take over the ball now. Again, they try to pass into that
side of the field being patrolled by defensive back Jacobs but he snags
his third interception of the game! No, wait! This one is going to be
called back because of an interference penalty on one of Jacobs' Green
Bay teammates. Jacobs will have to settle for those other two interceptions he made earlier in this game...that is, if he doesn't come up with
another steal...and I wouldn't put it past this former thievin' redskin
[ouch! but that would be the order of the day at the time].

And so the final score in a major upset is the Green Bay Packers
29, the Chicago Bears 20...Indian Jack Jacobs...playing the entire
60 minutes of the game... has a successful individual debut with the
Packers...Jacobs sure showed his teammates what they need to do be
successful in the National Football League this season.

As incomprehensible, as beyond imagination as that play-byplay seems, it is factually true, and Indian Jack Jacobs would go on to even greater glory. He would do that in the northern third of what the First Nations of North America call Turtle Island.

Canada is a long way from where "Okies from Muskogee" come from, and unfortunately, where relocated Creek Indians ended up coming from because of President Andrew Jackson's Indian Relocation Act which made five First Nations give up all of their traditional lands (and this thief's face is on the American $20 bill?).

Jack Jacobs was born on August 7th, 1919 near Holdenville, Oklahoma. A full-blood Creek Muskogee, Jacobs was proud of his Indian heritage but he didn't wear it on his sleeve. It was enough that being known as "Indian Jack Jacobs" would make people aware of the pride he carried inside so he didn't feel a need to share a lot of details about his Indian heritage all the time.

The first sign that little Jack Jacobs was special is a well-known local legend about how he escaped from stepping barefoot on a copperhead snake when he was just a young child. Word quickly spread that little Jack was "quick as a snake."

Jack Jacobs first realized he was good at games when he was better than everybody else at a stickball game that was the main sport of the Creek people.

Football was the big game in Muskogee, Oklahoma, and in his time, the big star at Muskogee High School was that Creek kid they called Indian Jack Jacobs.

Called a "passing and punting fool," Jacobs was just as well-known for his durability as his skill. Indian Jack never missed a game in high school and played both ways, as well as punting, so basically, Jacobs never left the field throughout his high school playing days. He was all-state and his journey into five Halls of Fame starts with the Muskogee High School Hall of Fame.

Jack's sister, Anna King, has fond memories of her brother but they don't include much about his exploits on the football field. Anna mostly remembers how competitive her sibling was while growing up together.

"He was mischievous, and I remember how he would wash our faces with watermelon rind," recalls King. "He was rough and tumble, whether it was against his opponents in boxing or fights with other neighbourhood children at the waterhole. Yet he was such a little thing as a young boy.

"And it wasn't passing a football around that was his first priority when he got home from school like the other boys. He was more concerned about playing a card game called Pitch. If he was losing, he would stay up all night until he won a game. I used to ask him, 'How do you stand to lose a football game?'

"Jack had that kind of motivation to win at anything."

One high school football teammate, George Ernest "Sonny" Roberts, recalls Jacobs as an all-around athlete who managed to parlay his boxing hobby into a Golden Gloves championship.

"What I remember most is when Jack got these two sets of boxing gloves for Christmas," Roberts remembers. "He told me to put two of them on and he put just one glove on and then proceeded to knock me all around the bedroom with one hand."

You just gotta be good when your opponent knows you are always going to be throwing your right.

Roberts says Jacobs was also a city champion in golf.

Jacobs, like most young American men, served his time in the military. A very handsome man, Jack was always impeccably dressed (a "clothes horse," according to Army mate Claude Arnold, also a Sooner teammate). Almost always flashing a bright smile, Jack exhibited a personal magnetism that could only be enhanced by a uniform (army or athletic).

Jack Jacobs received scholarship offers from about a dozen major college football powers but he wanted to stay close to home so he chose the Oklahoma Sooners.

Jacobs is always listed in the top ten of any list of greatest quarterbacks in the illustrious history of Sooners football (certainly he remains the most successful alumni—the one who had the most success as a pro, because Sam Bradford hasn't surpassed him so far—more on that later).

Jacobs lettered at QB, defensive back, tailback and halfback, as well as punting, and it was his success at running and kicking the football in college which undermined his historic status as a pivot. While Jacobs would end up as one of the most prolific passers in the game of football and revolutionized the game, he used his arm as much to cradle and catch the ball in college so the college passing records went to other guys and Jacobs became best known as this amazing kicker.

Nowadays, kickers are often these little, white soccer players who come from offshore countries, rarely get any dirt on their uniforms, and certainly shed little blood. Their contributions are often overlooked except when they miss a winning field goal on the final play of the game. But when they make that field goal, it is as if they were always expected to do so, so any glory is grainy and fleeting.

Back in the college days of Jack Jacobs, the kicking game was much more important. First of all, they hadn't figured out how much more sense it made to pass the ball and football games were often low-scoring affairs with offensive strategies based on three cracks at the line, clouds of dust and then punt. The punt was also used to reverse the fortunes provided by field position—again something which was much more important in low-scoring defensive struggles.

Even the "quick kick" was a major offensive weapon back then. Such as in one game against Maryland, when the Sooners were mired deep in their own end and it was tempting to concede two points with a safety touch, rather than punt and have their opponent in field position for a touchdown or field goal. But on third down, Jacobs got off a booming punt which advanced the ball 81 yards down a 100-yard field. That produced an instant change in field position and the Sooners went from there to a 14-0 win.

Jacobs got off on the right foot by starting his college career with a 65-yard kickoff return against Southern Methodist University. His passing skills were described as "a quick scoop of the arm above the head, with powerful wrist action—like a baseball catcher's peg to first base when the runner has strayed off the bag."

"If Jack Jacobs had played for Bob Stoops (coach) at Oklahoma, he might have thrown 40 touchdown passes in a year. But he was stuck in a run-first system under Bud Wilkinson," says sportswriter Kenton Brooks.

And so Jacobs holds the OU punting record by averaging 47.84 yards per punt in 1940. He maintained a phenomenal career average of 42.10.

But one sign of his passing prowess to come is the fact that he maintains the record for completion percentage in a game (100 per cent) after going 8 for 8 against Kansas in 1941. Jacobs accumulated the most offensive yardage (junior and senior) in '41 and as a defensive back, Jacobs is tied with seven other players for record number of interceptions in a game with three (1941 OU vs. Marquette).

Jacobs was extremely proud of his Indian blood, privately. The only way Jacobs acknowledged his Native American background publicly was through his nickname, which he embraced (such practices were not so frowned upon as they are today). Before the NFL draft, he said, "I figured I would always play ball with the Redskins. That would be a natural; an Indian playing with the Redskins, wouldn't it?" (Jacobs wasn't drafted by Washington but would play for the Redskins later in his career).

Jacobs was obviously unaware that the term "redskin" was derived from the practice of demanding a piece of red skin to be attached to scalps to prove Indian bounty hunters had actually killed an Indian in order to collect a $100 payment offered to early settlers to "clear the lands" of indigenous people. Many First Nations leaders decry "redskin" as a racist term and object to the use of sacred spiritual and political symbols such as headdresses, songs/chants and dances as infantilized cheers by Washington fans. But widespread knowledge about such issues just did not exist publicly in Jacobs' time in Washington. It would be unfair to criticize Jacobs for not speaking out against such practices just as it would probably have been unwise for him to raise the issue.

Jacobs was picked in the second round of the 1941 NFL draft by the Cleveland Rams. He began his professional football career in 1942 with an auspicious debut—replacing all-American Parker Hall at left halfback and ripping off an 85-yard punt. In all, Jacobs played six seasons in the NFL for Cleveland, Washington and Green Bay (missing

1943-44 due to World War II). He led the NFL in punting in 1947. You can look it all up.

By 1950, there were a lot of pro players who believed the NFL was under-paying them, and a large number of them joined a flight of players to the Canadian Football League. When Ralph Misener, resident of the Winnipeg Blue Bombers, waved a cheque in the amount of $6,000 in front of Jack Jacobs' face, along with a promise Jacobs would play quarterback and no other position unless it was extra duty, Jack headed north of the border.

The author of this book being a Winnipeg homeboy, I am proud that my hometown provided the professional football team for Jacobs to star for while he was supposedly on the "downside" of his career (not that we would have known that by the way he played here)...

The Winnipeg Blue Bombers have more than the best team nickname in all of professional football. They received that when *Winnipeg Tribune* sportswriter Vince Leah compared them to heavyweight champion boxer Joe Louis, the Brown Bomber. Leah remarked, "These are the Blue Bombers of Western football."

The Blue Bombers have a rich history, but their first taste of real success came when a Creek Indian was lured north by a lucrative contract that the fledgling National Football League refused to match.

Back in the 1950s, the Canadian Football League (CFL) was able to outbid the NFL for star players, like Billy Vessels, a star American college running back who led Oklahoma to the 1950 U.S. national championship. After being drafted by the Baltimore Colts, the 1952 Heisman Trophy winner chose to play for the Edmonton Eskimos. Rose Bowl winning quarterback and Most Valuable Player Kenny Ploen of Iowa, who won four CFL Grey Cup championships, Sam Etcheverry, the son of Basque sheep farmers who set (and still holds) all of the passing records at the University of Denver before bypassing the NFL to star with the Montreal Alouettes; Jack Jacobs and many others considered the CFL on par with or better than the NFL before American audiences fit pro ball into their weekend football fix (with Friday night lights on for high school football, Saturday afternoons for college ball and then ultimately Sunday afternoons got set aside for the pro game).

Indian Jack Jacobs was always proud of his Native American herit-age, and he was the only graduating quarterback from the powerhouse football factory that is the Oklahoma Sooners to complete a pass in the NFL until Sam Bradford, the Sooner quarterback who was drafted num-ber one overall by the St. Louis Rams in 2010, displaced him (the amaz-ing coincidence here is that Bradford is a registered Cherokee Indian, so Okee U's only two QBs to make the NFL are Indians whose ancestors were forcefully displaced from their homelands in the northern U.S. to Oklahoma through manifest destiny and that Indian Relocation Act of President Andrew Jackson).

The CFL could outbid the NFL for certain top players but the overall depth of the CFL was less than their counterpart down south (American athletes kick, catch and run right out of the crib while Canadians take their first steps on frozen water chasing a puck). But CFL rules, which mandated a certain number of Canadians on each roster restricted the number of "imports" (Americans) a team could play. So you still had to be a cut above to survive the import ratio and have a career of any worthwhile length in the CFL.

Jacobs arrived in Winnipeg on July 12, 1949. At that time, Winnipeg was a thriving prairie Canadian metropolis, the fourth largest city in Canada; the "Gateway to the West." Because of its location right in the centre of the country (the longitudinal centre of Canada is located just east of Winnipeg), the city was a gateway to pretty much everywhere else on the North American continent.

Winnipeg certainly had a thriving arts, culture and entertainment scene in 1949. The Royal Winnipeg Ballet and the Winnipeg Symphony Orchestra were worldclass and the city's numerous grand theatres hosted top productions and big name stars. Compared to the facilities that were available to accommodate major league sports, one might think the city was completely dominated by aficionados of the arts.

But Winnipeg was also a typically macho western Canadian prai-rie burg where sports fans are rampant. It just took a while for penny-pinching city fathers who used to throw nickels around like manhole covers to realize it was time for Winnipeg to move from the Wooden Age to the Age of Concrete.

So first, the 5,000-seat, rickety old wooden Shea's Amphitheatre would be replaced by the brick-andconcrete Winnipeg Arena (capacity 9,500) in 1955 (I mention this because Shea's contained the only indoor ice rink between Toronto and Vancouver, reinforcing once again the claim that Winnipeg was the premier prairie metropolis in central Canada).

Still, it took the arrival of a superstar who could fill the seats to overflowing at Winnipeg's old Osborne Stadium to prove the need for a new outdoor facility for football. And that star was a 31-year-old Indian who was supposed to be on the down side of his career when he arrived in Winnipeg.

Osborne Stadium was built in 1935 and was about the same size as a medium American high school stadium, seating 7,800 (OK, a small American high school stadium). While football cannot (and will not) ever compete with hockey for attention most anywhere in Canada, the facility that was built to replace Osborne Stadium was the biggest development in Winnipeg's sports history.

And it was all because of one man.

The smile that formed on Jack Jacobs' face when he first stepped on to the field at Osborne Stadium might have spread as wide as the Canadian Football League field he was salivating over. Sure, his joy was tempered by the small size of the grandstand, which was dwarfed by the college stadiums he had starred in, but this venue would be full and that had to be better than playing in front of 7,800 fans scattered throughout some of those huge NFL ballparks.

It was the wide CFL field that was most pleasing for a pure passer like Jacobs. He wondered why the CFL, which had a long history, much longer than the NFL, had remained a running league with this 65-yard-wide expanse between the sidelines (the NFL field is 50 yards wide). So much more room for his receivers to get open...so many more wide open spots to throw to! And with only three downs to make the ten yards needed for another first down, passing was a required option much more often.

By 1951, many people were thinking Jacobs invented the forward pass instead of just making it a much more integral part of all professional football. Canadian football had never seen any quarterback come remotely close to posting the kind of numbers Jacobs started putting into the record books.

First, he became the first pro quarterback to throw for over 3,000 yards in a single season in 1951. Jacobs was also the first to throw over 30 touchdown passes in one year with 33. He followed that up in 1952 by throwing 34 TD passes and the 2,586 yards he gained through the air was still considered an incredible season. Perhaps the best way to illustrate how remarkable Jacobs' achievements were is to remember that in this bleak era of passing, when quarterbacks often threw more interceptions than touchdowns, Jacobs had 104 TD passes and only 53 turnovers through the air during his CFL career.

No, the best way to illustrate the achievements of this northerly relocated Creek was the fact that his phenomenal exploits were attracting so many fans they had to build a new stadium in Winnipeg to house the overflowing crowds. Winnipeg Stadium, with more than double the capacity of Osborne, would always be better known as "The House That Jack Built."

The Grey Cup is the Holy Grail of Canadian football. It has become kind of a national championship because of a natural rivalry that pits the "best from the west" against the "least from the east" (it's "beast" from the east versus "lest" from the west when fans from the east refer to the match). The one game showdown for national bragging rights also became well-known as the "Grand National Drunk" in the 1940s and 50s.

Scalpers were selling $1 tickets for 25 bucks when the Calgary Stampeders and their fans travelled to Ottawa in 1948. Calgary's cowboy fans caused quite a commotion when they entered the lobby of the stately Royal York Hotel on horseback. The Royal York staff managed to get the imprint of a hoof in their guest book and the fans checked their horses at the elevators, so you could say they all got along fairly well.

Calgary beat Ottawa 12-7 in that Grey Cup game. The Stampeders won on a controversial play called "the sleeper"; aptly named because a Calgary player quietly lay down near the sideline hoping nobody noticed him. Sure enough, Norm Hill was uncovered and caught a touchdown pass from American import Keith Spaith before the Ottawa defenders noticed the Stampeders were a player short breaking their offensive huddle. The sleeper play is now called an "illegal formation" and is banned.

I offer the above to make a point. Ofttimes, championship games are decided by some unusual play or mitigating factor that is beyond the control of a team or a single player. But all too often, a player's career is judged solely by the number of championships he wins, and this is unfair. You cannot dismiss the careers of great quarterbacks like Dan Marino, Fran Tarkenton and Jim Kelly for failing to win a Super Bowl, because they had an enormous impact on the game overall. And thus we cannot judge Indian Jack Jacobs because he failed to bring a Grey Cup championship to Winnipeg. His overall impact on the game is a much better measuring stick for this great player's career.

Indian Jack Jacobs' first appearance in the Grey Cup was a dismal failure but the game was played under conditions that were less than ideal in a match that ended up being called the "Mud Bowl." Jacobs and the Bomber offence were completely shut down by the Toronto Argonauts 13-0. Jacobs led the Bombers back to the Grey Cup in 1953 but again, the Bombers were beaten, this time by the Hamilton Tiger-Cats, 12-6.

Despite those defeats, Jacobs' legacy in Canada was assured because he changed the philosophy of the CFL into much more of a pass-friendly league. In those four scant years, he became the all-time leading passer in Western Conference history by completing 709 of 1,330 attempts for 11,094 yards. The records Jacobs set would be surpassed (again, Jacobs only played four years in the CFL and that change in philosophy was bound to inflate passing stats year after year) but his influence on the game was truly historic. The modern era of the Canadian Football League was ushered in by the play of this unique QB.

While Jacobs was changing the face of the league, he was piling up awards and was named all-western quarterback twice. And there were certainly some breathtaking performances along the way.

In one game against Calgary in 1952, Jacobs threw an absolutely unheard-of six touchdown passes! During the next season, he went 31 for 48 against Hamilton (keep in mind that nobody had ever come close to trying close to 50 passes in a single game before!).

In November of 1953, Jacobs came off the bench to lead the Bombers to a thrilling come-from-behind win over the Edmonton Eskimos by firing three TD passes in the fourth quarter.

Even the annual game scheduled for the first Monday in September in Regina between the Roughriders and their prairie cousins from Winnipeg took its first steps toward becoming known as the Labour Day Classic after Jacobs led the Bombers back from a 22-6 deficit with less than 10 minutes remaining by throwing three late touchdown passes in the 1951 matchup.

But Jacobs turned the athletically ancient age of 35 by 1954 and it was time to hang 'em up. He spent 1955 scouting for the Bombers, then was a coach for the London Lords of the Ontario Rugby Football Union for a couple of years. Jacobs bounced around, working as an assistant coach with the Hamilton Tiger-Cats, the Montreal Alouettes and the Edmonton Eskimos, before returning home to the United States.

Before he left, Jacobs left Canadian football fans with some outstanding stories off the field as well, and one of the best involved legendary Winnipeg sportswriter Jack Matheson, who was a beat reporter covering the Bombers during Jacobs' heyday. I interviewed Matheson about a year before he passed away at the grand old age of 87, and he told me a tale about how he almost didn't make it to 30 because of a "misunderstanding" he had with Jacobs in 1953.

"Cactus" Jack Matheson is a legend in his own right. The longtime sports editor of the *Winnipeg Tribune* was the epitome of the ink-stained wretch, a bit of a curmudgeon, but he knew sports from the inside out, and was well-respected by his peers, sports fans, and even most of the players.

But not Jack Jacobs.

To the end, Matty could never figure out why he and Jacobs didn't get along. It certainly had nothing to do with the fact Jacobs was an Indian; Matheson went out of his way to support First Nations initiatives in Winnipeg, even coaching a team of media stars in an exhibition hockey game and cultural showcase to raise money for the local Indian and Métis Friendship Centre.

Matty's first "hint" that Jacobs didn't exactly favour him came the time he ordered some clothes from Holt Renfrew, a top local tailor, and got a surprise package when his order was delivered.

"Laurie Udow owned Holt Renfrew and he was a big Bomber booster. His clothes were considered the cat's meow so everybody bought from Laurie," says Matheson (who really used the phrase "the cat's meow" during our interview). "Players used to supplement their income from football by doing part-time jobs after practice and they got those jobs from business guys like Udow who supported the team. Jacobs worked in deliveries for Holt Renfrew and he handled an order of clothes for me.

"I was completely caught off guard when I opened the package and there was this note from Jacobs that read, 'You stink, Matheson!'

It was the start of something that didn't sit well between the two Jacks and it almost ended in tragedy with both men standing up and squaring off on a train one fateful day in 1953.

"We travelled by train in those days and the players and reporters usually shared the same cars so there was a lot more socializing and bonding," said Matheson.

Of course, this kind of closeness and contact was good and bad. A reporter could get some valuable insight to the players' attitudes and personalities but, at the same time, it could make it difficult to be objective in your coverage. Plus, you had to face the players you wrote about, sometimes critically, face to face. Things could get ugly after you pointed out a poor performance.

Things got uglier than Rob Ford on a Monday morning when the two Jacks squared off but it had nothing to do with anything that had been written.

It was all mostly fuelled by the demon rum (well, okay, beer...this was Canada, after all).

"Nobody knew where the beer came from," Matheson claims, a half century later with a nudge and a wink.

"Anyways, it sounded like a good idea at the time," Matty continued. "But I guess it really wasn't a good idea..."

The idea was to down as many beers as they could before the offensive line guys joined the party and started to inhale the brewskies two or three at a time. Time and miles began to fly by (or, "roll" by) and soon, as so often happens when boys binge on barley sandwiches, some vastly different opinions started to fly back and forth (it is so easy to get into an argument over sports, I mean, it's *natural*!) .

Matheson swears he would never say anything to Jacobs like, "I made you what you are and I can tear you down just as easily," which makes sense because young Jack (Matheson) was in his first year of covering the Bombers and veteran Jack (Jacobs) had already been the team's star for three years.

But when you got a rookie reporter swappin' spit with a veteran sports hero, it usually becomes time for the pen to take its leave before the sword cuts it in half. Matty might have been shuddering from a metaphor like that, as he used taking a pee as his pretext to get out of there. Jacobs followed and while he was explaining to Matheson how the ditch is where real men water the lilies and grabbing the young writer so he could get a "closer look," one Jack Matheson got very close to pushing up daisies.

"If it wasn't for Lornie Benson, I really would have been thrown off that train."

Benson was a rookie running back with the Bombers and it was only his intervention that prevented Matheson from being tossed into the Canadian countryside like one of those footballs Jacobs could fling 50 yards with the flick of his wrist. Matty is convinced that without Benson, he would have ended up in the wilderness wondering what happened when the booze wore off and he found himself all bruised and scraped up and a million miles from nowhere.

Then again, perhaps the problem was that Jacobs, who was rather a "dandy" when it comes to his own haberdashery, just didn't like Matheson's taste in clothing, and the note in that delivery box was only expressing his opinion about an ink-stained wretch's poor taste in tailoring. If so, Matheson might have met his end simply because he took some criticism about his dressing habits the wrong way, which led to an argument which, because of the way alcohol works, got exacerbated instead of explained.

It is certainly not that Jacobs or Matheson were big drunks, or that either had serious problems with alcohol. It was just one of those occasions when too many drinks went down and one thing led to another.

Eventually, they would learn to get along. Matheson certainly had a lot of respect for Jacobs' skills as an elite athlete and Jacobs came to respect Matheson for the great sportswriter that he was.

And what does that incident tell you about Jacobs' character?

Nothing much really, but it's a good story and these kinds of stories belong in books like this.

———————————

Jacobs was an electrifying talent, and his strong arm and pinpoint passes changed the way the Canadian game was played. Not only did Jacobs create an aerial circus in Winnipeg, his intensity on the field brought out the best in his teammates.

The Bombers had won just two games in 1949 (2-12) but with Jacobs leading the way, they finished first in the West in 1950 with a 10-4 record. The western Canadian final was a best-of-three series in those days and the Bombers lost a 17-6 thriller to Edmonton in the opening game. But Winnipeg roared back to win game two 22-12 and then routed the Eskimos 29-6 in the third and deciding game as Jacobs scored two touchdowns and punted for a 50-yard average.

And that put the Winnipeg Blue Bombers in the Grey Cup national championship game—that 60-minute showdown for national bragging rights. Unfortunately for the West, the Grey Cup almost always ended up residing in some trophy case in eastern Canada. The Bombers had only won the Cup twice in the first 50 years of the 20th century and were facing another powerhouse from Toronto, Canada's largest and richest metropolis (the Bombers had lost all six times they faced teams from Toronto in the Grey Cup during the 1930s and '40s).

The 1950 Grey Cup Game was either a total debacle or one for the history books, depending on your perspective. For sure, it was one of the most unusual and memorable football games played anywhere at any time.

It would end up being called "the Mud Bowl" because, after rain and snow pelted Toronto for weeks, the field at the University of Toronto's Varsity Stadium was a quagmire. And it turned out to be a total disaster for the Bombers.

Jacobs fumbled twice, setting up a pair of field goals by the Toronto Argonauts. Jack also had one of his punts blocked, and that led to the only touchdown of the game by Al Dekdebrun, so it turned out it was miscues by the Bombers star quarterback that led to all the scoring in the game, won by the Argos 13-0.

But really, nobody could be blamed for fumbling on a field that featured nothing but slipping and sliding around. The mud so deep that when Blue Bomber defensive tackle Buddy Tinsley went face down after a hit, referee Hec Creighton, worried Tinsley was drowning, rushed over and flipped the big lineman onto his back because his head was buried in a foot of water.

It made for a great headline, "Linebacker almost drowns on the field" but Tinsley claims he was just getting some rest. The season provided an auspicious debut for the Bombers "rookie" QB even though it did end up buried in muck.

Back in Winnipeg, team organizers and fans thought the entire mess was a debacle and they fired head coach Frank Larson and replaced him with George Trafton. It would be two years before the restructured Bombers would make it back to the big game.

According to another legendary Canadian sportswriter, Jim Coleman, Trafton didn't like Jacobs and doubted his ability. Trafton would make sardonic comments about quarterbacks being "slaves to the coach's plan" and had assistant coach Joe Zaleski design and call the plays. Jacobs was expected to execute the plan (which is the norm nowadays, but in the '50s, quarterbacks usually called the plays in the huddle). The free spirit that Jacobs was "refused to stay on the reservation" and improvised. Before long, Jacobs found himself picking slivers out of his arse on a pine bench.

It all came to a head on a brisk November day in 1953—the third game of the best-of-three Western final against the Edmonton Eskimos. Trafton left Jacobs sitting on the bench through the first half, which ended with the Bombers trailing 18-6. But Winnipeg football fans (and Jacobs) owe a lot to an activist executive named Ralph Misener, who stepped out of the stands and ordered Trafton to put the team's $6,000-a-year investment into the game.

Jacobs would lead the Bombers to a thrilling, come-from-behind 30-24 victory by throwing three touchdown passes in the final 30 minutes. It didn't start out very well, as Jacobs' first pass attempt was intercepted, but then he completed 14 for 243 yards and those three TDs, which were the margin of victory.

That put the Bombers back in the Grey Cup again, but this time, they faced a team from Hamilton, the Tiger-Cats.

This was the 41st rendition of the national classic and Winnipeg had won just twice, before but hopes were high.

The field was fine this time at Varsity Stadium, and 27,313 fans jammed in (the Grey Cup being Canada's biggest one-day sports spectacle offering a trophy second only in value to Canada's holiest of grails, professional hockey's Stanley Cup). Over 150,000 spectators had turned out for the Grey Cup parade through downtown Toronto, which featured 40 floats, 15 bands and even 12 Miss Grey Cup contestants. Okay, so this was still nowhere near as big as a Rose Bowl, but Jacobs and his fellow American players felt vindicated this show could overshadow the still majorly ignored NFL championship game (concepts like the Super Bowl were still a long, long way off).

The hoopla fit right in with the party persona that Winnipeg's dark, dashing quarterback had revealed to folks who got close to the team. The CFL championship had expanded to become "Grey Cup week" in Canada and players could get a good dose of fun in before they had to settle down on the weekend before the big game.

Toronto sportswriter Jim Coleman tells the legendary tale of a drinking party held one night in the Royal York Hotel. Coleman got involved in precautions Jacobs was taking to make sure matters didn't get totally out of control.

"If I pass out, make sure you lay me in my bed in Room 613," instructed Jacobs.

And, sure enough, Jacobs joined a rather large contingent of incapacitated players and journalists and fans who were left wandering and wondering who and where they were.

They decided to have some fun with Jacobs, so they stripped him to his shorts, laid him out on on his back in a bed in Room 613 of the Royal York and planted a lily in his hand as if he had passed away, not simply passed out. Only problem was that Jacobs had failed to mention he was staying in Room 613 of the King Edward Hotel five blocks away. It proved to be a less than nice surprise for some chambermaid at the Royal York but it was all part of the party that is the Grey Cup in Canada.

It was all in fun and everybody settled down on the weekend for the big game. Jacobs was a dandy, but he was also a consummate professional, and he never had a drinking problem on the level of an addiction requiring some sort of intervention, either during his career, or later on in retirement.

The game was dominated by Jacobs and the Bomber offence, but they would be undone by one big play here and another big play there. But that's football and not only do you have to make the big plays to win, you have to make them at the right time.

Jacobs led the Bomber offence on lengthy drives that produced some great stats that weren't matched on the scoreboard. In the first half, Jacobs engineered a 92-yard drive that was snuffed out by an interception by Hamilton's Vito Ragazzo. The Ti-Cats scored the only points of the first 30 minutes on a short run by quarterback Ed Songin and it was 6-0 (the touchdown was converted but TDs were only worth five points during those days.

In the third quarter, another long Bomber drive faltered at the Hamilton 28 when Dick Brown intercepted a Jacobs pass. Jacobs and the Bombers followed that up by driving deep into Hamilton territory again but this time a field goal attempt by Bud Korchak went wide. Winnipeg fullback Gerry James finally capped off another long drive with a one-yard touchdown run and the score was tied 6-all.

Hamilton got the benefit of a mistake by Winnipeg defensive back Geoff Cain, who went for an interception and missed, leaving Ragazzo to carry a Songin pass 45 yards through open field for five plus one and it was 12-6.

Time was running out and the Bombers got the ball on their own 10-yard line. Once again, Jacobs took the Blue and Gold on a long march and 98 yards later, they were on the Hamilton two. On the very last play of the game, Winnipeg's star receiver, Tom Casey, got open on the goal line and Jacobs fired him the pass. But just as the ball arrived (or just before), Ti-Cat DB Lou Kusserow hit Casey and he dropped the ball. Winnipeg fans screamed "Pass interference" (while Hamilton fans nodded "Well-timed tackle") and examination of the game films to this day are inconclusive. The officials didn't call a penalty on the play and Hamilton won 12-6.

And that was how the playing career of Indian Jack Jacobs in Canada ended. No professional championships but a slew of records and all-star honours (1950 and 52) as well as a Jack Nicklin Memorial Trophy as the Most Valuable Player in the Western Conference of the CFL in '52.

In all, Jacobs played 22 years of high school, college and pro ball without missing a season. He has been enshrined in the Canadian Football Hall of Fame, the American Indian Athletic Hall of Fame, Oklahoma Sports Hall of Fame, and the Manitoba Sports HOF.

Scouting and coaching throughout Canada provided an income for the next decade, and Jacobs even tried his hand at acting in the 1948 movie, *Triple Threat*.

And then Indian Jack returned home to see if he could still shoot fish with a bow and arrow.

Jacobs was a jock who was confident and sometimes cocky, but that's what you need to be in the world of professional sports. When you step away from the limelight, you become more of yourself, and Jacobs spent much of the rest of his life finding out what it means to be a Creek. For Jacobs, there was no better way to embark on the journey of discovery than to share that venture with his son, John.

"Indian Jack Jacobs was my father and he was very proud of his Creek heritage. As soon as I was old enough, Dad would take me to the Festival of Green Corn which featured what is often called pow wow dancing and all sorts of Indian games and ceremonies. I most enjoyed sitting with the Elders, who would speak about the history of our people and pass on details and even secrets which made me feel special. But as much as I was learning, my father was a much keener student. He would sit for hours, long after I wanted to try something different, and just listen to the Elders.

"And pray.

"Dad embraced his culture just like he cradled that football. The reason he was such a good Creek man in the end was the same reason he was such a good football player. He just loved what we were doing at the time.

"Dad would take me along with him on scouting trips, like when he worked for Minnesota Vikings coach Bud Grant at a camp in Winston Salem. Grant had won four Grey Cups as head coach with the Winnipeg Blue Bombers and this is where I learned about Dad's career up in Canada. He hadn't talked about his accomplishments all that much even though he was such a competitive guy. He didn't live in the past.

"We lost Dad way too early to a massive stroke or heart attack. We were raking leaves in the yard of our home in Greensboro, North Carolina when Dad raised his arm and pointed, 'Jay! Look at the squirrel' and that was it. He fell down and it was devastating because I was just 13 years old.

"I caught up with most of Dad's accomplishments because I was asked to accept the honours when he was inducted into various Halls of Fame. He is in six Hall of Fames and I even sat beside the son of Jim Thorpe at the Oklahoma induction. People always compare my Dad with Thorpe but I just honour two of the greatest Indian athletes who ever lived.

"Today when I run the mountain trails of East Tennessee and western North Carolina, I carry two things with me. My dad and God. That way, I know it is impossible to fail.

"Jack Jacobs lives on in the memories of many people, especially in Muskogee, where there is no doubt he was the best football player there ever was."

There is great achievement in representing the Creek nation at the highest levels of professional sports—providing an example and a standard of excellence on behalf of the people, and offering a role model for young people to emulate. Indian Jack Jacobs did that.

He had come full circle. The circle is complete.

"Long live my dad. Indian Jack Jacobs."—JOHN JACOBS

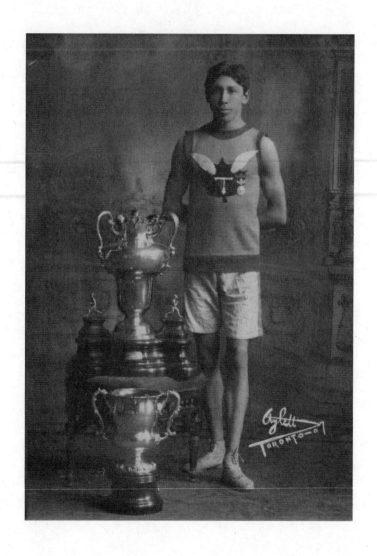

Tom Longboat

6

Longboat Left a Long Trail on the Land

The 49th parallel and the Rio Grande don't mean the same thing to First Nations as they do to the rest of North American society, so the fact that an indigenous person has been chosen the 20th century's top athlete in the United States, Canada and Mexico probably means more to those countries than it does to the First Nations, who really don't need to argue whether Jim Thorpe or Tom Longboat or some descendant of the Aztecs or Incas who now speaks Spanish is the greatest. A native of the Americas is definitely the greatest.

Longboat and Thorpe certainly gained a lot of notoriety for being chosen the best over such illustrious stars as Gordie Howe, Maurice Richard and Bobby Orr, and Babe Ruth and Michael Jordan and Jim Brown. So it is indeed quite an honour for the very best athletes over a 100-year period to be indigenous.

Tom Longboat was named winner of the Lou Marsh award by Canada's top national newspaper, the Toronto *Globe and Mail*, despite the that its fact one-time sports editor Lou Marsh once wrote that Longboat was "happy as a coon in a watermelon patch." The award wasn't an effort to patch things up. Longboat deserved the honour because he was the biggest star in Canada (and the United States) when it came to his specialty, and that was "running faster than everybody else," and for longer distances, too.

Longboat approached the world of competitive sports in a most humble manner. Born an Onondaga "Indian" in Six Nations Territory in the town of Oswegan, Ontario on June 4, 1887, Longboat knew he could run fast and it came in handy when he ran away from Indian boarding school at the age of 12. He wound up working at his uncle's farm, which was about the same thing as the residential school except he got paid instead of being free child labour for a work farm run by a bunch of priests and nuns.

It seemed like Tom Longboat never had to stop running unless he got lost. Family, friends and folks who lived in Six Nations knew he was fast and fastidious, and another local runner named Bill Davis helped with coaching.

But from the get-go, Tom was his own man and employed some unusual training methods (for the era). Mostly self taught, his training included running to nearby towns and back so he could gauge times and distances.

It was not unusual in those times for racing events of all kinds to be staged for the betting public; man against horse, horse against buffalo and so on. Tommy raced his brother to Hamilton, his brother driving a horse and buggy with a half-hour head start. This is the stuff legends are made of, and a legend was in the making.

Tom wondered how he might compare to runners outside his Onondaga world so one day in 1906 he showed up for the "Around the Bay" race sponsored by the Hamilton *Herald* newspaper. Wearing a droopy cotton bathing suit and cheap sneakers, he was almost laughed off the starting line. One *Herald* writer said his haircut looked like "it had been hacked off with a tomahawk." But the 19-year-old won the 19-mile race around a Lake Ontario bay in a time of one hour, 49 minutes and 25 seconds—a full three minutes faster than the rest of the world-class field.

The bookmakers had started Longboat off as a 60-to-1 long shot and one lucky bettor even managed a $2 bet at 500 to 1! When a fan wins a grand, especially back in those days when $1,000 was worth about $10,000 in today's dollars, the winner raises a hell of a ruckus, so any secret that was Tom Longboat was no more. He won the 15-mile Ward marathon in Toronto just a couple of days later, and then on Christmas Day '06, Longboat knocked two and a half minutes off the Canadian record for a 10-mile distance.

While these races were very important in Canada, the most prestigious long-distance test in North America at the time was the Boston Marathon. With sportswriters calling him "the Indian Iron Man" and "the Speedy Son of the Forest," even the bookies in Boston were hesitant to lay odds. In just a few short months, an Onondaga from Oswegan had become one of the favourites for the most famous marathon in the world. After this race, Tom Longboat would never go unnoticed again—which wasn't always a good thing.

But the legend began.

To start, Longboat beat the best time ever run at the Boston Marathon by a full five minutes! That is about a mile in distance. And he had to do that by running the last five miles uphill into a snow storm! (I can just see readers rolling their eyes remembering how their parents always told them the story about having to walk five miles to school in a blizzard, uphill both ways.) But there actually was a snow squall that blew in for the last section of the Boston Marathon, which is uphill.

Longboat even drew comparisons to Superman by out-running a freight train to win this race ("faster than a steaming locomotive"). That is because an actual freight train was barrelling down to cross the route and head off the runners at a level crossing so Longboat had to make a sharp right turn and out-run the train, dashing across the tracks at the first possible moment, and then return to the race course.

And yet he still beat the best time ever run at the Boston marathon by five minutes, setting a record (2:24:24) that wouldn't be beat until they made the course in Beantown easier. It was the fastest time for a marathon race in the history of the sport.

The victory in Boston was huge news back home and it was fuelled by national pride when a little girl gave Longboat a Canadian flag to wave at the finish line. When Longboat returned to Canada, it looked like the entire city of Toronto turned out for a big celebration in his honour.

As David Blaikie wrote in *Boston; The Canadian Story:*

A sea of celebrating humanity engulfed Longboat as he stepped from the train. The champion was placed in an open car; a Union Jack draped around his shoulders, and taken to City Hall in a torch light parade. Young women gazed at Longboat in rapture as bands played and fireworks exploded around him. A gold medal was pinned to his chest and the Mayor read a congratulatory address, highlighted by an announcement of a $500 gift from the city for his education.

But "legends are gardens where common men plant impossible dreams and harvest crops of make believe." Not everything was going so well in Longboat's personal life. He possessed a certain vulnerability to the corruptions of white society and Longboat was, after all, a young man with oats to sow.

He had been living and training at the West End Toronto YMCA but he got kicked out for missing curfew. Homeless, this drove him into the clutches of one Tom Flanagan, a flim flamman if there ever was one, who owned the Irish Canadian Athletic Club. The ICAC could put Longboat up for the night, but his days would soon belong to Flanagan, who became the inexperienced, naive young runner's trainer, manager and meal ticket (it works both ways, just sometimes one way more than the other).

For a time, Longboat flourished under Flanagan's training and continued to win races. The temptation was to turn professional, because this was a time before television, and society was much more enamoured with live track and field events than it is now. Professional match races were a huge attraction—sprints, middle distance and marathon match-ups that pitted mano a mano, one on one, were extremely popular because they provided so much pre-race banter back and forth to pass the long days of factory workers, office workers and even the idle elite. Arguing over "my guy can beat your guy" never gets tired.

And it was great for gambling on.

But the premier sporting event in all the world, then as it is now, were the Olympic Games, because this brought the best athletes from most every country on earth together to compete. Gold medal winners could count on a lucrative career of performance fees all over the world—rivalries replenished or created anew every four years by new meets and fresh meat.

The biggest problem faced by the athletes was retaining one's amateur status. The big con was that the official organizers of the Olympics were effete snobs who wanted to restrict the competition to the elite class who could afford to train like an Olympian needs to without having to worry about things like paying rent and eating. You weren't allowed to receive pay for playing any kind of sport but the prejudice and discrimination of the International Olympic Committee was so powerful and one-sided, the IOC could rule against someone for holding down almost any kind of job or earning any kind of income, and disqualify that person.

And so it was that Flanagan and his potential global star were torn between the lucrative incomes down the road that could be gained from glory at the Olympics, and the solid cash on hand they might be giving up because Longboat lost the race, or what seemed to be more likely at the time, he lost his amateur standing. There were various very powerful groups who didn't want this upstart star to show up their hopes, and the charges started flying in the calendar year prior to the Games and continued throughout the the early months of 1908 with the Olympics, which would stretch out over six months, to be played in Rome starting in April.

Longboat was the odds-on favourite to win the marathon, but he was an Indian with a slippery "mick manager" and there were plenty of powerful potentates who didn't want Longboat to compete in the big race that provides the glorious finishing touch to every Summer Olympic Games. Back in 1907, the New England Amateur Athletic Union had already declared Mr. Longboat a professional simply because they didn't want him to show up the Caucasian runners like he did at their Boston marathon.

The problems started for Longboat and Flanagan when Tom F. allowed Tom L. to stay in "Tom Flanagan's Grand Central Hotel" for free. Since Longboat also didn't appear to have a real job, what could he be except a man who was living off his winnings, and therefore, a professional?

Flanagan beat that back by setting Longboat up in a cigar business (yes, we can see the irony in an Onondaga being a "cigar store Indian") but that venture didn't work out too well. For some reason, however, it allowed Longboat to maintain his amateur status in the eyes of the IOC. (As the "owner" of a business, perhaps "income" becomes defined as the profits of your business and isn't recognized as "pay." Who really knows?)

Whatever the case, with protests appearing regularly against the Indian's amateur status, even from Canadian officials, and with the U.S. Amateur Athletic Union declaring him a professional and threatening to pull out all of their Olympic teams if Longboat was allowed to run, somehow Longboat was declared eligible by the IOC for the 1908 Games, now to be held in London, England because of the financial disruption caused by the eruption of Mount Vesuvius in 1906.

But it was obvious that something suspicious was up, and the 1908 Olympic marathon turned out to be one of the most controversial races ever run.

An interesting feature of the marathon that was developed at these Games that should be mentioned here because it played a huge role in determining who the winner of the 1908 race would be. It was in London where a standard distance was finally developed for the marathon that would eventually be used in every such race every time everywhere.

The scheduled distance for the marathon for the London Games was 25 miles, but the way things were in merry old England, with all its pomp and circumstance and nods to royalty at every turn, the course and then, of course, the distance from the start to the finish, was changed to meet the needs of the Royal Family.

First of all, the race was increased to 26 miles so the marathon could start at Windsor Castle, and then it was changed again at the request of Princess Mary so the start would be beneath the windows of the Royal Nursery. Then, to ensure that the race would finish in front of the King, the finish line was moved again by British officials, who were responding to American flag carrier (and shot putter) Ralph Rose's refusal to dip the American flag before the Royal Box during the opening ceremony ("This flag don't dip for nobody," said the burly American athlete). This final move was to "restore the importance of the monarchy."

As a result of these changes, the marathon covered a distance of 26 miles 385 yards (42.195 km), which became the standard length starting with the 1924 Summer Olympic Games held in Paris, France.

No matter the distance, Tom Longboat wouldn't make it and the reason why had charges of skullduggery flying around like shot puts and javelins landing in every direction.

Longboat was running a strong second as they entered the 19th mile when inexplicably, he just collapsed! With absolutely no history of ever faltering for even a misstep in his past, rumours immediately began to fly.

The fix was in, some of the bettors claimed. Longboat was a huge favourite for the race, so money wagered on the rest of the field was attracting great odds (and payoffs). However, when the Chief Medical Examiner, Dr. Michael Bulger, issued a statement that claimed Longboat collapsed because of the use of stimulants, fingers were pointed at possible purveyors of such drugs; which could either have given Longboat a boost he didn't really need (then again, some bettors like to make really sure) or knock Longboat out of the race with an overdose, which would cause the runner to faint or pass out.

There were plenty of bettors who could benefit from an upset, including Longboat's manager, if he used some "inside information" in some insidious way. And when Howard Crocker, the manager of the Canadian Olympic team flatly stated that, "Any medical man knowing the facts of the case will assure you that the presence of a drug in an overdose was the cause of the runner's failure," the reason why was fixed, but who fixed the race remained unknown.

It just didn't make enough sense for Flanagan to fix an overdose of drugs for his own guy because there were so many potential rewards for an Olympic gold medal marathoner down the road.

Drug testing wasn't near what it is today. From available records, it appears a doctor gave Longboat an external examination following the race (after the runner regained consciousness) "sort of like maybe" checked his pulse and blood pressure, peered into Longboat's eyes and said, "My God! This man appears to have been high!"

All of the medical statements simply state that the only reason Longboat passed out was from a drug overdose, without providing any scientific or medical information to support that conclusion (they didn't start drug testing until the 1968 Games in Mexico City after things got ridiculous when some members of the East German women's swim team showed up sprouting full beards and chest hair and posting times close to the men's results in the 200-metre freestyle...just kidding, but you get the idea).

So some bettors might have pulled off a fast one, but it was also extremely hot and humid on the day of the marathon, and the 35 degrees Celsius conditions could just as easily have caused all the staggering and stumbling around. So much so, the ending resembled a cross between the silent screen and a vaudeville show with the winner, Dorando Pietri of Italy, all 5-foot-2 of him, careening around the infield like Charlie Chaplin's little tramp or W.C. Fields on a bender. Fortunately for him, there were plenty of helping hands at the finish line, including Dr. Bulger, who was also president of the Irish Athletic Association (things just kept getting crazier and more controversial by the minute).

After running the wrong way, and completely collapsing at least four times, it seemed to be a matter of chance the little Italian would find the tape, except for the fact Bulger and Jack Andrew, the Clerk of the Course, each took Pietri by an arm, and with the good doctor massaging Pietri's heart to keep it beating, the Italian marathoner fell across the finish line first. That extra mile and some that had been added to appease the Royals might just have been enough to create that "wall" that many long distance runners like the diminutive Pietri fail to overcome. At least without help.

But even the *New York Times*, ignoring the obvious, got carried away with the fabulous finale, calling the race "the most thrilling athletic event since ancient Greece where the victor fell at the finish and with a wave of triumph, died."

Uh, *Times* people? Your "victor" might also have died if he hadn't been saved from his stagger and transported to his "triumph"; something I doubt the ancient Greeks would have stood for.

And neither would second-place finisher American Johnny Hayes. Obviously feeling he was cheated by a runner who should have fallen by the wayside like that Indian at mile 19, Hayes protested and was awarded the gold medal. Pietri, a pastry chef by profession, wasn't too disappointed because he had won the hearts of the fans and he would cash in big time on the professional racing circuit.

And so would Longboat. With nothing proven, everybody moved on and Longboat turned pro in November of that year.

But not with Flanagan as manager, at first.

Longboat finally rebelled against the heavy hand Flanagan was laying down, trying to mete out discipline, and they disagreed on the exact kind of training regimen Longboat should follow. Flanagan, hurting as much emotionally as financially, lashed out and was predicting that the Indian runner would squander his winnings ("native" that he was) and lose his edge without his guidance and discipline.

Maybe it was a case of "the devil you know," or perhaps it just wasn't time for Tom to take on the world without a white guide, but Longboat soon patched up his differences with his manager. Most important, Longboat was able to convince Flanagan that a runner knows his own body best and began to develop unique training methods that made much more sense and were so much more effective that they are in widespread use today.

Longboat's first major race was a marathon against Pietri, who some thought had actually won that Olympic marathon in London. And it is here that perhaps we see why the popularity that racing enjoyed back in the early 1900s has waned compared to now. Somehow, I just cannot see a packed crowd at Madison Square Garden sitting still for the kind of show the Indian and the pastry chef put on in December, 1908.

Not that it was the competitors' fault the promoters decided to put on a marathon in an arena which can only house a circular track, but the prevailing logic was that for a marathon to be a spectator sport, the audience was going to have to witness the entire race, not just the final laps after the runners entered the stadium or finish area.

So imagine this. Longboat and Pietri would circle that track 262 times in a race lasting two-and-a-half hours! Heck, I know I can't even watch long distance speed skating all the way through so I find other things to do until they reach the final stages of a race.

But the fact this one-on-one match race was popular is evident from the share of gate receipts that each runner was guaranteed—$3,750 apiece, which is well over $10,000 in today's money.

Pride was just as important though, so the spectators got a good show. Pietri led the race for most of the way before Longboat put on his, by now, signature finishing kick, passing Pietri at the 25-mile mark and sprinting well away to the win. Pietri, who was developing a signature move of his own, passed out and had to be carried from the track, this time avoiding the finish line.

A month later, they held a rematch in Buffalo, New York with exactly the same result, only this time, Pietri collapsed after just 19 miles.

It didn't take too long for the long-simmering dispute between Flanagan and Longboat to ignite into full flame again and this time, Flanagan left the relationship in a bad way. He sold Longboat's contract to an American promoter for a couple of thousand dollars. Just like any other race horse.

The major point of contention remained the difference in training methods the two men favoured. Flanagan was old school and his philosophy was "the more you train, the better you get." Longboat, who knew his body better than anyone else, liked to go hard one day, rest for another, and then add a day of "active rest" by going on long walks. Anybody familiar with modern track training methods will know that Longboat was on the right track again, and his training methods, which also included some weight training and time trials, are commonly used today.

Longboat was blessed with a natural talent for running, but he was also blessed with an innate knowledge of not only how to train, but also the very form for running itself. Competitors and fans alike ridiculed Longboat when, instead of raising his arms high up and down his sides when he ran, he dropped them into a relaxed style by his sides, but that is the style runners use today.

Longboat didn't lose much by leaving Flanagan, and he continued to win races. An intense rivalry built up between him and British distance runner Alfie Shrubb, the two runners trading victories and attracting a loyal following of fans who were fascinated by which style would win out each time. Shrubb tended to win at distances under 20 miles and Longboat could handle the longer races better, but the matches were unpredictable and that is what is most attractive about sports—never knowing who is going to win. That is why they run the races and play the games, and that is why sports betting is such a huge industry.

Longboat won a tidy sum of money throughout his professional career but he also spent freely on family and friends, and, never a shrewd businessman, he made a couple of bad business investments. Like many athletes, Tom Longboat had precious little left from his earnings when the legs gave out.

Tom's career off the track, however, took another exciting turn in 1916 when he volunteered for army duty during World War One. Tom's speed made him a natural for assignment as a messenger, but this was one of the most dangerous duties a soldier could have, running in and around and through enemy lines to carry messages from one post to another. But even Longboat couldn't outrun bullets and he was shot twice while posted in France. The first bullet cost him his first marriage.

Communications weren't all that good during WWI and word got back to the wife Tom had left behind that he was killed in action. Lauretta met another man and remarried and Tom was heartbroken when she chose to stay with her new man when Tom surprised her by showing up at her door after a second bullet ended his army career as a target in a shooting gallery. Fortunately, Tom would meet Martha Silversmith from his own reserve (Caledonia) in Six Nations, and their marriage produced four children. But anybody following Longboat's career had to be shaking their heads and wondering, "Is there anything that cannot happen to this man?"

Longboat's celebrity and service weren't much help to him financially after he returned from Europe, but he was an honest, hard-working man who had to bounce from job to job until he found steady work in Toronto. The fact he was a garbage man didn't seem to bother him, but it certainly said to the public he had "fallen a long way," especially when it became known he had pawned his medals when he was out of work.

Compounding this problem were the ever-present rumours of a drinking problem that all Indians had to deal with in those days; abstainer, teetotaller, social drinker or drunk.

The biggest problem that surfaced for Tom Longboat was that the media, the public rumour mill, and plain old gossipmongers love a story about the athlete who winds up destitute, most often with a substance abuse problem and even better if he ends up a charity case.

Yes, Tom liked to drink but, according to his daughter, Phyllis Winnie, he was a social drinker and never had a problem.

Unfortunately, in the days before television and other forms of mass media, few people really knew what celebrities actually looked like. And so there were more than a few Indians who would cadge free drinks by pretending to be the legendary Tom Longboat. The only way Longboat could fight back was to write letters to the editor in the newspapers explaining that these guys who were assuming his identity were "cheap, two-bit impostors."

Longboat's total public record was an intoxication charge in 1911 and a driving under the influence conviction 24 years later. Nothing to be proud of, but nothing spectacular for those days.

The race that Longboat couldn't win is one in which far too many Indians in North America finish last. The onset of diabetes is an often slow, creeping illness that spreads throughout the body with advancing age; first the legs go, and then the organs and ultimately, death. Longboat hated needles so his insulin treatments were not as regular as they should be for a man so used to the discipline of a training regimen.

Tom Longboat retired back home to Six Nations in 1947, where he passed away less than a year later of pneumonia. Tom was 61.

Most fittingly, a book written about Longboat by fellow distance runner Bruce Kidd was entitled *The Man Who Ran Faster than Everybody*. Who could imagine a better title than that for Longboat?

The memory of Tom Longboat lives forever. Not only because Canada issued a stamp bearing his likeness, not because he is Canada's Athlete of the 20th Century, and not because he has been inducted to the Canadian Sports Hall of Fame and the Indian Sports Hall of Fame.

The Tom Longboat Trophy is awarded annually to the top First Nations athlete in each province in Canada and it is the award most cherished by indigenous athletes throughout the country. The list of names on the Tom Longboat Trophy is a who's who for Indian sports since the award was initiated in 1951.

All of them striving to emulate the legendary Tom Longboat— a role model for all time.

George Armstrong

7

Hockey First for First Nations

Perhaps because hockey is so familiar with the traditional Ojibwe sport of baggataway (lacrosse) or maybe it is simply because hockey provides the most opportunities for native people to excel, hockey is the most popular of the contemporary sports producing the most successful and well-known indigenous athletes.

There are many theories about the origins of hockey. Nova Scotians claim the sport stems from a stick game that military leader Colonel Hockey used to keep his troops in shape. Folks in London, England say that a stick game played by kids who pushed around hock carts during a break looked a lot like the modern game. But when you consider that Mohawk warriors who competed at the hockey-looking-like sport of baggataway would yell, "Haw-Gee!" ("it hurts") when they got hit especially hard, I am inclined to go with indigenous claims that their culture provides the origins of hockey.

The stories of indigenous players who excelled at hockey are so many and varied they could fill a book. And so they did.

They Call Me Chief told the stories of First Nations, Métis and Inuit stars of the National Hockey League. The book was based on a successful documentary which outlined the passion, skill and fortitude of "warriors on ice" who overcame significant obstacle to achieve success. A review of these stories belongs in this book to bring these athletes together with stars of other sports and to provide an update on some of their stories.

Author's note: The word "chief" was used in the title of the book because almost every native player in the NHL was nicknamed "chief" without regard to the meaning of the title in the culture of First Nations. It was just the first word that came to mind and the consequences of its use are explained in depth in the book.

It starts with Fred Sasakamoose—the first recognized Indian to play in the NHL. Fred didn't have much more than a pot of tea with the Chicago Blackhawks but that's because the structure of professional hockey was so different back in the 1950s.

"Chief Running Deer on Skates" was a speedster with a booming shot who hailed from Ahtahkakoop First Nation (Sandy Lake) in Saskatchewan. He was called up late in the 1953-54 season but only played 13 games with Chicago, registering just six penalty minutes with zero goals and zero assists.

The potential benefits to Chicago's public relations department had been long desired. They finally had a genuine Indian in their lineup to match their logo, so they played "Indian Love Call" by Hank Williams when Fred first stepped onto the ice in Chicago Stadium.

Fred was good enough to play in the NHL but so were a lot of players who were mired in the minor leagues. This is because there were only six teams in the number one league and there is only so much room on each team's roster. At the same time, there wasn't that much difference in the calibre and the level of play, and the pay, between the NHL and the American Hockey League or even some of the senior leagues throughout Canada. Sure, the NHL was "the show," but sometimes it just wasn't worth the sacrifice.

In Freddy's case, he had made all the sacrifices on the ice to achieve the skill level required to star in the NHL, but the one thing he could not overcome was the loneliness; the time away from his family, friends and home.

It started with many hours skating on a pond on bobskates strapped by his grandfather on to moccasins made by his grandmother, so family was always nearby for young Freddie.

"My grandfather would cut two branches from a willow tree," Fred recalls. "He would carve one of them into a hockey stick and the other one into a fishing pole. I would skate around shooting pieces of ice and snow while Grandpa caught dinner."

But then Fred was taken away to the Indian Residential School at Duck Lake. The IRS system was a collaboration between churches and the Canadian government to assimilate native people, or as it was written in their policy manuals, "to destroy the Indian in the child." This dark chapter in Canadian history is a horror story of cultural genocide and physical and sexual abuse. Thousands of children died and many thousands more were physically and emotionally scarred by the experience, creating dysfunction which First Nations are struggling to deal with today. Despite an official apology by the Canadian government, some individual financial compensation and a Truth and Reconciliation Commission, the manifestations of Indian residential schools are ever-present in the economic and social problems First Nations are trying to overcome today.

Fred and his classmates spent half-days in the classrooms and the rest of their time slopping hogs and milking cows and tending fields in what was just as much a work farm using unpaid labour as it was a school. Fred escaped some of the abuse because the school was run by some hockey-mad priests from Montreal who could live out their fantasies through these Indian boys who won the Saskatchewan northern midget championship for them. Fred loved the hockey, but he was always so lonely that he begged his parents not to send him back to the school every year. But his parents faced being sent to jail if they kept their children at home so Fred was only able to enjoy Ahtahkakoop for two months every summer.

Finally, Fred reached age 14 and simply refused to return to school. Tension mounted as the season of the changing leaves came. Then one day, a huge black car carrying a couple of priests came barrelling down the dirt path that led to the Sasakamoose log homestead. Fred and his brother ran and hid in the bush.

To everybody's surprise, the priests didn't want Freddie to return to Duck Lake. They had made arrangements for Fred to join the Moose

Jaw Canucks of the Western Junior Hockey League, and Fred was off to "the big city."

Sasakamoose excelled in Moose Jaw and was chosen the "best player in western Canada" by the time he was 19. But while the "bright lights" of a small, prairie town only consisted of a traffic signal or two, Moose Jaw was as different from Ahtahkakoop as New York is to the Sudan. Fred's first language was Cree, and he saw few faces that looked like his or spoke the same tongue. Everything was different; the pace of living, the crowds on Main Street on Saturday afternoons (it was like walking around the big top at a pow wow), clothes, food; it was severe culture shock.

And loneliness. There was always that loneliness.

All Fred had was hockey, and the best player in half of Canada had everything the Chicago Blackhawks wanted. Fred, who was married by now, signed a contract with Chicago that was worth $6,000 a season, not a princely sum but enough to return home in the same kind of big, black car those priests used to pick him up; ironically, a Mercury DeSoto—named after the Spanish conquistador who specialized in "clever schemes for the extortion of native villages for their captured Chiefs," the explorer who was first to plant a white man's footprints on indigenous lands on the west side of the Mississippi River.

The culture shock he experienced in Chicago was exponential, so Fred figured that his wife Loretta would help ease the pain. But Loretta, who had once refused to move from one side of Ahtahkakoop to the other because she said she would get homesick, quietly but quickly said: "I'm not going."

Fred returned for Chicago's 1954-55 training camp but with radio announcers calling him "Saskatchewan-moose" and "Saskatoon-moose" and worse (Fred managed to shrug off most racial taunts except for one miscreant, who called him a "squaw-humper"—which hurt so much more because it was an insult directed at his wife), Fred's play suffered. The Blackhawks were going to send him to the minors but Fred asked to be assigned to a senior league team in Calgary so he could be closer to home. The Blackhawks complied, but they wouldn't pay for a plane ticket for Fred to go get Loretta and bring her to Cowtown to help him cope with the loneliness.

"So I took a taxi 700 miles from Calgary to home," Fred chuckles.

Despite the world-record cab fare and Fred's pleading, Loretta simply said: "I'm not going."

So, Fred Sasakamoose's NHL career was over. He still made a decent living "barn-storming" as a hired gun for teams throughout western Canada who could collect 25 cents a patron to come out and see "the only Indian to play in the NHL," but that also took him away from Loretta, family and friends. He began to abuse alcohol to compensate for that ever-present loneliness and it eventually became time to stay home.

Fred quit drinking and got elected Chief of Ahtahkakoop. He became a driving force behind the Federation of Saskatchewan Indian Nations; a lobby group which represents the rights of First Nations, on issues of sovereignty, treaty rights, land claims, social and economic development. He is now happily retired, living in a log cabin on the very site where he grew up skating on that pond. Fred keeps busy coaching the over 60 grandchildren and now great-grandchildren who have generated from Fred and Loretta's eight offspring. Fred also keeps busy conducting anti-alcohol and drug addiction workshops across Canada and the United States.

Fred Sasakamoose became a legend to the Indian people of western Canada. Tales of his exploits are still told around wood stoves and fireplaces and wherever children gather to learn about those who have gone before.

Imagine a grandfather sitting around a campfire surrounded by children and older youth hanging on his every word…

"Some white boys from town had been having considerable good fortune against our Rez team but they didn't know we had a secret weapon one game a while back. They dropped the puck and dem white boys raced after it like a pack of wild dogs but ol' Freddie Sasakamoose had dat dere bannock biscuit behind our net…Well, ol' Freddie just wound up and started stickhandling in and out and around 'dem white boys like they was… what do you call 'dem orange things they put out on the highways? Those cones? Yeah, pylons…he started skated around dem sonias (white men) like they was standing still!

"Meanwhile, Freddie's teammates went for a smoke…

"Now, Fred Sasakamoose wasn't one for making fun of other folks, but we had charged two bits a head for fans to come out and see the only Indian to play in the NHL and our community arena was jammed to the rafters…so Freddie skated back into his own end, let those boys pick up their jock straps, and he did it again just for show!

"So now there's just this scared little white guy dressed in real goalie pads covering his legs, not old magazines like our guy had to wear…

"Anyways, this little guy is shaking like a willow in a big wind as Freddie bears down on him, but instead of lettin' loose with that ol' thunderstick of his, Fred just backhands that ol' biscuit way up inna air, and goes and joins his teammates for that smoke!

"About a week later, just as that puck was coming down from the clouds, they all got back on that ice again, and Fred put on some more of the slickest moves you ever did see… I don't know if I really saw 'zackly what he did; his hands were so quick that if you blinked you missed it, and then Fred tucked that puck ever so gently into the corner of the net behind the corkscrew, which was what that little goalie had bin turned into…

"Dem white boys had their tails between their legs as they slunk offa da rez dat day, and the whole community was shining with pride for a long time.

"And that is a true story… I'm not lyin', I swear on my dogs…

And if I ain't telling the truth, may I be hit 'onna head by a puck falling out of the sky!"

The next two "Chiefs" to play in the National Hockey League were noted for their longevity and their legendary leadership.

George "the Chief" Armstrong of the Toronto Maple Leafs (not to be confused with George Armstrong Custer of the U.S. 7th Cavalry whose lack of longevity is legendary) is the longest-serving team captain in NHL history. NHL George led the Leafs to four Stanley Cup championships on his way to the Hockey Hall of Fame. The Leafs have officially retired Armstrong's Number 10 jersey—the highest honour a team can pay because it expresses the belief that there is no other player who could achieve as much success and honour wearing that sweater for the franchise.

Jim "Chief" Neilson enjoyed a 19-year pro career, appearing in over 1,000 games, mostly with the New York Rangers. One year, Jim finished second to the great Bobby Orr in balloting for the Norris Trophy, which is given annually to the best defenseman in the NHL. Jim was a stay-at-home-style rearguard who took care of things in his own end. He provided a steadying influence for up-and-coming superstars like Brad Park.

Jim's career even extended to the World Hockey Association, where in his final season with the Edmonton Oilers, he could be seen offering tips to The Great One—Wayne Gretzky.

Both Armstrong and Neilson are products of mixed marriages, but both have distinctively Indian features. Neither grew up on a reserve or was exposed to his First Nations culture, lifestyle and spirituality very much. At times, this created problems when their teams' over-zealous public relations departments tried to exploit their Indian backgrounds.

George Armstrong grew up in Falconbridge, Ontario. His father worked in the mines and his mother's family provided the Indian blood, which showed up in Armstrong's square, dark, handsome visage. Headline writers loved to use stereotypical images whenever they could:

"Chief Armstrong Scalps Bruins with Three Goals," "The Chief Expected to Sign New 3-year Treaty with Leafs" and "Chief Offers Peace Pipe to Canadiens Enforcer."

Armstrong rarely talked about his Indian heritage and did not grant any media interviews once he was able to scramble away from the spotlight of professional hockey in the early 1990s. This makes it difficult to gain insight into the man and his thoughts about hockey or life or his reluctance to embrace his native background publicly.

There have been rumours that George was ashamed one time at a public function put on by the Leafs when his grandmother showed up "shabbily dressed." It could just as well be that George's grandma had just dropped by for a casual, friendly visit and was unaware that the public event was going on, and George whisked her away so that she wouldn't feel out of place or be embarrassed. George won't let us know.

Jim Neilson faced similar situations, where reporters would ask questions about some aspect of native culture or history. The social, economic and political concerns of First Nations people in Canada are a major issue which need to be addressed and some media types might ask Armstrong or Neilson what they thought of the latest news about sovereignty or treaty rights or land claims...and housing and health care and infrastructure and clean drinking water and... Few would expect hockey players to be experts on complex socioeconomic issues but some reporters picked up on the fact that Armstrong and Neilson weren't intimately knowledgable about their people's history, or issues of the day.

This is, in no way, their fault, and there isn't any fault to find. Both players were very proud of the Indian blood that flowed through their veins and certainly were not ashamed of the way they looked. Neilson, while referring to the fact he was raised in a mostly white orphanage, explains simply that he "really didn't know much about it."

But with the teams' PR departments marketing these guys as "chiefs" and "warriors" and "braves," the insinuations and downright accusations they are exploiting culture start to fly like arrows across the road from Crowfair back in 1876 and unfortunately, most critics go after the players who are out in front of the public eye instead of the PR hacks who are behind the scenes avoiding the flack.

Neilson is a rather level-headed guy who probably wouldn't over-react in any situation, and he handled it all with grace and humour. But if pressure created by the lack of understanding of Armstrong's background and situation was a primary cause for one of the greatest leaders in NHL history to completely close off contact with the media, and through them, the fans who adored and respected him, it's a damn shame.

Perhaps the best way to handle Indian stereotypes created by the media is the way Neilson treated Red Fisher; a sports writer for the *Montreal Gazette*.

"Glen Sather had this cottage by a lake and Red Fisher coveted this Indian painting that Sather had. Sather (who was GM in Edmonton at the time) wouldn't part with that particular painting but he asked me if I would pose for a picture painting my house," Neilson says with a

sly smile. "Fisher got an 'Indian painting.' It was a picture of me painting my house."

Armstrong also played well over a thousand games during his 21-
year career and followed it all up by coaching the Toronto Marlboros
to a pair of Memorial Cup Canadian junior championships. George
then served, in turn, as chief scout, head coach and general manager of
the Leafs before retiring.

Neilson retired and worked for a while with the Department of
Indian Affairs, while catching up on knowledge about his Indian heritage.
He is retired and plays recreational hockey in Winnipeg whenever he can.

Reggie Leach was called "Chief" often enough, in the classroom at
school, walking down the street, or playing hockey. But Reggie is best
known as "the Riverton Rifle," because he sniped 384 goals in his NHL
career and he hails from the town of Riverton, Manitoba.

"My Indian family is from Berens River but I grew up in this hard-
living, Icelandic fishing village where drinking was considered 'normal.'
So I picked it up by the age of 12," Reggie says.

Surrounded by a sea of destruction, Reggie could see and feel the
devastating effects of alcohol close up.

Extremely close up.

"I lost one brother who froze to death in Riverton. I had another
brother who wrapped himself another a telephone pole and I had a sister who froze to death in a car…fell asleep. I had another brother who
strangled himself…"

And yet alcohol would be the curse of Reggie Leach's life, compromising whatever success he had in professional hockey, but then leading him to a cause and a career which would have more impact and
generate more benefits than anything he could possibly do with a stick
and a puck on a sheet of ice.

Reggie's hockey career started out in typical fashion for an orphaned
child trying to rise out of poverty. Reggie had loving grandparents who
raised him and his multitude of siblings but there was barely enough money
to go around for food and clothing, let alone luxury activities like sports.

So, Reggie didn't get his first pair of skates until he was 10 years old and they were a pair of size 11s. Reggie's adult skate size is a 7 so you could imagine how ill-fitting those humungous skates were on him as a kid. Instead of simply putting on an extra half dozen pairs of socks, Reggie had to stuff newspapers in the toes just to skate around. And still, he dominated his age group.

Then an "unidentified" local benefactor (some say it was the whole town chipping in) bought Reggie a brand new pair of skates and the next thing you know, the kid was playing for five or six teams in different age categories, scoring almost at will against players his own age, dominating higher age groups as he moved up the ladder against adults, where he was always competitive and often a contributor in local men's leagues.

In junior hockey, Leach was paired with Bobby Clarke, a small, diabetic kid who looked like he was raised in a mushroom patch. Despite their contrasting physical appearance, Clarke and Leach were like twins separated at birth and they terrorized the Western Junior Hockey League. After burning out the goal light behind the opposition net in the Whitney Forum ("The "Smelter"—which caused many an opposing player to come down with "Flin Flon flu" just before boarding the bus heading north), Leach and Clarke became the toast of the town; kids playing hockey strictly for the love of the game.

"The first car Clarkie and I ever bought was by chipping in together," Leach recalls with laughter. "A real piece of junk, we'd 'Fill up the oil and check the gas' when we pulled into a service station. But we didn't care. It was just so much fun because we were leading the league in scoring year after year and looking forward to our dreams of becoming pros coming true real soon."

They were drafted by different NHL teams, so Leach had to pass through the Boston Bruins system before joining Clarke in Philadelphia. An interesting side note: Leach avoided being called "Chief" by his teammates because the Bruins already had a "Chief" on their roster. Johnny Bucyk, a Ukrainian from Edmonton, looked so much like an Indian that his teammates had already taken to calling him "the Chief" long before Reggie showed up. So they hung the nickname "Little Beaver" on Reg (Little Beaver was a well-known midget wrestler who competed in moccasins and a headdress; apparently, the difference in weight and height between Reggie and the namesake they hung on him was not all that noticeable to his teammates).

Leach and Clarke repeated the success they enjoyed in junior when they were paired up in Philly. The "Broad Street Bullies" were a mix of size, strength, brute strength and skill that went unmatched as they won back-to-back Stanley Cups in 1973-74 and 1974-75, and then threw in a still record 35-game winning streak after that. The Flyers even caused the national team from the Soviet Union to walk off the ice during a high-profile tour when the Flyers were the only NHL team to beat them. The Red Army team was protesting broad, bully behaviour (which they were dishing out just as much) but when they were informed they wouldn't receive their share of the gate from the game, the Soviets returned to finish the match, which they lost 4-1.

But Leach, Clarke and the Flyers would have to make way for Métis star Bryan Trottier to take the New York Islanders on a four-year Stanley Cup run starting with the 1975-76 season. The Flyers didn't go quietly, and Reggie Leach became the only non-goalie to win the Conn Smythe Trophy given to the Most Valuable Player in the Stanley Cup playoffs while a member of the losing team. Reg earned that by scoring 19 goals in the post-season, to go along with the 61 he led the NHL with during the regular season.

And the most amazing thing about all this is that Reggie Leach accomplished a lot of it while he was drunk. Not sitting-at-a-table-spinning-yarns-and-spewing-spittle-drunk, not falling-down-trying-to-hail-a-cab-drunk, but as Reggie correctly points out, when you drink until five in the morning before a game the next day, especially a matinee, you are still pretty much juiced when you take to the ice and you would certainly blow over the limit on a breathalyzer.

"Alcohol was available everywhere in the NHL," says Reggie. "It was in the dressing room after the games, on the plane, in the hotel rooms, and all team functions. It was pretty much impossible to resist when you are used to drinking since you were 12 but aren't aware that you have a problem."

Reggie started to realize the negative impact that alcohol was having on his career, his marriage and his health in general. But every time he tried to quit, he was doing it for "somebody else."

"You can't do it for your family, the team, your friends...you have to do it for yourself."

"1984 was the most important year of my life," Reggie proclaims, with the passion of a man with the weight of the world of regret on his shoulders, but also with the hope and faith that many people who have overcome addictions and survived carry as a badge of honour.

"1984 was the year I retired from professional hockey, it was the year I got divorced, and it was the year I quit drinking."

Reggie hasn't drunk a drop of alcohol since 1984. He spends a great part of his life helping others avoid the same destructive path he followed, and find the way out that he found. Reggie Leach has conducted hundreds, if not thousands of workshops, for youth and children, as well as adults, about how to deal with alcohol and drug addiction.

Along the way, he re-established relationships with the people who were harmed by alcohol as much as it harmed him. Reggie and his son, Jamie, who enjoyed his own NHL career, have developed a unique hockey school that recognizes the fact First Nations people often cannot afford to travel to the centres where hockey schools are usually provided (often cities and other urban centres which are located far from rural and northern First Nations). So, Reggie and Jamie pack up their knowledge and skills and bring their school to the local communities.

Reggie Leach has dabbled in coaching. He was drafted (kidnapped?) by his neighbours on Manitoulin Island to coach their team, the Islanders. Reggie also takes great pride in sponsoring a hockey tournament each year in his name to raise money for local hockey development back in Riverton.

Reggie regularly attends Flyers alumni games and other social functions, but he doesn't need ex-teammates like Gary Dornhoeffer to step in and protect him when people innocently offer him a drink like they used to.

"Go ahead, Reggie, one drink won't hurt you," they would say.

"The hell it won't." Reggie knows.

"Drinking cost me my dream. My goal has always been the Hockey Hall of Fame but I didn't make it because of my drinking," Reggie says with regret.

There is a movement that is growing larger year by year and a petition to convince the powers-that-be that Reggie Leach rightfully belongs in the Hall. But there are more important things on Reggie's mind right now.

"It is our future generations who are paying for our mistakes that we made in the past," Reggie says. "We have to help them overcome our mistakes, otherwise, they will be doomed to make the same mistakes."

Well, at least we know this. Reginald Joseph Leach, the Riverton Rifle, deserves to be a Chief, in the real sense of the word.

Stan Jonathan has been described a a 6 foot 3 man who was placed in a compactor until he came out 5-foot-7. And so naturally, Stan's nickname was "Little Chief."

The tough little guy from the Six Nations Reserve, who would become an enforcer for the Boston Bruins, grew up as the sixth child in a family of 14 children. Stan learned early on he had to fight for his food at a crowded dining table, and if you were one of the late ones to arrive, you missed your spot in the back of the family pickup truck.

Stan learned his hockey skating on a slough behind his family's homestead in Six Nations, but he had to put in his time at school and summer jobs while dreaming of someday starring in the NHL.

One rite of passage to manhood for Mohawks in southern Ontario, Quebec and northern New York was "working the high steel."

The Six Nations of Mohawk, Oneida, Onandaga, Cayuga, Seneca and Tuscarora which comprise the Haudenosaunee are largely, or highly, responsible for building New York City. Their courage climbing and tight-roping the girders of skyscrapers is legendary.

Stan Jonathan worked the high steel when he was 16 and it provided a great lesson for hockey.

"When you make a mistake on the high steel, you don't get a second chance."

Despite once leading the league in scoring percentage/shooting accuracy, which divides the number of goals by the shots taken on net, with a 26.1 average, and despite his diminutive stature, Stan was destined to be a "Big Bad Bruin" like John Wensink, Terry O'Reilly, Ken Hodge and Fred Stanfield. All of these guys could score but they also "provided protection" for more gifted but gentlemanly playmakers like Bobby Orr, Phil Esposito and Jean Ratelle. It was quite a package, topped off by infamous hockey coach Don Cherry.

And so the Bruins looked to be on their way to the Stanley Cup in 1979 when they were leading the Montreal Canadiens 3-2 in the final game of the best-of-seven semi-final (tied three games apiece).

It was then that the Habs decided to send a "message," and the most famous fight in the history of hockey took place.

Hockey teams will sometimes resort to picking fights to "pick up their team" and the Canadiens had plenty of pugilists to pick from in their lineup, too, starting with Pierre Bouchard.

Even the name sounds like some mighty, huge lumberjack with a beard, wearing a plaid shirt with rolled up sleeves, carrying an axe etc.

"Bouchard was a monster," says Cherry. "He was about 6-foot-5, 260 pounds..."

"I was maybe 5-foot-6," Jonathan chuckles. "But I was 5-foot-8 with those high-heeled shoes we used to wear back in those days."

They didn't even wait for the refs to drop the puck. Jonathan and Bouchard just exchanged some "pleasantries" and the fight was on; both men hanging on to the other guy's sweater with one hand and throwing punches like pistons with the other.

"At the beginning, I was thinking, Boy! I think Stanley's bitten off more than he can chew this time!" Cherry recalls.

But Stan had a secret weapon he'd been carrying around since his childhood.

"Few people know, but Stan can throw with his left, as good as he can with his right," Cherry points out, demonstrating with his own beefy mitts, still formidable at 70.

"Coming from a family of 14, you had to get in there with both hands at the supper table or you didn't get anything to eat," Stan explains.

"Stan switched hands on him," Cherry says. "And he caught Bouchard with a solid left."

The mighty Habs defenseman went down like an oak, but the piston-like drive of Jonathan's arm did a lot more damage on the way down. The blood was splashing so wildly that linesman John D'Amico looked like Chuck Wepner (the boxer known as the Bayonne Bleeder) and that was just from trying to help Bouchard get up. Pierre suffered a broken jaw and or-bital bone, but Stan admits he didn't escape from the fight unscathed either.

"My head looked like a lumpy balloon for days after that one," Stan admits.

The Habs came back to win that game and went on to win the Cup, but ask most people who won it all in 1979 and they most likely won't be able to say. But ask them about the fight between Pierre Bouchard and Stan Jonathan during the playoffs and they will be able to re-create the scrap blow-by-blow.

"It was easily the best fight I've ever seen," swears Cherry. And, keep in mind that Cherry has produced a popular series of videos called "Rock 'em Sock'em Hockey," so he should know.

Stan had a satisfying career mostly playing for the Bruins and he remains a darling of the blue-collar, lunch-bucket crowd in Boston. He was often called an "Indian fighter." But in sharp contrast to those western heroes like Kit Carson who made their claim to fame by "fighting" Indians, Stan was an Indian and he sure was a fighter.

What most people don't know is how much of a fighter for Indian rights Stan Jonathan was throughout his career. Stan was a proud member of the Six Nations Confederacy and he fought to have the sovereignty of his nation recognized, as well as taking a personal stand against efforts to violate the Treaty rights of his people.

First of all, Stan knew that the Six Nations Confederacy was a political alliance with territorial jurisdiction that was established long before Canada and the United States divided themselves along the 49th parallel. Their nations extended from New York to Quebec and Ontario without the dividing lines that came later. Therefore, First Nations were allowed free access across the new border and this was set in accordance with what was called the Jay Treaty.

NHL teams that were located in the United States faced restrictions on the number of players they could have on their roster who were not American citizens. The Boston Bruins required green cards for Canadian players, but in Jonathan's case, they did not. This meant that Harry Sinden had what was essentially an open spot on his roster for an extra Canadian. But Stan Jonathan wouldn't allow his status as an Indian to be used in this way.

"I told Harry Sinden that I wouldn't allow him to bring in an extra player who might beat me out of my job, or replace one of my teammates who had earned his spot on the roster, by using my Indian status in this way," said Jonathan.

Jonathan was bringing public attention to the special status of First Nations, which some people confused with being just another ethnic group, like immigrants to Canada and the United States. These newcomers become citizens and inherit all the rights and responsibilities of American and Canadian citizenship (including honouring all treaties which are signed by their country; past, present and future).

Native Americans are unique. They are nations with special rights established by sovereignty, globally-recognized indigenous rights and those rights which were negotiated through the process of signing Treaties. These rights must be respected and defended with the same honour that Native Americans have shown by joining their Treaty ally, the American and Canadian armed forces, whenever they have been called upon.

In light of all this, it wasn't a trivial matter when Stan got into another tussle with Sinden over his right to sell used cars.

"I was offered this contract to do some used car commercials and Harry Sinden tried to tell me that I couldn't do that because I was only down there to play hockey and that we weren't allowed to do other work, but I knew from working the high steel that as a registered Indian I could work both sides of the border and I said to Harry, 'I'm going to do those commercials and you can do whatever you want but I have a right to do those commercials and to get paid for doing those commercials.'"

Harry Sinden came to the realization that the fearless fighter he had on the ice was even feistier off it, so again, Stan won the day.

And the people of the Six Nations Confederacy people continue to live and work freely in their territories, no matter whether they happen to be located in Canada or the United States.

———————————

Every fall, Stan Jonathan could expect to receive the same call from one of his relatives: "Hey Stan! I forgot to bring along enough bullets. Can you borrow me some? Oops! sorry, I forgot. You don't need bullets where you are, ha ha ha!"

"Stan! I just bagged a 12-point buck and I was thinking of you and how we used to go out every fall…and miss…whenever you shot at… a ha ha!…"

Training camp always takes place right in the middle of the fall hunting season. And Stan would get the call to report to a junior team, an AHL squad, the Bruins, or Pittsburgh, where Stan ended his career by playing a couple of seasons with the Penguins.

The only calls Stan Jonathan gets right now are "don't forget the bug spray" as he lives the autumn of his life enjoying fall hunts and the many grandchildren that he and Cathy, the love of his life and wife since his junior hockey days, have watched grow like their children before them. Some recent heart trouble has slowed Stan down, and he doesn't play as much senior hockey or join in the hunt as much as he would like.

"Little Chief" lives in Oswegan, Ontario in a house that begins with a door adorned with a stained glass turtle which honours Stan's clan. The circular living room is the centre piece of the house, and the "chandelier," a replica of the old centre ice score clock in Boston Garden, is the centrepiece of the living room. Jutting off in all directions are memorabilia of Stan's playing days, and pictures of his family, in equal numbers.

———————————

Bryan Trottier is a "half-white" (his term) who was born in the tiny town of Val Marie, Saskatchewan. Bryan Trottier is also undoubtedly the most successful native hockey player in NHL history.

Bryan hoisted the Stanley Cup over his head seven times during his career; six times as a player and once as a coach. He has won NHL scoring championships, trophies for being the top rookie and most valuable player, MVP in the Stanley Cup playoffs and is a member of the hallowed Hockey Hall of Fame.

And it all starts with the special relationship a young boy enjoys with his dog. Perhaps tired of getting into fist-fights at school because classmates taunted him with the name "half-breed," or because that didn't provide him with playmates to practice his hockey skills with, Bryan enlisted the family border collie, Rowdie to defend the net against his wrist and slap shots.

"Rowdie was a pretty good 'butterfly-style' goalie," Bryan recalls. "If he wasn't blocking the bottom of the net with his body, he was catching the puck with his teeth." "Rowdie died at the age of 17, there was not a tooth left in his head," Bryan recalls with sadness and a smile. After all, 17 in "dog years" is actually 68 in human terms, so Rowdie enjoyed a full life.

And Bryan developed a wicked wrist shot.

The Trottier family was quite typical for the western Canadian prairies—large in numbers and small in resources, living off the land as best they could. Being Métis, they had a musical bent, the old man played pretty much every instrument, so he taught one kid the fiddle, another the bass, this one the drums, that one to sing. Bryan learned guitar and drums like it was just part of growing up.

The family's musical training came in handy when Bryan's talent at beating Rowdie got noticed by some junior hockey scouts in Swift Current, SK. The Trottier family band would get a gig at the local hotel/bar in whatever town Bryan and the Broncos were playing so they could afford to attend the games and have a place to stay. After the games, Bryan would put down his hockey sticks and pick up some drumsticks, or a bass or a rhythm guitar, and entertain the locals while his teammates enjoyed their post-game in the more usual manner.

Trottier was a superstar-in-waiting but he wasn't drafted until the second round of the 1974 draft, going to the New York Islanders as the 22nd choice overall. The 21 picks ahead of Trottier include some no-names (Bill Lochead, Mike Naron, Bruce Affleck?) but the first round pick of the Islanders, Clark Gillies, reveals the experience and expertise the Islanders possessed at the time that would bring Mike Bossy, Denis Potvin and Billy Smith under the guidance of highly respected head coach Al Arbour and carry this franchise to four straight NHL championships.

Despite being a second-round pick, Bryan was offered the standard signing bonus at the time, and that was a car of the player's choice. Most players selected a Mercedes, or a Ferrari, a Cadillac at least. Bryan? He wanted a huge Chrysler New Yorker for his dad, because it was the only car he knew of that was large enough to ferry the Trottier family around.

Bryan Trottier was a leader on and off the ice. He served time serving his fellow players as president of the NHL Players' Association. He represented Canada at major international hockey tournaments, and then, because he has Indian status, played in a major tournament for the U.S. national team (this decision proved to be very controversial because some Canadian fans considered him a traitor but Bryan was adamant that he "wanted to give something back to the country he was making his living in"). Bryan is also a recipient of a National Aboriginal Achievement Award—the most prestigious honour a First Nations, Métis or Inuit can achieve in Canada.

I had the pleasure of working side by side with Bryan Trottier on a charitable, fund-raising event for the White Buffalo Spiritual Society of Winnipeg. The experience provided me with insight into the pressures and machinations that impact on sports celebrities, which are exacerbated when the player is a superstar whose core values can be exploited by hucksters and downright liars. But it also provided me with insight into the strength and desire to be fair which Bryan exemplifies in everything he does.

Bryan and I set about organizing an exhibition recreational hockey game between the Winnipeg Jets alumni and an all-star team of First Nations and Métis players from Manitoba (bolstered by Trottier and Stan Jonathan), with proceeds going to the charity. Bryan was very experienced and skilled at organizing public events like this, having donated his time throughout his career to support community organizations in need.

Bryan and I wanted to make sure that the players who were donating their time were treated properly. We both appreciated the fact that high-profile celebrity superstars like Dale Hawerchuk and Morris Lukowich have to take time away from jobs and families to support our requests and that they should be reasonably compensated.

There is always a conflict between the goals of the charitable organization to raise money and the expense they have to incur to raise that money. I have found that too often, the organizers of charitable events take an immense point of pride if they can get the celebrity to work for free (pro bono) or cheaply. I recall a charitable golf tournament which offered a round with a certain NHL superstar for $500. They sold 14 rounds and stood to collect $7,000. Since the NHL only requires that players be paid a minimum of $500 plus expenses, the organizer was most ready to pocket $6,500 for the organization.

In my opinion, this isn't fair. First of all, the popularity of the NHL player is a major reason the rounds sold so well, and I think it is only fair to compensate the player with an income which is at least comparable to the loss they are incurring from the time they are spending away from their career and family. We must find a middle ground that is fair.

Bryan and I decided to try and pay the players in "Legends and Legacies" a touch more than the minimum required by the NHLPA and we promised that to both the Jets alumni and the players who came from out of town to play. Well, long story short, the event made enough money to fulfill our promises but a representative from the charitable organization low-balled the players. Bryan was devastated but made up the shortfall out of his own pocket (and I was able to chip in later by selling off some memorabilia I owned—but certainly not as much as Bryan put out). That's just the kind of guy he is.

Bryan Trottier was inducted to the Hockey Hall of Fame in 1997.

Oh yeah, he holds the NHL record for most points in a single period, six points from four goals and two assists.

You can look it up (as Casey Stengel would say).

Ted Nolan had a successful on-ice career that was ended prematurely by a back injury but Nolan will always be more well known as a coach than as a player. The reason for that, coincidentally, is taking place right in front of my eyes as I write this.

It is February 19, 2014 and the Olympic Games in Sochi, Russia are in full swing. The men's hockey quarter-final is on and the Latvian national team is giving Canada a helluva go! The scored is tied 1-1 after two periods of play and absolutely nobody expected a game between these two teams to be ever remotely this close. Nobody even expected the Latvians to be in a playoff game in the later rounds where they would have a chance to be on the same sheet of ice as a top-level team like Canada.

Latvia versus Canada! A slaughter in the making, for sure.

But while the shots on goal heavily favour the Canucks, the Latvian players are finishing their checks like demons, crowding the front of the net and blocking the passing lanes, constantly disrupting Canada's plans and play. The Canadians have managed just one goal midway through the third period but the Latvian team matched that and they are getting some excellent scoring chances. If they manage to tie the game, anything could happen in sudden death overtime!

Speaking of unlikely scenarios, standing behind the Latvian bench is an Ojibwe man from Garden River First Nation in Ontario. And his name is Ted Nolan!

Yes, that Ted Nolan who was chosen Coach of the Year in the NHL in 1997 only to spend the next eight years out of hockey either because he was blacklisted by what he calls an 'Old boys' network' of racists or because, as prominent hockey analyst Don Cherry claims, he was a "GM killer." Either way, Nolan eventually worked his way back into the NHL by leading a junior team that was ranked 61st out of 61 teams in Canada to the championship game for the Memorial Cup in just one year. Nolan performed that miracle with the Moncton Wildcats the first time he was back behind a bench. He coached the New York Islanders for a while, getting that forlorn franchise back into the NHL playoffs after an absence of almost a decade, and now, after the break for the Olympics, he will be back with the Buffalo Sabres again; trying to turn around a team of no-names into another NHL contender like he did back in '97.

But speaking of no-names (or difficult names like Latvian goaltender Kristers Gudlevskis), Nolan has that Latvian goaltender kicking out 57 shots and now we are eight minutes away from forcing overtime where anything could happen. If Latvia wins, it will be the biggest hockey upset in the history of hockey anytime anywhere (forget the "Miracle on Ice"—this would be "Supreme Surprise in Sochi" or something like that).

It is as far from Garden River to Latvia as it is from Garden River to the NHL but Nolan made it by overcoming what he sees as the biggest obstacle First Nations face in trying to rise through the ranks in the sport of hockey.

Racism.

———

Nolan recalls his first experience with discrimination when he was a child growing up in Garden River.

"My mother would drop us off at the rink in the neighbouring white town in the morning and she would pick us up at the end of the day," Nolan remembers.

Ted and his brother Steve had to share equipment, so whenever one would come off the ice, the other would have to wait until his brother took off the gloves and helmet and passed over the stick and so on. Well, one day young Ted got over-anxious and jumped on the ice without the gloves and he fell down. A skate ran over his hand, cutting it deeply, and it began to bleed profusely.

"It sure was a long wait for my mom to pick me up that day because nobody would drive me to the hospital," Nolan recalls.

The racism Nolan experienced in hockey taught him some valuable lessons. He learned that if he wanted to be chosen for triple-A midget teams, he had to be three times better than the other players, all other things being equal (Nolan maintains that triple-A leagues are still run that way today). Nolan learned how to fight when he played junior hockey in Kenora, Ontario after hearing "all those welfare lines" and being called "wagonburner" and "spearchucker" (even worse was the inevitable spear in the ribs whenever the ref wasn't looking).

And so Nolan claims it was racism that kept him out of hockey for those eight long years after he threw that Jack Adams Trophy (Coach of the Year) down the stairs of his house. Who knows what really goes on in the hearts and minds of men?

One way to combat racism is to provide an alternative to the negative stereotypes that racism spreads, so while he was in exile from coaching, Nolan established an Aboriginal Role Model program with the Assembly of First Nations in Canada. Not only does this instil pride in the children and youth who look up to the positive images he provides, those images and the way those kids carry themselves go a long way to convincing people to take a second look at First Nations people, and themselves.

Ted worked his way back to the NHL, still enduring incidents like the time his junior Wildcats played the Chicoutimi Sagueneens and the PA system started playing music that got the local fans doing the tomahawk chop. Ted's players and his team did not have a First Nations background or theme so the taunts were obviously directed at him personally and he was left wondering if Chicoutimi wasn't the "Alabama of Canada" (a remark he made to the media in the heat of the moment).

But mostly, Ted knows the way to deal with racism is to educate and empower, so he introduced some indigenous ceremonies into his team's preparations and training, even using a "sharing circle" so that each member of the team had a chance to express himself at team meetings.

"The one who carries the wood is just as important as the one who brings home the deer."

Heck, sage was good medicine for travellers and players who had to endure a gruelling grind by bus, and who were welcome to believe in that power or not. It was just there for the taking, as it should be.

And always, he recalled the teachings his mother instilled in him while growing up in Garden River, which he has carried throughout his life.

"My mother, Rose, always made sure to take me to pow wows throughout Canada," Ted recalls fondly. "I had a nice outfit but I wasn't a very good dancer.

"In the summer, it was moccasins, in the winter time it was skates."

Nolan was raised to know that hockey is just as important a part of Ojibwe culture as pow wow dancing. And so Rose always found the time to get Ted and Steve to hockey practice and to make sure they had what they need to compete as they rose through the ranks. And that was not only equipment and meal money and the like. There is a certain attitude that winners need to have to make it.

Ted will never forget the time he was sent down to the minors after one of his first training camps with the Detroit Red Wings.

"I was going to quit," Ted remembers. "I had been thinking about a career with the RCMP (Royal Canadian Mounted Police) and so instead of going down to the farm team in Kalamazoo, I quit. I went home.

"My mother didn't say anything to me when I walked through the door. All she had to do was look at me, just for a few seconds, and all of the work I had put in all those years, and all of the support she had provided me with all those years, came flooding back. I turned around and got back on that bus and the rest is, as they say, history."

That history includes three years of solid NHL play in Detroit and Pittsburgh, and then on to a dynamic coaching career.

"Unfortunately, my mother was killed by a drunk driver," Nolan almost blurts out, like he can't bear to say the words unless he can get them over with quickly.

Rose Nolan was a born teacher and Ted knew she had been connecting the women of Garden River with empowering activities ranging from high school diploma equivalencies to ceramics classes to a university education. The teachings Rose had passed on to her son kicked in and the Rose Nolan Memorial Golf Tournament was born to raise funds to further Mom's good works.

The 2014 edition of the Sabres are a real work-in-progress and management is shaky at best, so how this turn behind the bench will turn out remains to be seen at the time of this writing. Three years before this latest stint in Buffalo, Nolan needed a map to find out where Latvia is, but here he is now in Sochi, Russia, standing behind 20 Latvians proudly wearing the crest of their ancient Baltic nation on the chest of their purple uniforms.

Nolan thinks back to his Ojibwe heritage and how a nation identifies itself through culture and language. So Ted thought it was important to speak the native tongue of Latvia; more to find identity than to communicate certain drills to the players during practice sessions.

It was important for the players to find their own identity in a country which had been taken over by Russia for much of the past century.

So Ted would only allow Latvian to be spoken in the dressing room and on the ice, by the players, and the players who served as his translators. Not Russian, which many of the players spoke because their homeland had been occupied by Russia for a hundred years; everybody had to speak Latvian.

"When you are a group who has been put down and under the rule of others, sometimes it is tough to find your identity," Ted explains. No matter if you are Ojibwe or Latvian.

"It's Latvia, so let's use your language," Nolan told the players. "You should be proud to be a Latvian. I am proud to be a Canadian. I am proud to be Ojibwe. You should be proud to be from whatever nation you are from."

And that pride surfaces every time the players communicate with each other in their own language. And when Ted Nolan speaks Latvian, it makes him part of the pride the players possess and that brings them all together with purpose.

Ted and his players can be proud of the way they played in Sochi but alas, Canada finally broke a 1-1 deadlock with just eight minutes to go in the game and held on for a 2-1 victory. Following the game, all the Latvian players credited Nolan with coming up with a strategy that stymied the Canadians for the longest time, and for "believing in them."

That was most important. Nobody had truly believed in this group of mostly cast-offs before.

Obviously, Ted Nolan is a player's coach first and foremost and this is one of the biggest reasons he has run afoul of management so often. You would think they would accept substance over style, results over repertoire, but alas, this is the NHL, and old boys and their way to play changes hard.

Nolan has no regrets. He is where he should be despite the fact he could have gotten there a lot more easily.

He was Coach of the Year in the greatest hockey league in the world—number one out of 30 vastly more experienced coaches, most of whom had much better players and way more resources. Anybody who knows anything about how coaches are compensated in the NHL expected the Sabres to make Nolan one of the highest paid bench bosses in the league, and lock him up for three years or more.

Yet they offered this proud Ojibwe man a one-year contract extension with just a small raise in salary.

Ted Nolan has always known what he is worth.

And now so do we all.

There are many other native stars in the NHL from First Nations on both sides of the border (but mostly from near that 49th parallel—the northern United States has the climate most conducive to hockey and the Canadian population is crowded along its southern rim). Some of the more prominent American-based stars of the past included Henry Boucha, who was the first (and only) player to wear a headband during games, and is still tied for the record for scoring the fastest goal at the start of a game (six seconds). Unfortunately, that headband couldn't protect Henry from a stick wielded by Dave Forbes that ended Boucha's career.

And Gary Sargent, who turned down a huge signing bonus from major league baseball and football scholarships from 15 major American universities, to pursue the sport he loved most—hockey.

On the Canadian side, fans in Vancouver will never forget Gino Odjick—"Chum Sa Bay" (Boy in a Man's Body), who will probably always hold the Canucks record for most penalty minutes, mostly earned protecting the "Russian Rocket," diminutive linemate and super sniper Pavel Bure—a Mutt and Jeff combination if there ever was one. Ironically, the "Algonquin Enforcer"'s career was ended by abdominal injuries that didn't come from a punch to the gut but from being stabbed by a car thief he had chased down.

Sadly, on June 27, 2014, Gino announced to his fans that he has just weeks to live after being diagnosed with the fatal heart disease "Amyloidosis." Gino made sure to mention that he was "just a kid off the Rez in Quebec but if he could make it the NHL, any kid can."

And then there was Ron Delorme, whom Don Cherry calls the best Indian fighter to ever play in the NHL; mostly because Cherry watched Delorme fight his three toughest players, Stan Jonathan, John Wensinck and Terry O'Reilly, each of them to a standstill, all in one game, first period, second period and third period. The respect was mutual. Delorme gave up his trademark way of celebrating a goal by pulling an imaginary arrow from a quiver on his back and shooting the opposing goaltender when he was traded to Cherry's Bruins.

Later, as a Scout, Delorme had to flee a pickup truck full of rednecks armed with shotguns when he was scouting University of North Dakota Fighting Sioux prospects during the time when one of the more heated battles over the use of that nickname was going on (please see Chapter 8—Mascots).

Ron was instrumental in starting an Aboriginal Role Model Hockey School in Canada after he experienced the kind of things Nolan experienced coming up through the ranks. Delorme saw too many examples of European players and Caucasian Canadians being drafted ahead of native players after they had all been seen going out for beers following a game (why weren't the drinking habits of those teammates ever questioned when they were doing exactly the same thing?). Delorme saw a lot of Russian players come over to America and crash and burn because they were given a free pass despite the fact they had been joining vodka-soaked family traditions for years.

Theo Fleury, a Métis from Manitoba, is one of the most notorious native players ever to play in the NHL. From starting the infamous "Punchup in Piestany" which got Canada bounced from the World Junior Hockey tournament (Theo was protecting fellow native Everett Sanipass) to leading the Calgary Flames in scoring and to a Stanley Cup championship, on to booze and drug-addled stints in Chicago and New York, side trips overseas to play with the Belfast Giants, his efforts to win an Allen Cup Senior hockey championship for a money-laden tribe in Canada and finally his efforts on behalf of sexually abused hockey players which drew on his experience with Graham James, who was convicted of assaulting players with the junior Swift Current Broncos, including Sheldon Kennedy, who has set up a ranch and a foundation to assist victims of sexual abuse, the type of work which Fleury has enthusiastically joined—whew! All of which makes for an incredible page-turner, which Fleury has done. His book, *Playing with Fire,* is a bestseller and is the basis for an HBO Canada documentary of the same name.

Jordin Tootoo has carved out a colourful career as the first Inuit to play in the NHL. From a trapline in Ranken Inlet in Canada's far North to Nashville, Tennessee is quite a trek but Jordin eased his passage by spending time with celebrity girlfriends such as Kellie Pickler (American Idol finalist) and beauty Jennifer Salvaggio. Tootoo is a compact scrapper who has registered two "Gordie Howe hat tricks" (a goal, an assist and a major penalty for fighting in one game). His middle name, Kudluk means "thunder" in Inuit.

Sheldon Souray made the celebrity and gossip pages without the female help. The handsome Métis from Elk River/Fisher Lake, Alberta has appeared as a model in *Esquire* and *GQ* magazines and appeared in the daytime soap opera *One Life to Live.*

"Ken Daneyko, my teammate in New Jersey, asked me how he could get in on some of the action but I had to tell Kenny that one prerequisite was a full set of teeth and he didn't make the cut," Sourray loves to tell people.

There are others—Blair Atcheynum, John Chabot, Wade Redden, Arron Asham, Jonathan Cheechoo, Craig Berube, Sandy McArthy and so many more. And there are many stories being told right now (from Montreal Canadiens number one netminder and Canadian Olympic team star Carey Price, Jordan and Brandon Nolan (Ted's sons), T.J. Oshie (first cousin to Gary Sargent and second cousin to Henry Boucha) and more.

The following is a list of native players and available figures on what they are compensated for their skills (obviously a far cry from the $6,000 contract Fred Sasakamoose signed with Chicago in the '50s).

2013-14 NHL COMPENSATION/NATIVE PLAYERS

Carey Price, Montreal (Dakelh)	$5,750,000
T.J. Oshie, St. Louis (Ojibwe)	$4,000,000
Rene Bourque, Montreal (Métis)	$4,000,000
Sheldon Souray, Anaheim (Métis)	$3,500,000
Jordin Tootoo, Detroit (Inuit)	$2,000,000
Vernon Fiddler, Dallas (Métis)	$1,800,000
Cody McCormick, Buffalo (Chippewa)	$1,000,000
Arron Asham, NY Rangers (Métis)	$1,000,000

(RECENTLY RELEASED)

Kyle Chipchura, Phoenix (Métis)	$800,000
Dwight King, Los Angeles (Métis)	$750,000
Jordan Nolan, Los Angeles (Ojibwe)	$700,000

(list compiled by Scott Taylor)

To various degrees, these "warriors on ice"—native stars of the National Hockey League have carried, and continue to carry, their culture with dignity and pride; offering role models and sharing their teachings and traditions with all who want to hear. The complete stories of many of these stars are presented in my earlier book, *They Call Me Chief*, which is based on a documentary of the same name.

Quite simply, the stories are interesting and empowering. And they a most enjoyable and enlightening way to spend your time.

8

Mascots

Mascot: "a person, animal or object adopted by a group as a symbolic figure especially to bring them luck." (*Merriam-Webster Dictionary*)

The very definition of the word "mascot" is dehumanizing in the way it reduces the status of a person to the level of an animal or an object. To use a group of people or an individual as a symbol without their permission is wrong. When that symbolic figure is used to "bring them luck" it conjures up the image of a slave master rubbing a negro's head or a gambler doing the same thing to a child before he rolls the dice. The most important point here is that if the person who is being used as a mascot objects to the practice, they should be heard and heeded. Yet the use of Native Americans as mascots and symbols by sports teams, corporations and advertising companies continues.

The use of Indians as mascots by sports teams and the associated controversy can be traced all the way back to the 17th century, because those mascots are based on stereotypes of Native Americans which began to be created as soon as the newcomers to America arrived. Most of the stereotypes were based on misinformation and misunderstandings, but misleading images were created and these are the the basis for the caricatures we see on baseball caps today.

It all started with "captivity narratives"—basically stories about the experiences of pioneer men, women and children who spent more time with Indians than what was considered normal for the time, at least in their imaginations.

The earliest known captivity narrative was written by Mary Rowlandson in 1682 and it established a basic four-part structure starting with conflict between settlers and Indians, capture by the Indians, ordeal at the hands of the captors, then rescue and return to Euro-American society. The more lengthy and widely-distributed captivity narratives were considered valid early North American literature.

The images of Native Americans covered a range. There were Fanny Kelly's vivid pictures of indigenous people who rejoiced in the killing of women and children, "barbaric" customs and treachery by the Sioux which helped convince settlers on the plains that military expeditions were necessary and that any sympathy for Native was misguided. And then there were Glenda Riley's accounts of women who came to an understanding of Native people and their increasingly desperate situation.

A case can be made that there were worthy attributes and some benefits to be derived from captivity narratives (see note 1 at end of chapter). But it is the misleading images of native peoples that were created by some captivity narratives that are relevant to this chapter.

Most of the more negative images stemmed from the captivity narratives that were written by bored housewives with too much time on their hands (and perhaps too many hormones stored up in their bodies when their men were out on the trail). There had been reports of Indians in the area and the housewife sat down at the kitchen table and penned a fantasy.

And what a wicked fantasy it was. First, there was a sneak attack. Poor old Grandpa couldn't fend off all the "tomahawk chops" that were raining down; thank God Grandma was too old to be of much use to the heathens, unlike our poor housewife hero. The narrative would carry on with tales of torment, ordeals of physical and mental suffering while she desperately clung to her virtue, but then all too often came the sexual misconduct that ranged from titillation to horrific (but not too explicit) ravaging that fed a prurient mindset prohibited by puritanical times. And then rescue and return to civilization, sometimes by escape or release, but most often resulting from a sly, brave series of actions by a hero white man.

These captivity narratives were passed around settlements, and the images of Indians as savage and war-like spread like wild fire. The captivity narratives led to the development of "dime novels."

In 1880, publishers Erastus and Irwin Beadle released a series of cheap paperbacks called Beadle's Dime Novels—their first series was called *Indian Wife of a White Hunter* and was written by Ann S. Stephens. The name and practice caught on with other publishers and dime novels were defined as "any quickly written, lurid potboiler, generally a pejorative to describe a sensational yet superficial piece of written work."

Dime novels were steeped in the pioneer lifestyle of homesteaders —outlaws and lawmen, and "cowboys and Indians." Most times, the stories involved heroic feats performed by white farmers, ranchers and soldiers against an "invasion" by hostile Indians, but the concept of a "noble savage" was also introduced; that stoic red man whose land has been stolen and his way of life taken away. Romance with a tall, bronze-skinned brave with raven hair and deep, dark eyes that burned from a handsome visage with high cheek bones was common.

In real life, the First Nations of the Americas, their numbers drastically reduced because of wars and new diseases they had no immunity from, were shunted away on reserves and reservations and had become the "forgotten American."

The image of Native Americans remained prominent through Buffalo Bill's Wild West Show, which crisscrossed the United States in the late 1800s, featuring Indians in buckskins, beads and headdresses, mounted on horseback and hunting charging buffalo. (Buffalo) Bill Cody respected Indians and his images were mostly positive. Inadvertently, however, he contributed to a stereotype that was being created by the entertainment world in general.

While both the cowboys and the Indians in the Wild West Show got out of their costumes when they dressed for dinner or went out for the evening, somehow the image of Indians remained cast in the past. As society evolved, cowboys became a thing of the Old West, but society clung to the belief that Indians continued to live in teepees and do rain dances and sit cross-legged around camp fires with their arms crossed and so on. Which is why Chief Knock-a-homa, mascot of the Atlanta Braves, would dance around a teepee dressed in traditional regalia after every home run, but if they used white folks as mascots, one would have to imagine a middle-aged guy in a leisure suit dancing around a motorhome.

Cody's show would prove to be tragically prophetic. His re-enactment of Custer's Last Stand ends with Cody arriving too late to prevent the death of General George Armstrong Custer and his men. But Cody manages to take the scalp of Yellowhand before the final curtain, avenging the 7th Cavalry's loss. Symbolically, this represents exactly what would happen after the Battle of the Big Horn in 1776—the last victory for the Indians, who were all hunted down and placed on reservations after that.

The image remained the same in so-called Hollywood "B" movies, where Indians on horseback circled wagon trains while sharpshooting little old grandmas in gunnysack dresses and white aprons picked them off with a rifle one by one.

Native actors were rarely used to play the Indian parts. Instead, olive-skinned Italian actors such as Sal Mineo were employed, and this gave rise to the term "Wopoho" The most well-known, true Indian actor was Jay Silverheels, who played Tonto, the Lone Ranger's sidekick. Tonto was a good guy with positive attributes but his dialogue was pidgin English ("me walk-um, mail-um letter" as every verb ended in "um"). His name Tonto translates roughly to "stupid" or "dolt," while Tonto called the masked man Kemo Sabe, which means "One who looks out from behind cover."

Away from the stage, Jay Silverheels and the Indians who performed in the Wild West Show combined modern and traditional lifestyles. Pictures of them reveal that they wore suits and ties when they went out amongst the general public, and their casual wear included jeans and cowboy hats, boots and moccasins. But that is not the image that was carried in mass media from movies to television to newspapers and magazines.

Along the way, native culture was infantilized in toys and dolls and games. Play sets would include miniature teepees and braves with bows and arrows; sort of an instant culture. Always simple. Always primitive.

Misleading stereotypes of Indians began to be used in advertising and brand names. Red Man tobacco, Thunderbird wine and Pontiac cars often featured the noble savage complete with headdress. There was little real experience with First Nations people to compare with.

———————————

Names are important, and so is historical accuracy. So many misconceptions have been created simply because society hasn't cared enough to get things right. And the image that is created can be not only misleading, it can be downright insulting.

The best example of a misleading impression involves the name of the revered Native American leader who is commonly known as Sitting Bull. When the white man first met this Hunkpapa Sioux tribal Elder and asked him his name, the man of great medicine said that his name stemmed from a prophecy which foretold he would become the "leader of a great herd" and that he would lead that herd into a sheltered valley before climbing up to a high vantage point to watch for predators while resting on his haunches.

"My name is 'Resting Monarch on the Plains,' from the prophecy," the great Indian leader said.

The white man thought about what he had been told, reconciled it with available images in his own understanding, and said:

"Oh! Sitting Bull."

"Sitting Bull" sounds more like an image from one of Gary Larson's *Far Side* cartoons while "Resting Monarch on the Plains" conjures up a vision of nobility and leadership.

Similarly, the name of another legendary Oglala warrior commonly known as Crazy Horse is a misnomer. His real name more accurately translates to "He Carries Inside the Spirit of his Horses," which quite rightly matches the free spirit this famed Indian (and wild horses of the west) are known for.

Even the origin of the name "Indian" provides an example of misconceptions which arise from superficial research and conjecture. The most common reason why the indigenous people of the Americas were named Indians was that Christopher Columbus was looking for India when he landed in what is now known as Puerto Rico and he mistakenly called the inhabitants there "Indians."

An alternative theory has been advanced that ol' Chris was so impressed by the spirit and physical nature of the Taino people he first met here that he was moved to proclaim they must have been made "from the body of God" or "du corpus in Deo" in Columbus's language. From "in Deo" comes the name "Indian."

Nice as that sounds, First Nations people generally object to being named by somebody else no matter how well-intentioned.

"We can come up with our own names, thank you very much."

That name "Indian" has gone on to mean many things to different people. To some, it conjures up images of failure, losers who have come to be marginalized by mainstream society. Others hold up the name with the pride of a people with a proud history and a deeply meaningful spirituality, culture and history.

Indians themselves hold vastly different opinions about the name. Some carry it with great pride, some have never known (or been known by) anything different and don't care to be, and others do not want to be associated with the negative stereotypes that have been created around the name.

Which makes it difficult for outsiders who wonder what to call the native people of the Americas. Canada seems to have settled on First Nations while the United States has found favour with Native Americans, but I have always tried to follow the advice I was given to "call the people by a name that they want to be known by themselves." So, there are Cherokees and Ojibway and Oneidas and the like. But that doesn't cover what to call native people generally.

Readers of the book will notice that I bounce around from Native Americans to First Nations to native people, indigenous people and Indians. This is because these are terms that the indigenous friends and colleagues I know find acceptable.

It is a quandary for sure. Even the most respected Native American leaders get tripped up when they try to figure out the name dilemma.

John Trudel, who has been very active in the American Indian Movement, rightfully points out that the word "Indian" was never uttered or heard anywhere on the North American continent before the white man arrived. So it certainly is not something the people used to call themselves, so Trudel asks why would they use that name now? At the same time, Trudel continues to identify himself with the American Indian Movement.

Trudel points out that tribes generally had a word that roughly translates to "the people" or the "human beings" but, just as "Anishnabe" means "the people" to an Ojibway, it means nothing to a Seminole.

Trudel is a brilliant man, a poet and a musician, an activist and a respected political leader. He correctly points out the real meaning of Crazy Horse's name in the excellent documentary film *Reel Injun* but then, as the film goes on, Trudel reverts to using the name "Crazy Horse" when he refers to the great Indian leader. Thus names like "He has the Spirit of his Horses" and "Resting Monarch on the Plains" and "Face like a Storm" (whom the settlers called "Rain in the Face") are not likely to replace those names which have become so common unless everybody stops using the old names and replacing them with the real ones.

The different images that people see when they hear "He has the Spirit of His Horses" and "Crazy Horse" can be misleading and negative. And this is the the crux of the matter when Native Americans object to the misleading and negative images that are created by inaccurate stereotypes.

Society should not feel shame or blame for not knowing what to call First Nations people because the issue is obviously very complicated. There is little wrong with ignorance, just choosing to remain ignorant. It is when people persist in using negative and racist stereotypes when they know better that problems arise.

The best way to know what to call the next native person you meet is to ask him or her what they prefer to be called.

Damn, it is simple, after all.

By far the most controversial and the most best-known use of Indian images has been as mascots by sports teams. It's a fascinating debate that is worth covering here as much for general interest as it is to empower people with useful information.

The original idea to name sports teams after Indian tribal names, symbols and terms stems from a rather positive image of Native Americans—people who were considered very brave (and fierce) and fought valiantly against tremendous odds, never giving up until the very end. These are the qualities that can carry a team to victory, and the mascots and logos are a constant reminder of the positive values the team should have. On the surface, this all sounds rather fine and many people have made the argument that the practice is a compliment or even a tribute to native people that should make them proud. Who wouldn't want to associate with a sports team with those qualities?

But what looks good to some may not look so good to others. There are a lot of mitigating factors to consider before deciding if this practice is okay or not.

The biggest problem with this whole issue has been the lack of consultation with the people who are being used as mascots. Sports teams, advertisers, automobile makers and most other organizations who employ native names and logos have mostly just assumed it would be all right. Sometimes it appears that the image they develop is positive and respectable, and other times, it is obvious the images are disrespectful and insulting.

First Nations people have been used as mascots by sports teams ever since the teams started giving themselves names. Warriors, Braves, Chiefs and just plain Indians are the most popular. The best way to determine if this practice is appropriate is by examining the history and rationale behind some of the known examples.

One of the most familiar mascots in major league baseball is "Chief Wahoo" of the Cleveland Indians. The design company that was hired by Cleveland owner Bill Veeck to develop a symbol of "pure joy and unbridled enthusiasm" assigned the project to a 17-year-old draftsman named Walter Goldbach. Completely unfamiliar with indigenous people or their culture, Goldbach drew from the commonly known image of a "noble savage" with high cheekbones and a huge nose. Goldbach said he "had difficulty making a cartoon out of this image."

Sportswriters quickly provided the mascot with the nickname Chief Wahoo. Goldbach objected strenuously, saying the nickname "Chief" was "all wrong."

"He's not a chief. He's a brave. He only has one feather. Chiefs have full headdresses," Goldbach proclaimed with a healthy air of authority.

His source for that nugget of knowledge about Native American culture?

Goldbach had been asked to give a talk to an elementary school class and one of the children "told him."

The latest word is that the Cleveland franchise will no longer be using Chief Wahoo as a logo or mascot but will continue to use the nickname "Indians."

Hands down, the most controversial nickname in all of professional sports is used by the Washington Redskins. The situation is muddied by the fact the image used by this NFL franchise is rather noble—a handsome warrior (in sharp contrast to some of the Washington fans, who dress up in cardboard hats adorned with chicken feathers and whack themselves in the mouth while yelling "Woo woo woo woo!" in a drunken stupor).

"We honour Indians," claims owner Dan Snyder, "by naming our team after them."

The debate is even more confusing because many Native American football fans agree with Snyder. It is common to find native people proudly wearing the red jackets of the Washington franchise, and feuding with their own leaders who are trying to get Snyder to stop using the nickname. Prominent aboriginal standup comedian Don Burnstick uses a routine: "You know you are a redskin when…" in his act (with apologies to Jeff Foxworthy) and he has named the hockey team he manages and plays on the Redskins.

The word redskin has deep historical roots which go all the way back to the first settlements in North America. That is because indigenous Americans have been hunted, killed and forcibly removed from their lands by European settlers since they arrived and this included the paying of bounties to speed up the process.

The paying of bounties began in the colonial period with, just for example, a proclamation against the Penobscot Indians in 1755 that was issued by King George II of Great Britain, known commonly as the Phips Proclamation. The proclamation orders: "His Majesty's subjects to Embrace all opportunities of pursuing, captivating, killing and destroying all and every of the aforesaid Indians."

The colonial government paid 50 pounds for scalps of males over 12 years, 25 pounds for scalps of women over 12, and 20 pounds for scalps of boys and girls under 12. Twenty-five British pounds sterling in 1755 would be worth around $9,000 today. With a school teacher's salary at just 60 pounds a year, the reward for exterminating Indians was very lucrative.

In order to prove that the bounty hunter had indeed killed an Indian, he had to bring in the head of said dead Indian, but soon the heads were piling up and so the government started accepting scalps as proof of prey.

All this began to cause settlers to look a little more closely at their neighbours, especially those with dark hair. When some of the scalps being turned in looked suspiciously like somebody who hadn't been seen around the settlement in a while, the government decided to demand that a "piece of red skin" be attached to any scalp that was submitted for bounty.

It wasn't a huge leap to start calling the indigenous people "redskins" and therefore, one of the origins of this nickname stems from a devastating practice of genocide. Kind of ironic when some people call Indians who object to this misuse of mascots "thin-skinned," ain't it?

Humankind has often been divided into four colours: white, red, yellow and black, and so it seemed to some a natural fit to call Indians "redskins," We don't know how African-Americans would react to being called "black-skins" because that hasn't been commonplace, but I doubt the reaction would be favourable.

The bigger problem is that most times when the term "redskin" is used it is in a negative context. Whenever you heard the word used in movies it generally referred to a person as primitive and war-like (e.g., "dirty, thieving redskin"). This is a racist epithet equivalent to "lazy, shiftless nigger." And we would never see sports teams called the New York Niggers and the Kansas City Kikes or even the Carolina Caucasians (how about the Carolina Crackers?) or the Winnipeg White Boys.

But we do see the Notre Dame Fighting Irish, complete with their logo/mascot of a short leprechaun dressed in green holding his dukes up ready for a fight. Quite often, this is used as an argument against the folks who protest the use of native nicknames.

"Irish people don't complain about being used as mascots."

And that is true.

So what? The Irish are free to disagree with Notre Dame's actions but they have chosen to embrace it. They would be perfectly within their rights to condemn the practice and make their case because they are the people who are most affected. And their opinions should be respected.

So that just provides even more support for the First Nations and Native American groups who are protesting against the very same thing. They have a different opinion on the matter and we should respect their opinion.

Many college teams (e.g., Stanford) have respected Native American wishes and changed their nicknames away from native themes, but few professional sports franchises are willing to make the switch. The National College Athletic Administration (NCAA) has encouraged universities to make the changes by threatening penalties such as sanctions, loss of bowl games, recruitment and scholarship restrictions, etc. The list of teams that have changed their names from anything derived from North American indigenous history and culture requires quite a scroll on the internet, yet there are still over 1,000 teams in the U.S. from high school to the professional level who retain indigenous-themed nicknames. The most reluctance to change occurs at the professional level, where there is a lot of money at stake because of lost sales of promotional items such as caps and jerseys. The process to change a nickname remains controversial and cumbersome and it will be a long time before the practice is completely discontinued, if it ever is.

The best example of how complicated and difficult it can be to get a team to change its name can be found at the University of North Dakota, who have used the nickname Fighting Sioux since the 1930s. This one has everybody fighting; Indians against whites, Indians against Indians, whites against whites, students versus students, faculty versus students and vice versa, citizen against citizen and well, you get the idea. This battle has literally been fought brick by brick.

The Fighting Sioux were originally called the Flickermen, but this was changed in 1930. For a long time, their uniforms featured the same logo as the Chicago Blackhawks, one professional team which has rarely encountered controversy over their logo. Generally, this is because the image is not particularly offensive but also because the team is named after the Blackhawks, an American military fighting group who were named after Chief Blackhawk; a respected native leader. Perhaps since Chief Blackhawk isn't around to object, or because the name honours an individual instead of turning a race of people into mascots, this NHL franchise has enjoyed relatively smooth skating through the general malaise.

Critics of the Fighting Sioux nickname called it a racist stereotype, while supporters maintained that it was inoffensive and a source of pride. Over the years, the debate proved to be a divisive issue at the University. The movement to keep the nickname and logo was led by UND alumni, sports fans, and athletic players and officials, the conservative right wing, as well as (for a time) the university administration. The campaign to change the nickname and logo was led by several Native American tribes, student organizations, the liberal left, and many UND faculty members.

In 1999, a bill was introduced in the North Dakota House of Representatives to eliminate the nickname, but that died "in committee." In 2000, 21 Native American-related programs, departments, and organizations at UND signed a statement opposing the continued use of the nickname and logo, saying that it did not honour them or their culture.

While all this was going on, one very prominent UND alumni was having fits. Ralph Engelstad, who claims that the education he received at UND is responsible for making him a multi-millionaire, is so grateful that he donated $100 million for the construction of Ralph Engelstad Arena.

Ralph, who played for the UND hockey team (so we can assume he wore that logo proudly over his chest) is not generally known for having a social conscience. He has housed a museum of Nazi memorabilia with a salute to Adolph Hitler in the Imperial Palace Hotel and Casino he owned in Las Vegas, including a painting of himself dressed in a Nazi uniform (captioned "To Adolf from Ralphie") as well as a painting of

Hitler with the reverse caption. He even hosted parties to celebrate Hitler's birthday at his casino that featured bartenders in T-shirts reading "Adolf Hitler—European tour 1939-45."

One of the conditions Engelstad placed on his donation was that the University keep the Fighting Sioux name indefinitely.

Faced with losing one of the largest donations ever made to a public institution of higher learning, some of the UND governors quite naturally felt they had a good argument for keeping the logo. While they wrestled with the ideology that public institutions such as UND are supposed to be immune to such pressures, one bright faculty member simply pointed out that "dear ol' Ralphie" is getting on in years (and reportedly not in very good health) so why not simply wait until he passes on?

When Engelstad heard this, he blew a gasket. Stubborn as a mule (there Ralph, how do *you* like it?) Engelstad placed thousands of Fighting Sioux logos in numerous places throughout the arena. Like, in every other brick in the walls, embedded in the backs of the 15,000 seats, inside the floor tiles, all to make physical removal of the logo very costly if attempted.

The arena opened in 2001. In order to be fair (as well as to show just how difficult and complicated the battle over Indian mascots can get), I offer Engelstad's own reasons for wanting to preserve the Fighting Sioux logo.

> Tradition is the gentle fabric woven through time and experience which generates meaning, character, and identity to one and all. The Fighting Sioux logo, the Fighting Sioux uniforms, the aura of the Fighting Sioux tradition and the spirit of being a Fighting Sioux are of lasting value and immeasurable significance to our past, presence, and future.
> —RALPH ENGELSTAD

Despite his Nazi leanings, Engelstad was a rather sharp fellow (after all, he was a multi-millionaire) and he took the additional step of placing the arena under private (rather than UND) management and stipulated that the Fighting Sioux motif be kept indefinitely. An Engelstad family trust continues to own the arena and rents it to the University.

The issue became further complicated when the debate reignited in 2005, following a decision by the NCAA to sanction schools using tribal logos and/or nicknames that the NCAA deemed to be "hostile and abusive," which included UND. The sanctions would not allow schools like UND to use their names or logos in post-season play and those schools would not be able to host post-season championships.

After an unsuccessful appeal to reverse the sanctions, UND started to pursue their legal options. On June 15, 2006, the Board of Higher Education elected 8-0 to authorize the Attorney General for the state of North Dakota to sue the NCAA for penalizing the UND over its Fighting Sioux nickname and logo.

In November 2006, UND was granted a preliminary injunction to prevent the NCAA from enforcing the rule.

On October 26, 2007, a settlement between UND and the NCAA was reached, preventing the case from going to trial. The settlement gave UND three years to gain support from the state's Sioux tribes to continue to use the Fighting Sioux nickname and logo. If that support was not granted at the end of the three years, UND agreed to retire the Fighting Sioux nickname and logo, remove most of the existing Fighting Sioux imagery in campus facilities, and pick a new nickname and logo to represent UND's athletic teams.

On May 14, 2009, the North Dakota State Board of Higher Education approved a motion directing UND to retire the "Fighting Sioux" nickname and logo, effective October 1, 2009, with full retirement to be completed no later than August 1, 2010. This directive was to be suspended, if, prior to October 1, 2009, the Standing Rock Sioux tribe and the Spirit Lake Sioux tribe gave namesake approval consistent with the terms of the Settlement Agreement. After extending the deadline for meeting this condition once, to November 30, 2009, the Board on April 8, 2010, unconditionally ordered UND to retire the Fighting Sioux nickname at the end of the 2010–11 season.

The North Dakota State Board of Higher Education announced on April 8, 2010, that the Fighting Sioux nickname would be retired after the 2010–2011 athletic season. The North Dakota State Board of Higher Education voted unanimously on Monday, May 10, to extend the deadline for the University of North Dakota to retire its nickname and logo to Aug. 15, 2011.

On March 11, 2011, by a vote of 28-15, the North Dakota Senate approved legislation ordering the University of North Dakota to retain its Fighting Sioux nickname and Indian-head logo. Governor Jack Dalrymple signed the Fighting Sioux bill into law the following week.

This law was subsequently repealed during a special session of the legislature in November, 2011.

On February 8, 2012, it was announced that supporters of the "Fighting Sioux" nickname received 17,213 signatures on a petition that sent the issue to a statewide vote in June. The university then resumed using the nickname.

On March 1, 2012, in a letter sent to the University, the NCAA reiterated its current policies concerning participation in NCAA championships and stated that the school risks losing the right to play postseason games at home if their athletes, cheerleaders or band display the nickname "Fighting Sioux" or the American Indian head logo. In addition, since "NCAA policy requires that student-athletes, band, cheerleading, dance and mascot uniforms and paraphernalia not have hostile or abusive racial/ethnic/national original references," any UND teams participating in postseason games that do not adhere to this would risk forfeiture of the game and "the NCAA reserves its right to seek reimbursement for expenses incurred."

On April 3, 2012, UND president Robert Kelley issued a statement warning about the negative consequences to UND if the statewide vote in June resulted in continued use of the nickname.

On June 11, 2012, the naming issue was up for a statewide vote, on the ballot as Referendum Measure #4, to keep or retire the nickname. A sizable majority, 67.35%, of North Dakota voters chose to retire the "Fighting Sioux" name and American Indian head logo.

On June 14, 2012, the state Board of Higher Education voted to get rid of the University of North Dakota's moniker and Indian head logo. The university is prohibited from adopting a new team name until 2015.

Whew!

All of this grief and emotion over the use of a mascot!

I am reminded of the time NHL scout Ron Delorme was literally chased out of a rural North Dakota town at high speed at the barrel of a shotgun when he inadvertently got mixed up in the UND scrap. Delorme, one of the First Nations alumni in the NHL, was scouting some UND players for the Vancouver Canucks and decided to stop for a drink at a restaurant alongside I-29 on his way back to Canada. Recognizing as an Indian, some local rednecks started picking a fight with Delorme because he was "a troublemaker who was making them lose their beloved Fighting Sioux logo." Ron was a pretty good scrapper in his playing days but even the NHL doesn't allow three-on-ones and the odds of one Indian against three prairie-fed country boys aren't so good, so he decided to hop in his rent-a-car and vamoose. Vamoose-ing would include speeding the wrong way down the Interstate to shake those big boys in their pickup truck who were actually point-ing a shotgun at him out their truck window.

As complicated as this logo controversy turned out to be with all of the personalities and opinions and court battles back and forth, most of the folks in North Dakota thought the issue was black and white. The use of another famous logo which has been in the headlines proved to be a very subtle argument.

The Atlanta Braves, formerly the Milwaukee Braves, previously the Boston Braves, were originally owned by George Preston Marshall, who also owned the Washington Redskins for a time. Marshall was a noted racist but there is no evidence he chose his nicknames based on that (most likely because nobody would think to would ask such a question back in the 1930s).

When the Braves were owned by Ted Turner, whose wife at the time was left-wing activist Jane Fonda, it was particularly embarrassing to be associated with an entity accused of racism. Turner made an attempt to pacify his Native American critics by financing a film project which produced some fine films about Native American heroes like Geronimo, but there was a bottom line we shall find that just would not allow Turner to change that name.

The problem here is that most people associate the word "brave" with positive qualities. We all want (or hope) to be brave when the need arises, right? So what could possibly be wrong with naming your sports team after a team which was used widely to refer to Indian warriors?

Even former president Jimmy Carter, whose home state capital is Atlanta, entered the fray one time when he was in Winnipeg for a Habitat for Humanity build and I asked him for his opinion on the matter.

"We awna (honour) Native Americans by cowlin' (calling) aw (our) team the Braves," President Carter claimed in his hard-to-understand southern twang, which is almost a foreign language in Canada (which allows me to mess with his quote).

If an American president isn't familiar with the argument I am about to present, it is doubtful most of the public would be. But, according to Professor Emma Larocque of the University of Manitoba, author of the highly-sourced book *Defeathering the Indian*, the term "brave" is actually a pejorative term.

"The American military began calling Indian warriors 'braves' because they wanted to convince their soldiers that their foe must be respected, but could be easily defeated because they were stupid and disorganized," Larocque says. "The U.S. Army was highly organized into generals and corporals and privates while Indians were foolish and disorganized; running around helter skelter with no sound, military-worthy plan.

"Oh sure, the Indians might be 'brave,' but without being organized to follow a good strategy for battle, they can be easily defeated."

And so "brave" fits in with all of the other derogatory things that are associated with being a mascot (I've already mentioned Chief Knock-a-homa, but then there's still the primitive and war-like image of the "tomahawk chop"). Suffice to say, the Atlanta Braves organization has faced the same criticism as their Cleveland counterparts, and NFL teams like the Kansas City Chiefs and that franchise in Washington.

There have been examples where the local Native American tribe has agreed to cooperate with the use of their image by a sports team; the most noteworthy example being the Florida State Seminoles, who work closely with the university to insure that the images are culturally appropriate and dignified. And this brings us ever closer to the solution to this quandary about using Indian images.

We can't close off this chapter without a discussion about the social and political impact this practice has on Native American people. Native American logos and nicknames create and maintain stereotypes of a race of people. When such cultural abuse is supported by one or many of society's institutions, it constitutes institutional racism.

The logos, along with other societal abuses and stereotypes separate, marginalize, confuse, intimidate and harm Native American children. The logos teach non-Native American children that it's all right to participate in culturally abusive behaviour. Children spend a great deal of their time in school, and schools have a significant impact on their emotional, spiritual, physical and intellectual development. As long as such logos remain, both Native American and non-Native American children are learning to tolerate racism in our school.

People say they understand why having a Native American as a mascot is offensive, but do they really? Oppression is prolonged cruel or unjust treatment or control. There are many examples of oppression happening in places that have mascots. In Minnesota, a pep rally is held where teachers and students dress up as "cowboys and Indians," and the cowboys yell "Go back to the reservation." In Kansas, a man who sought to remove the mascot was sent emails from students that threatened his home and the sexual assault of his wife.

Aw heck, when the local teams wins, the Indians look good, but when they lose they look bad. Who in the hell wants their social standing to depend on the fortunes of a sports team?

And we cannot forget that the nicknames and logos manifest themselves in cultural misappropriations and downright insults. Some of the costumes worn by fans belittle sacred religious and political symbols of First Nations.

For example, a headdress is a symbol of leadership which is not worn willy-nilly by just anybody who can paste one together. As Oneida comedian Charlie Hill used to say, "How would Catholics feel if we danced around wearing a Pope's hat and swinging rosaries?"

When you consider all of the controversy and division that the people of North Dakota went through over the use of the Fighting Sioux logo, you would hope that an easier way to decide whether or not to use them can be found.

And it can, in the form of one Dexter Manley, late of the Washington Redskins.

Dexter was a ferocious defensive lineman who played for the Washington NFL franchise, but who also happened to be the poster boy for all that is wrong with college sports.

You see, Dexter, despite being drafted out of a major American university (Oklahoma State), is functionally illiterate (which doesn't say much about the public high school system, either). One doesn't imagine Dexter reads much about social issues, and he probably isn't up to speed on sociology and politics and the rest of the disciplines which might govern the mascot issue.

But when asked what he thought about the use of the name "redskin" by the football team he was playing for at the time, Dexter simply answered, "If the people who are most affected by it don't like it, then we ought not to do it."

In other words, how would you feel if we used your name in a way you didn't like or approve of without your permission and consultation?

Should Dexter Manley lead us on this?

The image of Native Americans or First Nations can be a very positive one, full of character and spirit. There are many, many examples of courage and achievement by native peoples, including the stories of the remarkable people who are described in this book.

From captivity narratives through to sports teams, the image of Native Americans has been misrepresented and often exploited. When we examine the practice from its historical roots to the present time, it is obvious it is not fair and should be discontinued.

Unfortunately, while the development of many of these stereotypes might have been benign or because of simple mistakes, the motivation for continuing this practice is definitely purposeful and thus, the use of Indians as mascots won't be ending any time soon.

In the case of professional sports teams like the Atlanta Braves and the Washington Redskins, who sell millions of dollars in merchandise such as hats and uniforms and baby bibs every year, there is just too damn much money at stake. So much that Snyder has offered to set up a foundation to "assist Native Americans" and we recall that Ted Turner financed positive movies about natives.

Those initiatives cost a lot of money but that just reinforces the fact there is a lot of money to be made by exploiting these native images. And while Cleveland has agreed to drop the "Chief Wahoo" mascot, they will continue to use the nickname "Indians." To change is just too costly and there is just too much revenue at stake. It is interesting to note that nobody has ever offered to share the revenues with Native American groups but that would be fraught with complications, financial, cultural and political, that would render such a deal unfeasible.

A case can be made that these captivity narratives provided one of the first literary forums dominated by a women's experience, expressed by a female voice. A woman's will to survive proves stronger than her fear or grief. The narratives provided a forum for expression for a female voice in a male-dominated society and some of the women become cultural mediators between civilizations. The better captivity narratives would go on to describe the difficulty the woman would have being accepted back into white society because, no matter that her fate was outside her control, she was "tainted goods." And some of these female authors showed sensitivity and appreciation for the culture of the First Nations, as well as understanding and empathy for the economic and political disparity First Nations were dealing with. Some of their captivity narratives created awareness and support for native peoples of the Americas.

The captivity narratives are sometimes seen as early pornography, not only for the sexual content, but in a way that movies like *Mississippi Burning* are pornographic for the Ku Klux Klan. As much as the filmmakers want to expose the cruelty of southern racism, crowds of rednecks would gather to watch black men and women lynchings and rape scenes and beatings with glee, then shut down or leave the film before justice prevails.

This issue will remain with us a long time. I hope the information provided here empowers readers to offer informed, fair and balanced opinions about the entire matter.

9

Playing Our Own Games

Just like anywhere else in the world, the indigenous people of the Americas played "games" or sports before the Europeans arrived. While some of these games were strictly for fun and competition, or to encourage physical fitness, teamwork, sportsmanship and fair play, there was often a social, political and spiritual component to the games indigenous people play.

Rather than choose from the hundreds of different games that were played by the thousands of different tribes who lived in North America prior to European contact, I decided to try and find one game that might be representative of the type, structure, philosophy, practical and spiritual value of indigenous games that native people played before the arrival of white people to the Americas.

The Bone Game encompasses the cultural, social and spiritual aspects which underlie many other indigenous games. It is a fascinating interplay which incorporates competition, teamwork, discipline, fair play and all of the other benefits of good games, but also such complex but practical elements as conflict resolution, including possible wars between nations, building community, democracy, enhancing individual growth, and empowering the social, cultural and spiritual fabric of a community from the individual to the family to the nation to interactions with other nations.

Whew! All that in a game?

As you shall see, the Bone Game really is an incredibly complex but brilliant mechanism for growth, harmony and peace between individuals and nations. In disguise.

Before I get into the description and analysis of the Bone Game, I must make note of the fact that the modern games we play are most often referred to as "spectator sports" with good reason. While sports and recreation are an ideal way to have fun and to grow, to build those values of teamwork, discipline and fair play, the entertainment of spectators (fans) is a primary function of the modern sports featured in this book. The speed and power of Jim Thorpe was a sight to behold, the grace and accuracy of Notah Begay III's golf swing, the acrobatics of Wahoo McDaniel performed before huge crowds in arenas and stadiums throughout North America. Following the ebb and flow of competition, especially in tightly contested competitions, is thrilling entertainment. All of those same attributes can be applied to the indigenous games of the Americas...

Back in 1982, I had the tremendous honour of directing an Indigenous People's Performance featuring over 30 indigenous performing arts groups from around the world at the World Assembly of First Nations in Regina, Saskatchewan. It was proposed that we demonstrate some indigenous games during half-time of a Canadian Football League game.

Our indigenous performers were familiar with the traditional games of their people and we were rehearsed and ready, but the idea was scrapped at the last minute. During rehearsals, however, I was thrilled to watch thaka (Pima), basket games (Papago), bagattaway (Haudenosaunee), log-haul (Apache), hand games (Cree) and other indigenous games. The skill and grace of these athletes was a sight to behold, and it was entertaining to watch the teams compete back and forth.

There was no time to learn the social, cultural and spiritual aspects of these games back then but this book has provided me (and you) with such an opportunity.

Through the Bone Game.

It is obvious that without modern heat and air conditioning and other amenities, living conditions were far more difficult to cope with over 500 years ago. Harsh, cold winters, blazing hot summers, famine and war were a constant threat to survival. Anything that can help an individual, community or a nation to survive or even overcome the harsh realities of life was an asset.

Indigenous nations developed highly functional systems for food and shelter and other necessities of life. They carved out territory and had their own sovereignty, systems of governance, social structures and so on. The people weren't perfect—there were good and bad; however, behaviour that was disruptive to the harmony of the tribe was discouraged because the tribe needed everybody working together cooperatively in order to survive. If a person would not conform, the worst punishment was to be banished because it was near impossible to survive alone in the wilderness.

So mostly, there were structures and processes in place that would encourage everybody to contribute and work together in harmony. An excellent example of this can be found in the Bone Game, which was even used to keep peace between nations.

From time to time, disputes might arise between tribes (and families, factions or individuals). War was always an option but like all good people, First Nations deeply believe in the sanctity of human life, and like most normal people, they aren't very fond of bloodshed and crippling injury, either. However, both sides must save face, assert the sovereignty of their nation, maintain their territory, and keep their pride. If there is another way to resolve their differences, both tribes would most likely choose to do so. And if that way involves processes which empower the members of the tribe, including rituals of personal and group transformation for the better, it is more than welcome and the tribes are even more likely to choose this course of action.

The Bone Game provides this mechanism.

At first look, it appears to be a simple shell game, and whoever can "find the bean under the right cup" wins. But the stakes in the Bone Game are so high, and the procedures leading up to the competition so complex and empowering to the deepest human potential, it becomes obvious that modern society could immensely benefit from a Bone Game today.

In lieu of mortal combat with losses of life on both sides, alternative stakes are developed through the game. For example, one tribe might wager 30 ponies and the other bets their entire supply of winter wheat. Of course, in the end, one tribe will win and one will lose, but the stakes are often so high the experience transcends simple winning or losing.

What does it mean to win, if you are taking away another tribe's means of hunting for food? Or their entire source of food in a hostile climate? What does it mean to lose such important goods? Each individual, and the tribe as a whole, is involved in the decision, and this makes everybody explore fundamental issues and develop a sense of what is truly essential in life.

That starts by learning how the Bone Game is set up and played.

Each tribe forms a team that will represent it in the Bone Game. The minimum number per team is five, because there are five ritual roles that must be filled to begin the game. Finding a way to break down a large group into the small team that will represent the tribe is the first step of the Bone Game and it varies from tribe to tribe.

It is the process the team goes through to prepare for the Game that is a master stroke in empowerment, inclusion, transformation and almost every other buzz word of the so-called new age.

A whole whack of decisions have to be made before the guessing part of the game takes place. First of all, the team must create what is called a team Power Object, which is a device that will be used to focus group attention throughout the Game.

Each person on the team brings an object of some personal value to the first meeting. They sit in a circle with their objects in front of them and take turns describing the value or meaning of his or her object.

For instance, the first person might say, "This is my wallet. It is a gift from my grandfather. He made it from wild game he caught and it carries a message of life. The only picture I have of my grandfather is in the wallet, and there is also quite a bit of money in it, heh heh!"

The next person might put a stone in front.

"I carry this stone from my sacred vision quest. It has power to heal and to provide wisdom."

And so on.

Then the objects are passed to the left around the circle, one at a time, until each person has examined every object. The objects are then passed around again, but this time, if someone feels the object is not suitable to be the team Power Object, it is placed on the ground outside the circle, removing it from further consideration, until only one object remains in circulation. This becomes the team Power Object.

It is in how the Power Object is used where we find most of the benefits to be derived by the individual participants. They go through a process that provides an outstanding opportunity for participants to experience, explore, develop, and share deep aspects of themselves in a very short period of time. The ritual enlivens the individuals, it helps them get in touch with imagination, intuition, inspiration, creativity, and insight, and it creates powerful bonds between them. Many lessons are learned from this game about the differences between competition and cooperation, fear and courage, separateness and unity, timidity and power, deception and honesty, attachment and transcendence.

Again, this sounds very complicated but it all results from some simple, but highly respectful and inclusive, processes.

The person whose object was chosen the Power Object begins each cycle of sharing. When he or she is finished speaking, the object is passed to the person on the left and so on until everybody in the circle has had a chance to use the Power Object.

Whoever holds the Power Object has the full, undivided attention of everyone in the group. The person can share thoughts, tell a story, sing a song, do a standup comedy routine, perform some improv, simply hold it and remain silent for a few moments, confront someone, or do anything else until she/he is finished. That person has the total focus of the group until he/she passes the Power Object to the next person on the left.

If someone else in the group wants to comment or speak while another member holds the Power Object, that person has to raise their hand and wait to be recognized by the holder of the Power Object. The person holding the Power Object can never be interrupted, for any reason whatsoever, without first choosing to recognize and then give permission to another person to speak out of turn. The holder is not obliged to recognize someone else.

What a powerful way to use and move personal energy, intellect and emotion! People seldom have the undivided attention of their fellow citizens, the time to search for their words, or the opportunity to creatively and fully express themselves to completion. The point of this, and the profound understanding of Native Americans, was that the "Great Spirit" resides equally in all of us. Every one of us has the capacity to speak truth, to share wisdom, to counsel and advise, to heal, to know ourselves in depth, to touch the depth in others. A receptive and caring atmosphere, mutual respect, and the freedom to express ourselves in our own unique way encourages the unfoldment of our deepest human potential.

There are several other ways the Power Object is used but every decision must be made by consensus. That means that everyone must either agree with, or not object to, a proposal presented to the group. If someone who holds the Power Object makes a proposal, such as what is to be given to the other tribe if they lose the Bone Game, it must be voted on by all group members. Thumb up means yes, thumb down means no, and open palm, face up, means a person has a neutral position or no stand on the proposal at hand.

The team bends over backwards to insure that all voices are heard. Everybody who votes against a proposal is given an opportunity to express their reason(s) for their negative vote, beginning with the first negative vote to the holder's left, and moving around the circle in clockwise fashion, until everybody in the circle has spoken. Those who are in favour of the proposal or are neutral have no voice at this time.

At the end of the sharing, the Power Object holder can make the proposal again, or amend it to include new information provided by the group. Then the vote is taken again. After the second vote, if there is still dissension, the proposal is dropped and the Power Object must be given to the next person in the circle. And on it goes until they develop a proposal that everybody agrees with (e.g., "We have to provide the evening meal for the other family for a month").

It is the responsibility of every person to express his or her thoughts, feelings, intuitions or disagreements openly and honestly. Voting by consensus assures that everyone has the opportunity for equal power in the decision-making process.

Another task using the Power Object is the creation of the group name. The Power Object passes around the group and anyone who wishes can share a favourite name and its relevance to the group or to the game. After everyone has spoken, names are voted on, one at a time, until consensus is reached.

Now the team must determine which of the five roles each member will fulfill. This is like picking the players to play the positions on a team and some consideration is given to the particular skills of each individual, their character and, of course, their ability to fulfill the duties of the particular role.

The similarities with modern sports teams here are obvious except for the way in which players are chosen for certain roles. While a hockey coach might decide to move a forward back to defence and a baseball manager might change who is batting cleanup from day to day, the entire Bone Game team is involved in selecting who "plays what position" (or assumes which of the roles).

There are five ritual roles that must be filled within each team (two negotiators, two hiders and one pointer). These roles are also filled on the basis of consensus. A role is announced, the description of the role is made, and then those who feel they want to fill the role speak up, one at a time, passing the Power Object clockwise around the circle until everyone has spoken. All interested persons present their credentials, background, or reasons they feel they are appropriate for the job. Then, by voting on the basis of consensus, the role is filled.

There are two negotiators per group. One negotiator per group is verbal and can speak to the verbal negotiator of the other team. But each group also has a silent negotiator, who is an ally and consultant to the verbal negotiator when these transactions are taking place. The silent negotiators remind the verbal negotiators about the spirit of their team, its wishes, intent, strategies, etc., but away from the line at which negotiations take place. The silent negotiators also report to their team

what they saw take place between verbal negotiators. They can inter-
pret mood, information, or their sense of the other team as portrayed
through the actions of the other verbal negotiator, but they never speak
to anyone on the other side.

Negotiators can never make decisions for their group. They only
transmit information. If and when a decision is called for, the negotiators
must return to their group where, by consensus, the decision is made. Even
the place where the negotiators meet to discuss and exchange information
must be negotiated and voted on within each group. All communication
from one team to the other must be channeled through the negotiators.

The negotiators from each team meet to exchange information, then
return to their teams to discuss issues and make decisions. Each group
can either accept or reject the other team's stakes, proposals, whatever.
The outcome of team deliberations is communicated to the other team
through the negotiator, and the work goes on and on until it is time
to play the game. But once the stakes of one team are accepted by the
other, no matter what else follows, that team cannot change its mind
or renegotiate stakes again.

And once the two teams form to play the Bone Game, no further dialogue or conversation can occur between members of opposing teams,
until the game is done.

The stakes are real. Whatever an individual or group bets, the relevant person(s) must be willing to deliver the bet upon losing the Bone
Game. The negotiating, decision making, proposing and voting are all
critically important parts of the Bone Game ritual. It cannot be rushed
or short circuited.

After the Power Object and the group name are chosen, the ritual
roles are filled, the stakes are agreed upon, and the place where the Bone
Game will occur are decided upon, it is time to play the game itself.

Each group has chosen two Hiders (by consensus, natch). The Bone
Game derives its name from the fact that Native Americans play the
Game with four "magic bones". These were carved or painted bones,
small enough to fit within a person's closed hand. These bones were
magic in the sense that the whole tribe had energized or protected them
with caring, attention, special chants and so on.

Two of the bones are worth one point each if found by the Pointer of the other group, and two of the bones have no point value. Through negotiation, it is decided which group will hide first and which will point first. The pointer tries to guess where the bones are hidden within the four closed fists of the other group's two Hiders. The Hiders go away from the line of play and decide who will hold which bones where and how. For instance, one Hider might hold one point bone in one hand and one worthless bone in the other, and the second Hider might do the same. Or one Hider might hold both magic bones in one hand and nothing in the other, etc. Before the beginning of the first round of play, each team must show their valued and worthless bones to the other team so that there can be no dispute when the Pointers do their choosing.

Each team selects one Pointer. This person's job is to go to the line of play when it is time, and point with his or her index finger(s) to two of the four closed hands of the Holders of the other team. The Holders of the other team must immediately show the contents of the selected hands and, if a point or two is made, this information is transmitted to each team by the negotiators.

Each team comes up with their own unique way of helping their Pointer choose well and their Hiders hide well. The persons chosen for these roles often say they have some special gift, to help them find or hide the bones. Each team stands silently behind the actual line of play and only the negotiators can speak at the line, and only to each other. The Pointer can take as long as he or she needs to tune into where the magic bones might be held before actually making the guess. After the guesses are made, it is the other team's turn to guess. The other team can guess right away, or go away from the line of play to prepare for their turn. Whichever team collects seven points first is the winner.

Because of its meticulous and ultra-inclusive nature, a Bone Game is often not completed. The decisions are complex, the stakes can be hard to decide upon, the roles can be hard to fill—all on the basis of consensus. Time can run out before the seven points are won.

But, from the moment the two teams form, the magic, mystery and wisdom of the Native American experience profoundly impacts all participants as they touch the depths within themselves, and each other. The

Bone Game is a dynamic and powerful experience. It delivers a truly transformative experience for all who play it and, for this reason, deserves to be incorporated into the politics, culture and human dynamics of modern society.

Imagine if we used a mechanism like the Bone Game to resolve disputes. I know it is naive and idealistic to think that nations or even individuals would resolve their differences in such a long, drawn-out and complicated way that is oblivious to political and economic considerations, but the processes included in the Bone Game are worthy of consideration in and of themselves.

The decision-making by consensus, the inclusion of every voice to deliberations, the empowering of all members of the group; to include all of these steps when resolving a conflict enhance the benefit to be derived far beyond simply settling a dispute.

Indigenous groups throughout the world, particularly the Maori of New Zealand and native groups in Canada, use many of the processes of the Bone Game in what they call "restorative justice." The sharing circles and the meetings between victims and perpetrators are all part of a process to get everything out in the open so that wounds can heal and the community can function more smoothly.

At the beginning of this chapter, I claimed that a well-played Bone Game can be a spectacular spectator sport. From what I have written so far, it certainly doesn't look like that but let's call that team preparations prior to the big match (like football practice). Once a Bone Game gets going, it can turn into a swirling, melodic, exciting showcase of skill and deception.

Tribes have incorporated singers, drummers and dancers into the play, (somewhat like cheerleaders). Their job is to move about singing haunting rhythms and swirling around the field of play with colourful outfits and intricate moves (which can be compared to the the gymnastics presented by attractive cheerleaders that have been known to distract players during a football game).

The players also take advantage of the music and rhythms to bounce up and down and contort their bodies while sitting cross-legged, crossing their arms and waving them around, opening and closing their hands and tossing the bones back and forth, hiding them behind their backs one minute and up in the air the next, lulling their opponent into a visual routine which they use to hide the bones to the point where it is impossible to follow where a bone is or isn't.

The entire Game turns into an intricate cultural showcase of swiftly moving dancers, drumbeats, haunting and melodic chants and rhythms, with players waving their arms and bodies all in time; all with a goal to deceive the opponent into guessing wrong when it comes to the location of the Bones, which score, the points and ultimately decides who is the winner of the Bone Game.

And often, when the stakes aren't too high, the Games are just fun to play and to watch.

———————————

There are many more indigenous games that can be explored in your local library or on the worldwide web and if you do so, you will find that usually more than simple competition and physical fitness underlie these games. The Haudenosaunee played bagattaway to prepare warriors for battle and the seed ball games of the tribes in the American Southwest were a ritual related to a good harvest. Whatever you find behind these games, there is almost always an easy extrapolation that can be made to the modern world and this, at least, gets us thinking of different ways to handle things.

Which is often a good thing.

"For as long as the sun shines and the grass grows, and the river flows."

10

"The First 500 years are Always the Toughest"

It is pretty obvious from what I write about First Nations people/ Native Americans that I'm one of those "goddamn Indian lovers." Yes, I do support much of what native people have to say, but this doesn't mean that I walk around pretending or assuming that they, or I, are right about everything. One of the seven sacred teachings is respect, and I truly embrace other opinions, so long as the person offering them has done some homework and is familiar with whatever subject or issue we happen to be exchanging information about.

I love learning new things, including information that is contrary to what I know or believe. And I often "stand corrected" when other people provide me with convincing arguments that are more accurate or truthful than what I have to say.

On the other hand, there are people who are so vain that they think they have the answers to all of the world's problems without doing any research or studying the issues in any way. Common sense is fine, as far as it goes, but there are so many subjects which demand further study and so many times you will change your mind through that further study.

I have my opinions on native history and current affairs and I express them often as Editor of *Grassroots News* (Manitoba's oldest and largest First Nations newspaper), my regularly appearing column in the *Winnipeg Free Press*, and a weekly column on Troy Media. Many of the internet responses I receive are well researched and well thought out, and they enlighten and empower me with new information and other points of view. These responses are equally split between agreeing and disagreeing with me.

I also receive many knee-jerk reactions that are racist or ignorant. All too often, the responses are written in anger, or with a mocking or condescending tone. Some are downright insulting.

We don't need to do this. The Elders say we must guide people gently to a higher understanding, and while perhaps sometimes I am more forceful than I want to be, my most basic goal is to empower people with information so they can make fair and balanced choices about social and economic justice and equality.

This is what I hope to accomplish with the information I have provided in this book. I only ask that you take the information into consideration and, of course, feel free to agree or disagree. Just please support your arguments or opinions with research and please offer them in a kind and gentle way.

In this spirit, I offer this chapter, which is my brief account of the history between indigenous people and the newcomers to North America in order to provide a rationale for the empathetic slant that flows throughout this book. This chapter is based on 40 years of experience working with First Nations political, business and cultural leaders, and the research and reading I have done during this time.

There are many people who would argue with what I have to say and I welcome that. Because of limited space, I have drawn some general conclusions and there are many, many exceptions to the rule. When what I have to say is broken down into specifics, there are even more arguments, but overall, the general conclusions that I have made hold true.

At least to me.

———————————————

The basic history of Canada and First Nations is dominated by the signing of treaties. This not only established and affirmed the sovereignty of First Nations, there are obligations which both parties share as signatories to the treaties.

In other words, we are all treaty people.

First Nations leaders maintain that the treaties were not a "real estate transaction." That is, First Nations did not agree to sell or in any other way give up their rights to the land in exchange for what was promised in the treaties. First Nations maintain the treaties were "an agreement to share"—in the sense that First Nations would move on to smaller tracts of land called Indian reserves in exchange for certain things.

What those "certain things" are has always been hotly contested. Some literal translations of certain treaties claim the obligation of the Canadian government (on behalf of the Crown—the original signatories) is restricted to $5 and a sack of flour for each Indian each year. These people also claim that it is written in some treaties that the Indians ceded all lands and rights to resources and so on. One thing that everybody agrees on is that Indians have paid their taxes in advance and that First Nations will never pay taxes to another government.

First Nations maintain the treaties are to be interpreted by the "spirit and intent" in which they were signed and they have won support for this position from Canada's highest courts. First Nations leaders could not read or write English but common sense tells us that nobody would be foolish enough to sign away massive territories and rights in the kind of one-way deals some people claim treaties are. By traditional First Nations custom and law, most of these leaders were bound to only sign treaties which are "good for seven generations," so it is unlikely their intent was to sell off the future of their children. Most were wise and knowledgable leaders who ran good governments at the time.

Land is the centre of First Nations culture and spirituality and is of primary importance (even Hollywood Westerns will give you an idea of how strongly Indians fought for their land). As respected

Saskatchewan Elder Pauline Pelley said, "We are nothing without our land."

Few could envision a future of hydro-electric power, massive forestry and mining operations, modern agriculture and all of the other immense wealth that has been derived from the lands which First Nations occupied prior to European contact. If we are all treaty people, and the treaties are an agreement to share, the Canadian people have benefitted much more from the treaties without fulfilling their agreement to share—fairly and certainly not equally.

While the treaties may be subject to interpretation and mis-interpretation, they are the official, governing documents which were negotiated between the First Nations and representatives of the Crown/Canadian government. Unfortunately, the Canadian government then huddled together in Ottawa and developed what is known as the Indian Act without any consultation with First Nations leaders.

The treaties obligated the Canadian government to set aside mon-ies for education (to learn the ways of the white man), health care (the medicine chests shall be full), economic development (ploughshares) and so on. This was first known as "Indian monies," but instead of transferring these funds directly to the First Nations who signed the treaties, the Canadian government set up the Department of Indian Affairs (DIA) to implement the Indian Act.

And so almost all of the money that was supposed to go to Indians went to white bureaucrats to run the DIA, and they hired their white contractor friends to build shoddy housing and infrastructure, and struck deals with white churches to operate Indian Residential Schools (IRS) which were a horror story of physical and sexual abuse governed by a philosophy to "kill the Indian in the child" and so on and on and on. This is certainly not what the First Nations expected when they signed the treaties.

And so First Nations in Canada have experienced over a hundred years of poverty and neglect while Canadians enjoy one of the highest standards of living in the world. The social and economic disparities between mainstream Canada and First Nations are always cited whenever Canada presents itself as a modern, democratic, liberated country to the world.

It is so ironic that Canada looked down upon the United States for its treatment of black people in 1960 while at the very same time, Indians were shunted away on reserves and in residential schools, could not leave the reserve without a pass and were even denied the basic right to vote.

But things are changing. First of all, Canadians and their government have recognized that the Department of Indian Affairs and the Indian Act do not work. And secondly, First Nations have begun to assert their sovereignty and they have won numerous battles for treaty rights and land claims in the courts. First Nations leadership has made education and economic development a priority and there has been some significant progress.

There is a long way to go but recently, First Nations gained control over the education of their children and increased funding to achieve success, and First Nations are developing equity partnerships with resource companies so that profits and jobs can be developed locally and recirculated within First Nations. These developments are far from perfect but they are a sea change from the way things were just one generation ago.

The experience of the Indian Residential Schools and years of poverty and neglect are manifest in the dysfunction Canadians see in First Nations and in the ghettos of their cities. It may take two or three more generations for First Nations people to achieve their rightful and equal place in Canadian society but the tide is turning.

Having provided this admittedly one-sided summary of Canada's history with First Nations, there are plenty of arguments against what I write and many, many exceptions to the rule. But I can rightly claim the following.

All First Nations people in Canada want is the rights and resources to raise their children in safe, healthy homes and communities. They want to pursue careers and they want their children to be educated and achieve better. They want to embrace their culture, traditions and spirituality in peace and freedom as sovereign nations with a historic relationship governed by treaties with their partner nation Canada. And if Canadians live up to their obligations under the spirit and intent of the treaties, the wrongs of the past can be undone and there is a positive future ahead.

I personally have been blessed with the opportunity to work and play with First Nations people throughout my life. I have been enriched with spirituality, love, knowledge, friendship and so many other things that I cherish most highly.

I would never say all Indians are good people and First Nations are right about everything they claim. Just like any other group, there are good and bad.

There is a gift we have been given by First Nations people and it is something I think we should try to carry with us every day.

First Nations Elders say that we must live our lives by seven sacred teachings: respect, love, goodness, truth, courage, humility and knowledge (Don: this only six). It may take most of a lifetime to fully understand and appreciate this gift and we might still fail every day. But as long as we keep trying, and people allow us to keep trying, we can try to live with this gift every day.

I have seen many wrongs perpetrated on First Nations and I know the majority of Canadian people want to change things for the better. I hope this book has made a contribution to empowering people with information so they can make fair and balanced decisions about social and economic justice and equality.

As for the history between the United States and Native Americans, there are similarities and there are differences between what has happened in the u.s. and what has happened in Canada. I am not experienced enough with the situation in the u.s. to offer a meaningful contribution to the discussion between Native

American leaders and the American government except to wish for the same kind of justice and equality we are trying to achieve in Canada.

Kyle Lohse

11

"Too Many Stars and Not Enough Space"

Besides hockey, the sport in which Native Americans have achieved the most widespread notoriety has been America's favourite pasttime—baseball. The superstars may be few and far between when compared to other ethnic groups such as Caucasians, Blacks and Hispanics who have excelled in the major leagues, but the Native American stars certainly enjoyed some interesting, and some would say, "colourful" baseball careers.

Baseball was introduced to North American Indians by merchants and missionaries when the game was taking root throughout the United States in the late 1800s. Many Indian tribes who were captured and placed on government reserves spent their idle time while incarcerated playing baseball. The great Apache warrior Geronimo played baseball while being held captive at Fort Sill, Oklahoma. No stats are available on his batting average, but Geronimo led a team of Chiracahuas to victory over a team of soldiers in one highly publicized game.

In addition to prisons and reservations, the u.s. government had a policy of placing a large portion of Indian youth in government boarding schools. One positive byproduct of this policy was that baseball was often part of the school curriculum.

In 1886, the Carlisle Indian Industrial School in Pennsylvania founded a full baseball program that produced a lot of Indian players who went on to careers in the pro leagues. The list includes such notables as Frank Jude, Mike Balenti, Louis Leroy, Hall of Famer Charles Albert Bender and Jim Thorpe, the world's greatest athlete.

Unlike the exclusion of black players in the major leagues, professional baseball had no official segregation policy regarding Indians (you might recall black actor Richard Pryor trying to pass himself off as an Indian to get into the major leagues in the movie *The Bingo Long Travelling All-Stars and Motor Kings*). However, walking through the front door of the exclusive club that was pro baseball was not the same for an Indian as it was for whites, who were easily accepted by members. Indian players also had to put up with blatant racism and stereotyping from the fans as well as the journalists who were covering the games. There has never been a defining moment of reception for Indian players like the one Jackie Robinson, experienced when he broke the so-called "colour barrier" by becoming major league baseball's first African American player.

One small victory for the Indians was that they weren't under the kind of gag order Robinson had to play through because he had been told he had to be the kind of player "with the courage not to fight back." This allowed future Hall of Famer, Native American pitcher Charles Bender (inventor of the slider) to answer one group of racial taunting misanthropes with, "You ignorant, ill-bred foreigners. If you don't like the way I'm doing things out there, why don't you just pack up and go back to your own countries!"

Racism took its toll in more insidious ways and truly damaged some potentially great baseball talent. Louis Francis Sockalexis, nicknamed the "Deerfoot of the Diamond," was the big league's first high-profile American Indian player because his abundant skill attracted widespread attention (and some adulation). Sockalexis played in the National League for only three seasons because he just couldn't cope with the mean-spirited vindictiveness and outright, undeserved hatred, spending his all too short career (1897-1899) as an outfielder for the Cleveland Spiders.

An account of Sockalexis' early experience in Cleveland was chronicled in columns written for the *Sporting Life* newspaper by Elmer E. Bates and published in May of 1897:

> War whoops, yells of derision, a chorus of meaningless "familiarities"
> greet Sockalexis on every diamond on which he appears. In many

cases these demonstrations border on extreme rudeness. In almost every instance, they are calculated to disconcert the player... It was during a pandemonium of "ki yis" directed to his ears that he yanked down the drive that saved Thursday's game, and it was to the accompaniment of a thousand derisive voices that he banged the ball to the fence Friday for a home run...

All eyes are on the Indian in every game. He is expected not only to play right field like a veteran, but to do a little more batting than anyone else. Columns of silly poetry are written about him, hideous looking cartoons adorn the sporting pages of nearly every paper. He is hooted at and howled at by the thimble-brained brigade on the bleachers. Despite all this handicap, [Sockalexis] has played good steady ball.

Born on October 24, 1871, Sockalexis was from the Penobscot Indian Island Reservation in Maine, where his grandfather was Chief of the Bear Clan. It was clear at an early age that the boy had special athletic talent and the kind of arm that would have pro scouts drooling. Sockalexis could throw a baseball clear across the Penobscot River, just like George Washington threw a dollar across the Potomac, and often entertained crowds at the Bangor Race Track by playing catch with his father across the entire track (take that, George!).

After completing high school, Sockalexis fashioned a slick .444 batting average in his freshman season at the College of the Holy Cross in 1894. Sockalexis transferred to Notre Dame for more competition and in 1897, the Fighting Irish baseball team played an exhibition game against the New York Giants at the old Polo Grounds. Every time Sockalexis took the field he had to deal with heckling, taunts, and racial insults, as did other members of the Penobscot tribe who had made the long trip from Indian Island to see him play.

Amos Rusie, a future member of the Baseball Hall of Fame, pitched that day for the Giants. Before the game, Rusie had promised reporters that he would strike out Sockalexis. Louis stepped up to the plate and got sweet, rapid revenge by homering off Rusie's first pitch.

Louis's career at Notre Dame was short and sweet because he was expelled for excessive drinking. Despite his issues with alcohol,

Sockalexis signed a major league contract on March 9, 1897 with the Cleveland Spiders.

But drinking had become an all too common way for many young Indian men to deal with the culture shock, racism and loneliness caused by their interaction with white society. Soon after he made his major league debut, Sockalexis, reportedly drunk, jumped from the second-story window of a brothel and severely injured his ankle. Evidently, the injury did not affect his play too badly because in the five games after the incident, he pounded out nine hits in 18 at-bats.

In his first season with the Spiders, Sockalexis hit for a .338 batting average, with three home runs and 42 RBIs or Runs Batted In (so, more properly, RsBI). In 66 games, Sockalexis also stole 16 bases. This was a very good performance for a rookie and foretold a bright future.

It was a destiny that would fail to materialize.

Sockalexis' three home runs does not sound like much by today's standards, but one must keep in mind that this was the "dead ball era" which ran from the beginning of major league baseball to the early 1920s. It all had to do with how hard and durable the ball was (or would end up).

During this time, it was not unusual for a baseball to be in play for 100 pitches or more, causing it to endure quite a pounding which softened it up a lot (a ball was not taken out of play by the umpire until it literally started to unravel at the seams). Have you ever tried to hit a flaccid mound of leather-covered mush?

Baseballs were relatively expensive and fans were even required to throw back balls that had been hit out of play. The longer the ball was in use, the more abuse it suffered, the softer it became, and the more difficult it became to hit for distance.

There were other factors that influenced hitting in the "dead ball" era, such as discolouration. It is harder to see a dark, dirty baseball coming at you day or night. And all the scuffing on the ball cover from hours of play gave the pitchers a distinct advantage in gripping the ball to throw their junk pitches. On 13 occasions between 1900 and 1920, the league leader in home runs had fewer than 10 round-trippers for the season, so Sockalexis' three homers as a rookie was quite respectable.

But drinking was Sockalexis' nemesis—limiting his pro career to just two more pedestrian seasons that aren't worthy of note, and his great career potential was never to be fulfilled.

That doesn't necessarily mean this story doesn't have a happy ending. Because after Louis Sockalexis finished with the majors, he returned home to Indian Island where he enjoyed passing on his love of baseball to younger players by coaching junior teams. Who is to say that starring in the spotlight of major professional sports is always better than the love and friendship of family and friends while enjoying the exact same pasttime?

Not all of the early Indian pioneers in baseball succumbed to racism or turned to alcohol to cope. Some even thrived with the financial opportunities that a professional baseball career could offer a man at the turn of the century. Charles "Chief" Bender, a Hall of Fame pitcher, was one of them, as he explained in an interview with the *Chicago Daily News* in October 1910.

> The reason I went into baseball as a profession was that when I left school, baseball offered me the best opportunity for both money and achievement. I adopted it because I played baseball better than I could do anything else, because the life and the game appealed to me and because there was so little of racial prejudice in the game. There has scarcely been a trace of sentiment against me on account of my birth. I have been treated the same as other men.

Despite some indignities, Bender felt that being a major league player afforded him more opportunity than he might have found in any other profession.

Charles Albert Bender was born on May 5, 1883 in Crow Wing County, Minnesota (near Brainerd of the movie *Fargo* fame and often referred to as the home of Paul Bunyan). His mother was part Ojibwa and he spent his childhood on the White Earth reservation, until at age 13 he was placed in the system of schools for Native Americans, including the Carlisle Indian Industrial School.

Bender's talent was so obvious and vast that he skipped the minor leagues and jumped straight from semi-pro ball to the big leagues, where he enjoyed a long and remarkably productive career, becoming one of the top pitchers of his era. Bender won 212 games during his 16-year major league career with such notable teams as the powerhouse New York Yankees, including such highlights as leading the American League in winning percentage for three seasons and throwing a no-hitter in 1910, a rare feat which was long considered the high-water mark for great pitching in the major leagues.

By the time Bender retired from the game, he had racked up 1,711 strikeouts. He also pitched in five World Series Championships (also leading the Philadelphia Athletics to a couple of World Series titles), going 6-4 in ten starts with an ERA of 2.44, winning two games apiece in the 1911 and 1913 fall classics. He pitched 3,017 innings during his career, with an almost obscenely low earned-run average of 2.46.

Connie Mack, the legendary Philadelphia manager, raved about Charles Bender: "If I had all the men I've ever handled, and they were in their prime, and there was one game I wanted to win above all others, Albert would be my man."

At 6-foot-2, Bender was an intimidating force, and he possessed a reliable fastball, an exceptional curveball and excellent control. But another weapon in his formidable pitching arsenal was something considered illegal today but an accepted part of the game at the time: the so-called "talcum pitch."

Talcum was a foreign substance similar to baby powder that, when rubbed on a baseball in a proper manner, would cause the ball to drop sharply as it approached the plate, just as if it fell off a table. Bender also developed a variation of the "talcum pitch" but without a foreign substance involved. He is widely credited with the invention of a pitch called the slider, or "nickel curve," as it was called in Bender's day.

The slider is an amalgam of a fastball and a curve, incorporating the best features of both. It is a pitch that breaks laterally and downward with a velocity somewhere in between that of a curve or a fastball. The break on the ball is shorter than that of a curveball but with more speed to make timing it very awkward for hitters of any generation.

Bender and his slider are also credited with prolonging a starting pitcher's career in an era when relievers weren't used nearly as much. Bender had to come up with something so he wouldn't have to rely so heavily on his fastball, which is known to lose velocity and effectiveness with an aging arm. This was added value for the slider.

Bender was one of the "big name" players the upstart Federal League signed when a group of wealthy businessmen had success for a few years competing with the National and American Leagues.

After retiring as a player, Bender continued to work in baseball for various pro teams as a scout, manager, and coach. He made a handsome living on the sport that he loved right up until his death in 1954. His long and accomplished career was formally recognized through his election to the Baseball Hall of Fame in 1953.

Like many other Native American athletes, Bender was given the nickname "Chief," but he was more than ready to stand up for his rights, his dignity and his native culture. Bender considered the use of "Chief" in such a cursory and unthinking manner to be derogatory and inaccurate, founded in racism and stereotypes. In retaliation, Bender refused to sign his autograph with anything other than "Charles Bender."

Ironically, in the Baseball Hall Of Fame where he is rightfully honoured for a distinguished career, he is called "Chief" Bender.

Sigh.

Opposing Bender's Athletics in 1911 was New York Giants catcher John Tortes Meyers, a member of the Cahuilla tribe in Riverside, California. Meyers made his big league debut in 1909, after hitting an astonishing 29 home runs during the month-long spring training season. Meyers hit .332 in 1911, .358 in '12 and .312 in '13, as the Giants reached the World Series in all three seasons. Manager John McGraw call Meyers "the greatest natural hitter in the game."

Meyers' .291 career batting average is the highest among catchers to play in the "dead ball" era (1900-1919). Outspoken on Indian affairs during and after his playing days, Meyers chronicled his own career and the achievements of other Native American athletes as a columnist for the *New York American* newspaper from 1912-14.

In a column on teammate Jim Thorpe, Meyers wrote: "It would be false modesty on my part to declare that I am not thoroughly delighted with the fact that my race has proven itself competent to master the white man's principal sport."

Two years after his death, Meyers was inducted to the American Indian Athletic Hall of Fame at Haskell Indian Nations University in Lawrence, Kansas.

Moses J. Yellow Horse, a Pawnee, was the dominant Native American player during the roaring '20s, and he was followed the next decade by John Leonard Roosevelt Martin, the St. Louis Cardinals outfielder more commonly known as "Pepper" Martin. A member of the Osage tribe from Temple, Oklahoma, Martin was also known as the Wild Horse of the Osage for his aggressive base running and all-out style of play. One of the more high-profile Native Americans to play in the majors, Martin was a member of the Cardinals' infamous "Gas House Gang" teams of the 1930s.

A four-time All-Star, Martin led the National League in stolen bases three times and posted a .298 batting average during his 13-year career. In perhaps his finest hour, Martin led all hitters with a .500 average, racking up 12 hits in 24 at-bats in the Cardinals' victory over the heavily-favoured Philadelphia Athletics in the 1931 World Series. "Pepper" Martin was inducted into the Oklahoma Sports Hall of Fame in 1992.

A classic example of the kind of derision sportswriters got away with in those days can be found in the way Rudy York was treated in print. York, who was part Cherokee, was plagued by inconsistent fielding early in his career. So the press, perhaps thinking they were somehow being clever, labelled York "part first baseman and part Indian." This is especially cruel when you consider the fact that York's skill with the bat earned him seven All-Star game appearances and he led the entire American League with 34 home runs and 118 RBIs in 1943. But the inclination remained that anything York did wrong was due to his being "part Indian."

The absolute absurdity of racism can be found in the example of Jimmy Claxton; a rising star with the Oakland Oaks of the Pacific Coast League, who didn't seem to be hurt at all by the fact he was part Indian.

But when the powers-that-be in baseball found out Claxton was also part-black, he was kicked out of the league.

Ironically, Claxton was originally from British Columbia in Canada, where there was little discrimination against blacks but Indians were shunted aside.

You almost feel sorry for somebody who had to keep track of who to hate when and where. An acronym commonly used by mobile phone users who text messages is the only accurate way to describe all this.

WTF?

We can't leave "old-time ball" without highlighting the career of Allie Reynolds. Among the most successful pitchers in World Series history, this New York Yankee's seven World Series game victories are equalled only by Hall of Famers Red Ruffing and Bob Gibson, and rank second only to Whitey Ford's ten. Yet Reynolds started out in track and field and was only converted to a baseball player and pitcher when he was observed throwing the javelin by Oklahoma A&M's baseball coach.

With the Yankees, Reynolds pitched for six World Series championship teams in seven years, including five in a row from 1949 195353 during the Yankees dynasty days. During his eight seasons in the Bronx, Reynolds compiled a 131-60 record for a remarkable .686 winning percentage.

Reynolds was born in 1917 on the Indian reservation in Bethany, Oklahoma, His mother was a member of the Muscogee (Creek) tribe. During his time with the Yankees he was known alternately as "Chief" and "Superchief"—a reference that was a double entendre including his Native American origin and a railroad train model that was very popular at the time.

Reynolds didn't like it but it provides an interesting example of a cultural dichotomy when you go by the way former teammate Bobby Brown explained it.

"The Santa Fe Railroad had a crack train called the Superchief that ran from California to Chicago, and it was known for its elegance, its power and its speed," said Brown, while acknowledging that Reynolds did not appreciate the nickname because of what the title "Chief" stands for in his native culture.

"We always felt the name applied to Allie for the same reasons as that super train. When we talked with him, we called him Allie, but when he wasn't in the room, he was referred to as the Chief because we felt he was the one at the top, the real leader."

———————————

There are three Native Americans who have made a big splash in baseball's modern era. One of them who entered the major leagues with a helluva buzz is Joba Chamberlain.

Hanaga (First Son—Ho Chunk) grew up in Lincoln, Nebraska near the Winnebago Reservation—home of the Ho Chunk Nation. His given name was Justin Chamberlain, but a young cousin had problems pronouncing his brother Joshua's name and when Justin and his father Harlan heard the little guy stammer out "Joba," they thought it sounded great and Justin's legal name was changed to Joba Chamberlain. A member of the Buffalo clan, Joba grew up dancing at pow wows and playing sports.

Joba was an exceptional athlete, starring in most high school sports, especially baseball where he dominated from the mound with blazing heat, and from the plate, batting well over .500. But finances (or lack thereof) delayed college. Chamberlain spent some time working as a maintenance man in Lincoln to support his family before he entered university.

Chamberlain led the University of Nebraska-Kearney with 49 strikeouts and four complete games in just eight starts as a freshman, before transferring to the U. of Nebraska-Lincoln where he led the Cornhuskers to their first College World Series win. Chamberlain had a 10–2 win/loss record with a 2.81 ERA for the year, and his 2005 stats included five double-digit strikeout games. During the 2004-2005 college off-season Chamberlain pitched for the Nebraska Bruins of the National Baseball Congress. He started six games in 2005, recording a 5–0 record and a 1.59 ERA.

Chamberlain was drafted 41st overall by the New York Yankees in the 2006 Major League Baseball draft. Before the 2007 season, Baseball

America ranked Chamberlain as the fourth-best prospect in the pitching-rich Yankee organization, and the 75th-best prospect in MLB, while ranking his fastball as the best in the Yankee farm system.

Chamberlain was promoted to Triple-A, and made his first start the next day, striking out ten in five innings and earning his first Triple-A victory. While the Yankees still saw him as a starter in the future, Joba made his first relief appearance the next day, striking out the side in one inning and hitting 100 miles per hour on the radar gun three times. In another relief appearance, he struck out two batters in a 1–2–3 eighth inning, then pitched two innings and struck out five batters the next day. It would always be difficult to decide whether Joba should be employed as a starter or used in relief, and it has affected Chamberlain's performance throughout his career because it requires vastly different ways to physically train for the different roles in the off-season as well as to mentally prepare for an upcoming season.

Chamberlain's career in the major leagues has had its highs and lows, alternating between becoming a regular reliever and/or starter with the Yankees, stints in the minor leagues, time off due to injuries and pretty much everything else that can happen to a baseball pitcher. At last word (2014), Joba Chamberlain had signed a $2.5 million contract covering one year with the Detroit Tigers. Anybody will tell you that for any pitcher to survive for seven years in the highly competitive world that major league baseball has become because of the ridiculously high salaries they pay nowadays, he must have a lot of talent and desire.

Back to that reference I made about entering the major leagues with a buzz, Joba Chamberlain will always be best known for a crazy incident which took place during the American League Division Series with the Cleveland franchise now known as Indians. It was Joba's rookie season, and these were the major league playoffs, so there was pressure enough. He didn't need heat-seeking, Yankee-destroying missiles turning him into a giant sugar cube.

It has already become one of baseball's legenday stories. Chamberlain was pitching in the bottom of the eighth with the Yankees leading 1–0 when suddenly, a swarm of small insects dispatched from over-polluted Lake Erie attacked the field like a Biblical plague, blocking out the lights, home plate and the hand in front of your face on a tropical, breezeless night.

But somehow the gnats didn't bother the Cleveland players, who have experienced such visitations before. Casey Blake smiled and called them their "small pterodactyls." Cleveland hurler Fausto Carmona pitched right through them as if they were old friends and didn't flinch once.

Joba, with bugs camped out on his neck and lined up along his eyelids, was repeatedly sprayed down with blasts of insect repellent, which had no apparent deterrent effect on the midges, who were absolutely driving Joba to distraction. He ended up throwing two wild pitches, yielding the tying run. Cleveland went on to win the game 2–1. The Yankees would then lose the Division Series against Cleveland in four games in the best-of-five series.

It is a testament to Joba's character that he refused to make excuses for giving up that tying run without giving up a hit.

"Bugs are bugs," Chamberlain grumbled afterward, mostly at himself. "It's not the first time I had a bug near me. You just keep your mouth closed. No excuses. I let my guys down. Disappointed is an understatement."

Chamberlain refused to blame the gnats, but Yankee manager Joe Torre had gone out in the eighth inning to crew chief Bruce Froemming, asking if maybe this was a good time for a delay because the insects were as thick as a blanket out on the field. Froemming, despite noting that Torre was gnat-ily attired, told the Yankee bench boss to bug off.

"There are bugs in baseball."

But "there's no crying in baseball," as Jimmy Dugan, Manager, Rockford Peaches , infamously proclaimed in the 1992 movie "A League of Their Own" when a player on his womens professional baseball team didn't handle his managerial style of barking at players when they make a mistake in the manner to which he was accustomed.

On October 18, 2008, at 1:00 a.m. Chamberlain was arrested near Lincoln for suspicion of driving under the influence, speeding, and having an open container of alcohol in his vehicle. His arrest was captured on police video, which later aired on the "Drivers 13" epi-sode of *truTV Presents: World's Dumbest...* Joba didn't disagree, and never tried to downplay or diminish his bad choices. He stood up like a man, pled guilty to drunk driving, and was sentenced to probation on April 1, 2009.

And that is the kind of man Chamberlain wants to be for his one son, Karter. Not the DUI part, but the courage to stand up for his ac-tions good or bad, and do what you can to do good in this world. Joba is fulfilling his dreams of being a big league star and the best that he can be on and off the field. This is also what drives the Dream Big Foundation—Joba's organization which fosters positive development in native children and youth.

When Kyle Lohse toed the rubber for the St. Louis Cardinals in Game 3 of the 2011 World Series, it marked the first time that a Native American pitcher started a Series game since New York Yankees hurler Allie Reynolds won Game 6 in the 1953 Series. Prior to Lohse, reliever Chamberlain had been the last Native American pitcher to appear in the World Series, making three relief appearances against the Philadelphia Phillies in the 2009 Fall Classic.

A member of the Nomlaki Wintun American Indian tribe from Chico, Calif., Lohse didn't start out looking like he would even have a major league career. Drafted in the 29th round by the Chicago Cubs in 1996, Lohse was traded to Minnesota in 2001 and had spot success but was even sent down to the minors in 2006. Lohse bounced around from Cincinnati to Philadelphia before he finally found his groove in St. Louis during the 2008 season when he went 11-and-2 with a 3.39 Earned Run Average (ERA).

That provided Lohse with a $41 million, four-year contract exten-sion which he paid off with a 16-3 won-loss record to lead the National League in winning percentage at .842. By the year 2013, Lohse was commanding a 3-year, $33 million reworking of his contract with the Milwaukee Brewers, and the 2014 season appears bright as he heads up a strong rotation.

———————————

Jacoby McCabe Ellsbury was born on September 11, 1983 in Madras, Oregon, steeped in his Native American background. His father, Jim, worked as a forester for the Bureau of Indian Affairs and his mother, Margie, was an early-intervention specialist on the Warm Springs Reservation near Madras. Margie, a full-blooded Navajo, descended from a famous 1-th century tribal leader, Granado Mucho. She was raised on the Colorado River Reservation on the Arizona-California border—home to the Mohave, Chemehuevi, Hopi, and Navajo tribes.

Jacoby Ellsbury was always fast. Once, after cornering a young deer in the woods near his home, Jacoby, 11 years old at the time, was able to run down the deer and loop a rope around its neck.

"I always knew I was fast from a young age."

Deer-roping notwithstanding, Jacoby's favourite sport was baseball. He played Little League ball in Arizona, where he visited his grandmother during the summers. She taught her grandson traditional Navajo songs while he stayed with her. Jacoby's raw speed cannot be taught.

In high school, Ellsbury was a flawless baserunner. In four years, nobody can recall Jacoby being thrown out on the base paths, or ever stopping at third base. His speed and acceleration were completely intimidating.

In the spring of 2002, Jacoby was offered a full ride to several West Coast schools, including nearby Oregon State. That June, he was also drafted in the 23rd round by the Tampa Bay Devil Rays. After weighing his options, he decided to take the scholarship. He would play three years at Oregon State.

"I weighed the pros and cons of both, and college outweighed the pro ranks at the time and I'm definitely glad I made the choice to come to Oregon State because I'm a better player for it."

Jacoby batted .330 with seven home runs in his first season and earned Freshman All-America honours. The star centre fielder was described as the first "bona fide, drop-dead, first-round draft pick" Oregon had ever had.

Then Jacoby Ellsbury made a trip to Boston to watch a Red Sox game and he was blown away by the atmosphere of Fenway Park. He bought a Boston cap and brought it home to Oregon. Later, after the

Red Sox made their amazing comeback in the playoffs against the New York Yankees to break the Curse of the Bambino (Boston hadn't won the World Series since their owner sold Babe Ruth to the New York Yankees to finance a Broadway play), Jacoby started wearing the Boston cap before each game.

Perhaps because of his Cape Cod League exploits, Jacoby was on the Red Sox radar and they both got their wish when he ended up drafted by Boston.

Jacoby signed for a $1.4 million bonus with the Bosox and began his pro career. After standing out in the minors, Jacoby played in 26 games for the Red Sox in 2006 and was a revelation. All told, he batted .353, torching righties and lefties equally. He slugged over .500, with 11 of his 40 hits going for extra bases.

It wasn't long before Boston fans realized the Red Sox were a different team with Ellsbury in their lineup. When they swept the World Series against the white-hot Colorado Rockies, Jacoby sparked the team with his defence, base running and hitting. In 11 postseason games, he batted .360 with nine hits and a couple of stolen bases.

"You can be in the league your whole career and never make it to a World Series. For me to do it in my first year and be part of a World Series Championship team is very special," Ellersby said.

Since then, the career of Jacoby Ellsbury has been filled with big victories, agonizing defeats (which only come at the Division playoff or World Series level) and honours, while marking some obscure marks (stroking the only single to score three runs in post-season history, the first pure steal of home for a Red Sox player since 1994, stuff like that). Jacoby's quick acceleration and pure speed has resulted in stolen base records and lots of triples, lots and lots of triples, and batting averages routinely over 300.

Only a severe rib injury in 2010 could cause Jacoby to have a dismal season, lowering his batting average below .200 for the first time in his career. Boston fans kept their fingers crossed for a bounce-back season from Jacoby in 2011 and what they got exceeded even their wildest expectations.

Ellersby revealed his resilience by playing the entire year, leading the league with 732 plate appearances and 364 total bases, winning his first Gold Glove and finishing second in the MVP voting by just 38 points to pitcher Justin Verlander. Prior to the campaign, the Red Sox were one of the only teams without a member of the 30–30 club. Jacoby changed that with 32 homers and 39 stolen bases. He also notched career highs with 212 hits, 119 runs, 105 RBIs and a .321 average. Jacoby is also well-known for playing errorless in the field, winning numerous Gold Glove awards.

And that is the kind of career Jacoby Ellsbury has had. Some down times due to injuries, and then mostly sunshine whenever he was healthy. Along the way, Jacoby tied the knot with his girlfriend, Kelsey Hawkins.

Jacoby led the Red Sox to another World Series title in 2013 and most people figured he would play out his career as a superstar in his beloved Boston. But in a shocking, shell-shocking, turn of events, Jacoby decided to test the free agent waters after the 2013 season and the Red Sox, with a hot prospect, Jackie Bradley Jr. in the wings, decided not to get into a bidding war. In turn, Jacoby signed a seven-year contract with the Red Sox's most reviled rival, the Yankees, worth more than $150 million. The team announced that he will play centrefield in 2014 so if Jacoby can remain healthy, he stands a chance of adding his name to the team's long list of luminaries who have manned centrefield at Yankee Stadium—including Joe DiMaggio and Mickey Mantle. So much for joining the ranks of Ted Williams and Carl Yastrzemski on the Red Sox Wall of Honour, something that had been expected for a while.

Ellsbury's deal includes a $21 million option for the 2021 season, with a $5 million buyout. If the option is exercised, the deal would be worth $169 million over eight years. Louis Sockalexis and Allie Reynolds just rolled over in their graves.

And perhaps not just because of the huge salaries paid to modern-day baseball players. One can't help but notice that Chamberlain, Lohse and Ellsbury do not include incidents of racism or discrimination when they tell their stories. The social climate in baseball has improved dramatically from the old days, when Indians were heckled and jeered when they came to play in the major leagues, and blacks were not even allowed to play MLB at all.

North American society has gotten better, too. Nobody would claim we have achieved social and economic justice and equality, far from it, but things aren't as blatant and utterly ridiculous as they were in the past.

It is interesting to note that society was always a couple of steps behind baseball, Jackie Robinson could play on the same field as his teammates but he couldn't stay in the same hotel. Neither could Lou Brock. But they aren't keeping Pedro Martinez and Barry Bonds out of the finest hotels these days.

Sports demands teamwork and is built on sportsmanship and fair play. Society should be, too. It is when good men are forced into situations where they have to pull together that barriers get broken down.

"If we're good enough to stop bullets, we're good enough to use the same washrooms."—phrase used by black G.I.s when they returned home from World War II.

Until 1984, no First Nations citizen from Canada had ever won a gold medal at an Olympic Games. Mohawk Alwyn Morris finally broke through by winning the two-man, 1,000-metre kayak event at the Summer Olympic Games in Los Angeles, but that wasn't what made Morris's victory most notable...

The gold medal win by Morris is more widely recognized for his pose from the podium which reveals Alwyn holding up an eagle feather; the symbol of truth for Canada's First Nations. Morris was paying tribute to the honour, friendship and life of the Kahnawahke Mohawk Nation that he represents, and has been compared to the so-called "black power salute" which was made by sprinters Tommie Smith and John Carlos at the 1968 Games in Mexico City. Historical analysis reveals that all of these athletes were representing essentially the same thing— a gesture of human rights more than anything and in retrospect, their actions have gained almost universal support and acclaim.

In Canada, the eagle feather is recognized as a sacred spiritual and cultural symbol representing truth (a person cannot lie when he or she is holding an eagle feather). For example, First Nations citizens use an eagle feather to swear an oath instead of a Bible in court cases. Possessing eagle feathers is illegal in many places but exemptions have been made for natives despite the fact that this majestic bird is an endangered species because of over-hunting and environmental damage to its habitat. This acceptance was not gained easily, but it is now generally accepted that First Nations people will not abuse this sacred privilege.

When Alwyn Morris held that eagle feather aloft from the medal podium at the 1984 Olympics in Los Angeles, he was holding aloft the hopes, pride and sense of accomplishment of Canadians in general, and First Nations in particular. The Kahnawake Mohawk followed his gold medal performance in the two-man 1,000 metre kayak event with a bronze medal in the 500-metre event.

The eagle feather represents honour, friendship and life. Mr. Morris has done much to symbolize all three.

After 13 years with the Canadian National Canoeing Team, Alwyn served as a role model for the National Native Alcohol and Drug Abuse Program. His poster for the program, featuring the famous medal pose, encouraged Aboriginal youth to dream, succeed and never give up.

A recipient of the Order of Canada in 1985 for outstanding service and achievement, he has established the Alwyn Morris Education and Athletic Foundation and continues to coach kayaking, canoeing, and hockey for the youth of Kahnawake. He has served with the Canada Games Council, the Canadian Sport Secretariat, and was a Special Policy Advisor for Aboriginal People and the Constitution.

Alwyn Morris received a National Aboriginal Achievement Award in Sports for both his accomplishments and the light of his example— the highest honour an Aboriginal person can achieve in mainstream Canadian and First Nations society.

There was a time in Naomi Lang's young skating career when she thought she would have to give up her dream of becoming the first of her Kanuk tribe to become a top figure skater. The costs of skating put a strain on her mom and brother; Lang recalls buying bargain clothes and sleeping on a mattress on the floor until she was 18.

"There's no one that tells you that this is going to cost $60,000 a year at the high levels," says Lang's mom, Leslie Dixon. Dixon moved Lang and her brother to Michigan when Naomi was eight. There she raised them as a single mom on a nursing salary while her ex-husband remained in California. Just as Naomi's skating career was taking off, Dixon prepared her daughter, then a high school senior, for having to give up her skating dream.

But Russian Peter Tchernyshev happened to be searching far and wide for a skating partner, and he had spotted Lang skating at the 1996 U.S. Figure Skating Championships in San Jose, California. Soon after, Tchernyshev held tryouts. As soon as he saw Lang's graceful ballet movements, he knew he had his partner. Dixon fondly recalls Tchernyshev telling her, "If she will agree to skate with me, I'll cancel the rest of my tryouts with all the other girls."

He also offered to pay her way if she'd be his partner and move to New York to start training for the Olympics. Thirteen years later, they're still skating together in shows, though no longer competing. In fact, Lang says that if she skates without Tchernyshev, she feels as if she is missing her right arm. With Tchernyshev living in Russia, the two choreograph their performances by video, chatting on Skype, and they skate together only when they meet to perform

Lang's skating partner of 13 years was born halfway around the world and they have won the United States Figure Skating Championships as a pair for five consecutive years, from 1999 to 2003, which made them eligible for Olympic competition.

Russia is always well-represented at the Olympics and so is the United States. But in Lang's mind, she remains the exception, not the rule. In 115 years of Olympic Games and over 11,000 U.S. Olympic athletes, only 14 have identified as Native American. And she is one of only two females among those 14. Lang is a minority within a minority, fighting for a chance for herself, and then for a way to bring similar opportunities to others like her.

"On a lot of reservations, what you'll hear from these Native kids is, 'We want to be active. We want to be healthy,'" says Crystal Echo Hawk, a Pawnee Indian who helps Lang run an organization that fosters young figure skaters in Indian country. "But they don't have the access and opportunities."

Lang says one of the secrets of her success is believing in herself and picturing herself on the podium. And when she's not skating in shows, raising her kids or—most recent achievement—running in marathons, she is drawing up plans for her Native American Skating Foundation.

"I don't think Native Americans really have a chance," says Lang, pointing to a complete lack of infrastructure for aspiring Native skaters. "So I've been trying to start this program to get kids out of their reservations and into something positive."

When Lang started ice skating at the age of eight, Leslie Dixon remembers telling her daughter "to always have a kind heart" since "Winning wasn't the most important thing." So when Lang's first coach suggested the budding skater enter a competition, Dixon discouraged it. "Mainstream sports are so competitive and it's like every man for himself and I've seen people want to win at any cost," she says.

The competitions haven't scarred the mind of Leslie Dixon's daughter, and Naomi Lang continues to have a kind heart.

It was February 8, 2002 when five Utah tribes, the Ute, Goshute, Shoshone, Paiute and Navajo/Diné, led the opening ceremony at the Salt Lake City Olympic Games with traditional dancing and drumming in full regalia. With the announcement of each tribe, hundreds of Native people danced and marched into the rink. They clasped American flags and eagle feathers in the same hand, their feet tapping and lifting from the ice in unison, bells and shells jingling, multi-coloured feathers whooshing. And leading each tribe was a tribal Elder on horseback.

Naomi Lang still struggles to find the words to describe the honour of being chosen, at the age of 23, to present gifts to the five Utah tribes at the opening ceremonies.

"And then you just see these horsemen coming at you, over the ice, they're walking on the ice," Lang recalls of a Goshute Nation leader who welcomed her in his traditional language. "It was like you were transported back, way back to the old days."

"You don't just go call someone Pocahontas or do oh-oh-oh-oh because it's just stereotyping Native Americans," she says of being mocked while wearing traditional regalia on Grouse Mountain during the 2010 Vancouver Olympics. "And I always get mad. Always. I'm like, 'Don't do that. Because that's not right. Don't ask me if I live in a teepee.'"

May 1 is a feast day on the Pueblo/San Felipe reservation just north of Albuquerque, and traditional dancing is one aspect of this celebration. In his 38 years, Notah Begay III estimates he has danced in 30 of them. It's just one of Begay's customs to honour his people and remember his ancestry. "If you can't go through life knowing who you are and what you come from and what that means," he says, "then you're perpetually lost and looking."

Baseball keeps Joba Chamberlain a little busy in the summer, but he always tries to make it to the powwows on the Ho Chunk reservation in Winnebago, and in his hometown of Lincoln a few hours south. "I dance traditional," Chamberlain says, referring to one of three styles of men's powwow dancing in which the dancer carries his head held high, proudly and with an air of distinction.

"It's special to see and it's fun to go, and it's a workout, too," he says. "When you put all your regalia on, it gets pretty warm." He has his own handmade regalia, including a chest plate and two roaches, a type of intricate headdress.

Naomi Lang (Maheetahan—Morning Star) is a member of the Karuk tribe of California and grew up attending powwows, idolizing the twirling grace of shawl dancers and eating homemade Indian fry bread. She recently attended a powwow in Arizona, where she now lives with her husband and two children. "The beans and the cheese and the lettuce and—oh!" she says, her hands on her heart as she recalls her recent fry bread experience. "I had like three fry breads. Don't tell my partner. Shhhh."

"My Native American heritage was always a part of my life and it's always been significant, and as I've gotten older, it's become more significant," Chamberlain says. "As I got older, I appreciated it more. I think we all play a part from the beginning to the players playing now.

"Opportunities on the reservation are few and far between, so I think for kids to see that there are Native Americans out there that maybe had it different growing up, but still have a chance to play and can show that we are talented, it's good to see that there are some current players right now that can give hope and faith to those kids on the reservation. They should never lose hope of their dreams because their opportunities aren't as vast as they are in a big city. Kids seeing Jacoby and myself, doing as well as we are and being the people we are, is even more important. They can have people they can look up to, people can look up to either of us as a baseball player, and a person, and a Native American."

And then there are so many, many more.

Just off the top of my head, the name of Angela Chalmers springs to mind, the runner from my home province of Manitoba who brought so much glory to her Birdtail Dakota First Nation and the nearby town of Brandon. For about five years, it seems we were reading about one of Angela's exploits in the newspaper every month or so as this Olympic bronze medalist and three-time gold medalist at the Commonwealth Games become a sports celebrity and role model for so many children and youth around here.

And then I recall the Firth twins out of British Columbia—sisters from the Gwitch 'in First Nation who dominated cross-country skiing by winning Canadian championships by the dozen and coming so close in four Olympic Games in sports that are so thoroughly dominated by the Scandinavian countries. The were brought to my attention through a field report for a documentary series our company used to produce which focused on how these ladies passed on the outdoor lifestyle and culture of their people of northern B.C. and the Northwest Territories.

So many like this…

And all the others I have missed, including some kind of acknowl-edgement of those outstanding athletes who, for one reason or another, were unable to fulfill their enormous potential, but grace our recrea-tional hockey leagues, fastpitch and softball leagues, and the many other sports we enjoy together. For example, Manitobans will never forget McKay United—a Métis fastball team which consisted solely of mem-bers of the infamous McKay family, and dominated competitive and recreational fastpitch tournaments in Manitoba for decades (they just kept producing more and more stars for McKay United).

And then there are all of the outstanding athletes who compete in the North American Indigenous Games (NAIG) which have been held eight times in various cities in the United States and Canada since they were founded in 1990. About 10,000 athletes took part in the 2006 Games, with more than 1,000 tribes represented. In addition to sporting events, the Games included a parade and a variety of cultural performances. The 2014 Games are scheduled for July 20-27 in Regina, Saskatchewan.

But mostly, I just wish there was more space.

INDEX